TALENT

3

STUDENT'S BOOK

Clare Kennedy

with Ciaran Ward and Teresa Ting

CAMBRIDGE
UNIVERSITY PRESS

CONTENTS

CONTENTS

STARTER A

Festivals

Grammar: adverbs of frequency; present simple v present continuous
Vocabulary: music genres

1 🔴 [1.02] **Read and listen to the text. Then answer the questions.**

1 What is WOMAD?
2 MandyV writes about different kinds of events at WOMAD. What are they?
3 Why is the festival *global*?

MandyV's big blog

Thursday: A muddy field in Wiltshire, England

Hi from WOMAD! We come here every year. We usually just stay for a day but this year we're camping – so we've got more time. It's very easy to miss events because there's so much going on, so this time I'm making a list.

There are so many cool acts, it's difficult to decide. WOMAD is a really global festival because there are performers from all over the world. I definitely want to see Imarhan. They're an African band and they play a mix of jazz and blues. It's great dance music and there are great lyrics, too! We like dancing to Kachupa, too (they're a folk-rock band from Italy).

What else? I'm looking forward to visiting the *human library* this year. The *books* are people, and they tell true stories about their lives. What a cool idea!

Food and music go together at WOMAD. Cooks from all over the world give demonstrations – in fact right now someone's singing and cooking Mexican food at the same time. It smells so good, I need to try it out! So bye for now!

Festival Facts

- The letters WOMAD stand for World Of Music Arts and Dance.
- 30–40,000 people visit British WOMAD every year.
- About 900 performers come from about 50 different countries.
- The main festival is in the UK, but there are WOMAD festivals in other countries too, for example Spain, Chile, Italy, Australia and New Zealand.

VOCABULARY: Music genres

2 🔴 [1.03] **Listen to six pieces of music. Write the order you hear. Which ones do you like?**

.... blues

.... classical

.... electronic

.... folk

..1.. jazz

.... pop

GRAMMAR GUIDE

Adverbs of frequency

- We <u>always</u> ***watch*** TV on Friday nights.
- I ***don't*** <u>often</u> ***get up*** early on Saturdays.
- What ***do*** you <u>usually</u> ***have*** for breakfast?

But ...

- I ***am*** <u>often</u> hungry.
- You ***aren't*** <u>usually</u> fed up.
- ***Is*** he <u>always</u> late?

➡ See **GRAMMAR REFERENCE** Workbook page 111

3 Rewrite the sentences adding the adverbs in brackets.

0 Clare is tired. (*always*) **Clare is always tired.**

1 Do you play tennis? (*often*)

2 It doesn't snow. (*usually*)

3 I'm wrong. (*never*)

4 We go out on Monday nights. (*sometimes*)

5 Is Sam bad-tempered? (*sometimes*)

6 We have pizza on Fridays. (*often*)

7 Does Joe wear the same T-shirt? (*always*)

8 Jed plays in a band. (*sometimes*)

GRAMMAR GUIDE

Present simple v present continuous

We usually **come** *for the day.*
(We use the present simple for habits and things that are generally true.)

This year we **'re camping***.*
(We use the present continuous for actions in progress at the moment of speaking.)

With state verbs:
It **smells** *so good.*

➡ See **GRAMMAR REFERENCE** Workbook page 111

4 **[1.04] Complete the dialogues. Choose the correct option. Then listen and check.**

1 **A** What kind of music ⁰ (*do you like*) / *are you liking*?

B Hmm, I ¹*don't know / am not knowing* really – I ²*listen / am listening* to all kinds. But I ³*hate / 'm hating* background music in cafés – it's horrible.

A Yes, I ⁴*agree / 'm agreeing*! I ⁵*don't like / 'm not liking* it either.

B It's really hard to talk. I ⁶*don't understand / 'm not understanding* why they have background music.

2 **A** Hey, what's funny? Why ⁷*do you laugh / are you laughing*?

B I ⁸*watch / 'm watching* a video. A dog ⁹*rides / 's riding* a bike. Look!

A Oh, I ¹⁰*don't think / 'm not thinking* that's very kind. I ¹¹*feel / 'm feeling* sorry for it. Poor thing!

B The dog ¹²*seems / is seeming* happy! And it ¹³ *gets / is getting* a biscuit every time it does a complete circle.

5 Complete the dialogues with the correct form of the verbs in brackets.

1 **A** Look! Tom .... (*stand*) over there!

B Oh yes! And he .... (*wave*) at us.

2 **A** Hi! I .... (*often, not / see*) you at the bus stop!

B I .... (*know*). Dad usually .... (*give*) me a lift on his way to the office, but he .... (*not / work*) today.

3 **A** I .... (*write*) a shopping list. .... (*you / need*) anything?

B No, thanks. I .... (*not / think*) so.

4 **A** Where's the bus? It .... (*usually, not / be*) late.

B You're right. I .... (*often, not / wait*) very long.

6 Complete the text. Write the present simple or present continuous of the verbs in brackets.

Celebrate Edinburgh

Edinburgh is the capital of Scotland. I ⁰ **don't live** (*not / live*) there, but I ¹........................ (*think*) it's really cool, and I ²........................ (*go*) there every year. Why ³........................ (*I / love*) it so much? Because of the amazing Edinburgh Festival. Every August the population ⁴........................ (*increase*) as thousands of visitors ⁵........................ (*arrive*) to watch all kinds of performers – from classical musicians to rappers, from ballet dancers to street entertainers.

In this photo the musicians ⁶........................ (*perform*) in the street. They ⁷........................ (*look*) fantastic! The audience are lucky because it ⁸........................ (*not / rain*). It's often wet in Scotland! In this one they ⁹........................ (*watch*) a fire eater. He ¹⁰........................ (*do*) a weird dance at the same time. He's either very brave or crazy!

Champions

Grammar: past simple v continuous; time expressions with past simple, *while* and *when*
Vocabulary: sport

7 Which of these statements do you agree with?

1 I can't stand sport at all.
2 I support a team but I don't play much sport myself.
3 I love sport!

8 ▪ [1.05] Read and listen to a text about two sports stars. In what ways are they the same?

The Two Ellies

Ellie Simmonds won her first two Paralympic medals for swimming when she was 13. That was in Beijing in 2008. Four more medals followed four years later, in London (she was studying for school exams while she was training!). Then, in Rio in 2016, she added another two. Not bad for someone who was still only 21!

Back in 2012, 11-year-old Ellie Robinson was watching when the other Ellie won gold. The two Ellies have the same disability – restricted growth (they are both about 1.2 metres tall). The younger Ellie was a swimmer too – and now she had a new hero.

Fast forward to Rio 2016. A tiny figure approached the pool. Ellie Robinson was wearing a huge coat, and she was holding her arms out straight – gangster style. Back home in the UK, her classmates were watching on a big screen. Along with the crowd (and Twitter!) they cheered as she swam to victory.

9 Answer these questions.

1 How many medals did Ellie Simmonds have in 2016?
2 How old was Ellie Robinson when she was in Rio?

VOCABULARY: Sport

10 ▪ [1.06] Match the sports below to the symbols. Then name the people and the verbs. Then listen and check.

- basketball
- climbing
- cycling
- diving
- football
- horse riding
- rowing
- running
- skating
- skiing
- ~~swimming~~
- tennis

sport		person	verb	sport		person	verb
0	swimming	swimmer	swim	6			
1				7			
2				8			
3				9			
4				10			
5				11			

GRAMMAR GUIDE

Past simple v past continuous

past simple	past continuous
Ellie Simmonds **won** her first two medals **when** she was 13.	Ellie Robinson **was wearing** a huge coat.

Simultaneous actions:

*She was studying for school exams **while** she was training.*

Interrupted actions:

*Ellie Robinson was watching **when** the other Ellie won gold.*

 See **GRAMMAR REFERENCE** Workbook page 111

11 **Write the past continuous of the verbs in brackets.**

1 Who won? I ...**wasn't watching**... (*not / watch*),
  I .... (*check*) my phone.
2 Sorry I'm late. I .... (*look*) for my wallet.
3 It .... (*rain*) hard and people
  .... (*hurry*) home.
4 The accident happened because the driver
  .... (*use*) his mobile phone.
5 I saw you at the station yesterday. Where
  .... (*you / go*)?

GRAMMAR GUIDE

Past simple: Regular and irregular verbs

Regular: *watch**ed** – call**ed** – walk**ed** – jump**ed***

Note the spelling of these forms:

*phone**d**; rob**bed**; travel**led**; cr**ied***

Irregular: *be* → ***was / were**; come* → ***came***

 See **GRAMMAR REFERENCE** Workbook page 112

12 **Write the past simple of these irregular verbs. Then check on Workbook page 109.**

0 do	***did***		
1 get	7 put	13 have	19 sit
2 hit	8 feel	14 lie	20 take
3 make	9 go	15 see	21 tell
4 fall	10 leave	16 hear	22 win
5 give	11 read	17 lose	23 write
6 learn	12 find	18 send	

13 **Use the prompts to make sentences in the past simple.**

1 The match / start / at 3:30 and / finish / an hour ago. We / win!
2 The police officer / stop / us because our bikes / not have / lights. He / tell / us to walk home.
3 I / leave / my bag on the bus but somebody / find / it and / give / it back. Lucky!
4 We / go / to France last summer. What about you? Where / you / go?
5 I / drop /my little sister's favourite cup and it / break. She / cry / and I / feel / awful.

14 **Complete the text with the past simple or past continuous of the verbs in brackets.**

Climber Joe Baxter tells us about his worst — and best — experience.

It ⁰ ...**happened**... (*happen*) two years ago, in Scotland. My friend Jimmy and I ¹ .... (*climb*) Ben Nevis*. Everything ² .... (*go*) well when suddenly, without warning, a rock ³ .... (*hit*) me on the head. I ⁴ .... (*wear*) a helmet but I ⁵ .... (*fall*). I ⁶ .... (*land*) on a ledge and ⁷ .... (*pass*) out. When I ⁸ .... (*wake*) up it ⁹ .... (*get*) dark. I ¹⁰ .... (*try*) to keep calm when I ¹¹ .... (*hear*) a helicopter. They ¹² .... (*send*) a man down to rescue me and soon after that I was safely in hospital. It ¹³ .... (*be*) a scary experience, but I ¹⁴ .... (*learn*) a good lesson. What ¹⁵ .... (*I / learn*)? I can trust my friend Jimmy!

* Ben Nevis is the highest mountain in the UK. It's 1,346–metre high.

New beginnings

Grammar: present perfect and continuous; *been* v *gone*; time expressions
Vocabulary: transport

15 Describe the pictures. Guess what the text is about.

16 [1.07] Read and listen to the text. Why did Mo leave his home?

A hard journey

This is Mo. Six years ago, he was a normal, happy 13-year-old with big plans. He dreamt of becoming a doctor. Then war came to his city, and everything
5 changed. Mo managed to escape from Aleppo, along with his parents and little brother. Suddenly, they were refugees. Together they travelled 150 km through Syria to the border with Turkey. It was a very
10 dangerous journey. Most of the time they were on foot, but sometimes they travelled by lorry, hiding in the back with other terrified people. They continued through Turkey and then went on, by boat, to Greece. It's a short
15 distance, but the boat was small and held too many people. They were lucky to survive. A lot has happened since then. After two long years in refugee camps, the family flew to the UK and started a new life in
20 Bradford, in West Yorkshire.
'It was a big culture shock at first,' he told me. 'And it was so cold! But we've been here for four years, so we've settled in now. We've been lucky.'
Mo has never given up his dream, and 25 he hasn't wasted any time. He's been studying hard and he's learnt fluent English. In fact, he's just taken three A level exams (and he's already passed 8 GCSEs). 30
'I haven't had the results yet, of course, but I've applied to medical school,' he explained. 'My dream hasn't changed.'

British students take national exams called GCSEs (General Certificate of Secondary Education) when they are 16. They take further exams, called A (Advanced) levels, when they are 18.

VOCABULARY: Transport

17 PAIRWORK Which of these methods of transport do you use? Put them in order (1 = often, 6 = never / almost never). Then compare your answers.

I *often go to town by bus*. I *never travel by boat*.

- [ ] train
- [ ] bus
- [ ] tram
- [ ] the tube / underground
- [ ] ferry
- [ ] boat
- [ ] motor bike

- [ ] taxi
- [ ] lorry
- [ ] van
- [ ] plane
- [ ] car
- [ ] ship
- [ ] bike

GRAMMAR GUIDE

Perfect tenses

Present perfect

I've applied to medical school.

(Past activities connected to present and recently finished – time period continues.)

Present perfect continuous

He's been studying hard.

(Activities started in the past and continuing.)

 See **GRAMMAR REFERENCE** Workbook page 112

GRAMMAR GUIDE

Past participles: Regular and irregular forms

Regular: *walk – walked – walked*

Irregular: *drive – drove – driven*

Been v gone

Jack has **gone** *to France.*

(He's in France now.)

Jack has **been** *to France.*

(He isn't there now, but it's part of his experience.)

➡ See **GRAMMAR REFERENCE** Workbook page 112

18 Complete with the past simple and past participles of these irregular verbs. Then check on Workbook page 110.

0	be	**was / were – been**						
1	drive	....	6	fall	....	11	forget	....
2	fly	....	7	hide	....	12	give	....
3	go	....	8	lie	....	13	write	....
4	see	....	9	take	....	14	tell	....
5	come	....	10	do	....	15	sing	....

19 Write the present perfect or the present perfect continuous of the verbs in brackets.

0 Sam ...**has been packing**... (*pack*) for his holiday all morning but he ...**has forgotten**.... (*forget*) to book his ticket.

1 Wake up! We .... (*just / arrive*). You .... (*sleep*) for the whole journey!

2 I .... (*be*) to London twice but I .... (*not / be*) to Paris yet.

3 .... (*you / see*) Katie? .... (*she / text*) you? She's very late.

4 Oh no! I .... (*miss*) the bus, and it .... (*just / start*) to rain.

5 We .... (*wait*) for hours. .... (*the plane / land*) yet?

6 My parents .... (*have*) the same car for ten years. It .... (*never / go*) wrong.

7 The baby .... (*cry*) for hours. We .... (*try*) everything!

8 I .... (*know*) Jamie since we were both five. We .... (*always / be*) best friends.

20 Look back at the text on page 8 and underline examples of *just*, *already*, *yet*, *since* and *for*. Then choose the correct answer.

0 We use (*just*) / *yet* to show that an action has recently happened.

1 We use *already* / *yet* when an action happened sooner than expected.

2 We use *already* / *yet* for an action that we expect to happen soon.

3 We use *for* / *since* to talk about when a past activity started.

4 We use *for* / *since* to talk about the duration of an action.

21 Complete with *just*, *yet*, *already*, *for* or *since*.

0 Hey! I've ....**just**........ had a text from Joe! Look!

1 I don't want to watch that film. I've .... seen it three times.

2 Have you chosen your subjects for next year .... ?

3 Amy has been interested in history .... she went to Istanbul.

4 Hurry up! You've been getting ready .... ages!

5 Don't tell me the end of the story. I haven't finished the book ....

22 Rewrite the sentences so that they mean the same.

0 We've lived in this apartment for six years. We moved to this apartment ...**six years ago**.... .

1 My dad's been a teacher since 2015. My dad .... for .... years.

2 How long ago did you meet Ben? .... known Ben?

3 They built our school in 1900. Our school has been here ....

4 They started dancing hours ago and they're still dancing. They've ....

5 She started working on that chapter this morning. She's .... all day.

My future

Grammar: future simple and first conditional; degrees of certainty
Vocabulary: jobs

23 Have you thought about what to do when you leave school? What are your options?

---

http://www.focusonapprenticeships.com

Focus on ... APPRENTICESHIPS

Traditionally, apprentices trained to become skilled workers like plumbers, electricians or mechanics. However, these days there are many other apprentice schemes, for example for lawyers, accountants and engineers. Apprentices earn money while they learn how to do a job. They often go to college or university part-time. Their companies pay the tuition fees, and when they qualify, they already have a job.

In the UK apprenticeships are becoming a popular alternative to university; university courses are very expensive and students graduate with a very big debt.

I'll go to university if I pass my exams. If I don't get the right grades, maybe I'll try again next year. I won't know for sure until I get my results in August. I think I'll probably be OK.
Rosa

My sister's a student. When she graduates, she'll definitely owe a lot of money to the government. And unless she's lucky she probably won't even get a job at the end! On the other hand, she loves her subject, she'll get a degree – and she's having a great time!
Maya

I'm not sure about university. It's very expensive and it won't guarantee a job. I'd like to be a lawyer. I think I'll apply for an apprenticeship. That way, I'll start earning money as soon as I leave school and I'll learn lots of relevant skills.
Josh

24 [1.08] Read and listen to the text. Decide if the sentences are true (T) or false (F). Correct the false ones.

1 There are more apprentice schemes these days than in the past. ☐ T ☐ F
2 Apprentices don't study because they are working. ☐ T ☐ F
3 Rosa is planning to go to university. ☐ T ☐ F
4 Maya's sister hasn't graduated yet. ☐ T ☐ F
5 Josh thinks university is worth the money. ☐ T ☐ F

VOCABULARY: Jobs

25 Find the names of six jobs mentioned in the text. Use them to complete the notes.

0 _accountant_: someone who prepares financial records
1 ....: someone who works with gas and water
2 ....: someone who works with electrical things
3 ....: someone who designs machinery or roads
4 ....: someone who works with legal problems
5 ....: someone who repairs cars

26 Write your own notes about these jobs as in the previous exercise.

0 carpenter: *someone who* ...

1 pilot	4 builder	7 surgeon
2 soldier	5 actor	8 vet
3 architect	6 lecturer	9 dentist

GRAMMAR GUIDE

Future simple and first conditional

future simple
It **won't guarantee** a job.
She**'ll get** a degree.

first conditional
I**'ll go** to university **if** I **pass** my exams.
I **won't know** for sure **until** I **get** my results in August.
When she **graduates**, she**'ll** definitely **owe** a lot of money to the government.
Unless she**'s** lucky, she probably **won't** even **get** a job at the end!
I**'ll start** earning money **as soon as** I **leave** school.

Degrees of certainty:

- *She'll **definitely** owe a lot of money.* (100% sure)
- *I'll **probably** be OK.* (90% sure)
- ***Maybe** I'll try again next year.* (50% sure)

 See **GRAMMAR REFERENCE** Workbook page 115

27 Use the words below to make sentences in the future simple.

> tell you • ~~be a doctor one day~~ • stop now and relax • probably / go to the cinema • go to school today • maybe / go to Spain

0 He's a medical student. **He'll be a doctor one day.**

1 She doesn't feel well this morning.

2 They're thinking about a holiday.

3 I've been working for hours.

4 We're hoping to go out tonight.

5 Sorry. It's a secret.

28 Complete the questions.

0 What books ......**will I need**...... for next term? (*I / need*)

1 When .... our exam results? (*we / know*)

2 .... food at the party? (*there / be*)

3 .... me at the station? (*anybody / meet*)

4 How .... ? (*the story / end*)

5 How old .... on your next birthday? (*you / be*)

29 Complete with *if, unless, when, until* or *as soon as.* More than one answer is possible.

0 Jenny will be very upset ....**if**.......... she doesn't get good grades.

1 .... I leave school, I won't waste any time – I'll look for a job .... I can!

2 .... our team wins the match, we'll definitely celebrate.

3 We'll be broke .... we get jobs soon.

4 I think I'll wait .... I'm 18, and then decide what to do.

5 You'll never understand .... you ask questions.

30 [1.09] Write the future simple or present simple of the verbs in brackets. Then listen and check.

Becky I'd like to be an architect. But I
0 ....**won't have**.... (*not / have*) enough money to go to university unless I ¹.................... (*get*) a part-time job. If I ².................... (*do*) that, there ³.................... (*not / be*) time to study. Help!

David My dream is to be an actor. I want to go to drama school. It ⁴.................... (*be*) so cool if I ⁵.................... (*get*) in. The trouble is, I probably ⁶.................... (*not / be*) successful – it's very hard. Maybe I ⁷.................... (*not / apply*).

Stu I've got a university place for next year, but I'm worried about my mum. She's disabled and I usually help my dad look after her. If I ⁸.................... (*leave*) home, he ⁹.................... (*probably need*) to give up his job. It's a horrible problem.

31 Look at exercise 30 again. Match the replies to Becky, David and Stu. What do you think they should do?

0 Go for it! You'll never know unless you try! **David**

1 If you borrow the money, you won't need a part-time job.

2 If you talk it over together, I'm sure you'll find a solution.

3 If you don't get in, there will be another chance next year.

4 I think your parents will be happy if you're happy.

5 If you qualify as an architect, you won't have any more money problems.

Cheap clothes

Grammar: subject and object questions; direct and indirect questions
Vocabulary: shops

32 Describe the photos and look at the title of the text. What do you think it is about?

---

http://www.susiejacksonreports.com

SUSIE JACKSON REPORTS Ethical Fashion – What Is It, And Why Does It Matter?

We all love a bargain, especially when we're clothes shopping – but why are some clothes so much cheaper than others? I asked ethical fashion designer Tania Roberts.

Can you tell me where these cheap clothes come from? Who makes them?
A lot of the clothes in high-street shops come from factories in poor countries.
5 Wages for the workers are very low there.

But they have jobs. That's good, isn't it?
Yes, it is, except often their lives are terrible.

What do you mean?
They work very long hours and often the conditions aren't safe. Worst of all, quite young
10 children often work in those factories. They should be at school but their parents don't earn enough.

That's terrible! Next time I buy clothes, I'll want to know if the workers had fair pay and good working conditions – so what can I do?
Look for a fair-trade label on your clothes. OK, you might pay more but it's worth it.

15 **But I've never seen a fair-trade label on clothes! Do you know where I can buy them?**
It's not very easy at the moment, it's true.
But more and more independent shops are taking an interest, as well as some high-end designer shops and department stores.
20 You can also research it online. Try googling *ethical fashion* and you'll be surprised. If you care enough, you can find out.

---

33 🔊 **[1.10] Read and listen to the text. Decide if the sentences are true (T) or false (F). Correct the false ones.**

1 The article is mainly about factories in poor countries. T F
2 Tania Roberts says that factory workers often don't get enough money. T F
3 If you see a *fair-trade* label, you'll know the clothes are expensive. T F
4 You can buy *fair-trade* clothes only in a few shops. T F

VOCABULARY: Shops

34 Match the shops to the descriptions. Can you think of local examples?

0 a chain store
1 ☐ corner shop   2 ☐ delicatessen
3 ☐ department store   4 ☐ supermarket

a a shop that has branches all over the country
b a very large shop that sells lots of different kinds of things
c a small shop that sells basic, everyday things
d a large food shop where the customers walk around
e a shop that sells special *luxury* food

GRAMMAR GUIDE

Subject and object questions

Subject questions:

- 'Who *likes fashion?' 'I like fashion.*'
- '*What caused the accident?*'
  '*The rain caused the accident.*'

Object questions:

- '*Which jacket do you like?' 'I like* **the blue jacket**.'
- '*Who did they ask?' 'They asked* **the teacher**.'

 See **GRAMMAR REFERENCE** Workbook page 116

35 **Complete the questions. Which ones are subject questions?**

1 **A** What ⁰ _did you buy_ (you / buy) yesterday?
   B I bought some new shoes and a T-shirt.
   A What colour **1** .... (be) the T-shirt?
   B Red.

2 **A** Where **2** .... (you / go) at the weekend?
   B I went to a rock concert in London.
   A Wow. Who **3** .... (pay) for the ticket?
   B My parents. It was my birthday present.

3 **A** Which cake **4** .... (look) the nicest?
     What **5** .... (you / think)?
   B The chocolate one!

4 **A** Who **6** .... (you / wait) for?
   B I'm waiting for Harry.
   A Oh. Who **7** .... (be) Harry?
   B He's my brother.

36 **Write the questions. Start with *What*, *Which* or *Who*.**

0 ' _What are you reading_ . ?' 'I'm reading **a sci-fi book**.'

1 '......................... ?' '**English** is my favourite subject.'

2 '......................... ?' 'I chose **the blue dress**.'

3 '......................... ?' '**My uncle** taught my sister to drive.'

4 '......................... ?' 'Jack gave his mum **some flowers**.'

5 '......................... ?' 'I was chatting to **Bernie**.'

GRAMMAR GUIDE

Direct and indirect questions

- *What's your name?*
  Could you tell me **what your name is**?

- *What do you think?*
  Would you mind telling me **what you think**?

- *Who did you see?*
  Can you say **who you saw**?

- *Are you ready?*
  Could you tell me <u>if</u> **you're ready**?

- *Do they live here?*
  Would you mind telling me <u>whether</u> **they live here**?

- *Has it started yet?*
  Do you know <u>if</u> **it's started yet**?

 See **GRAMMAR REFERENCE** Workbook page 116

37 **Write the direct or indirect questions. Use expressions from the Grammar guide. More than one answer can be correct.**

0 How old are you?
   Could you tell me how old you are?

1 Could you tell me where the post office is, please?

2 How long does the journey take?

3 Do you know what the weather is like in Istanbul?

4 Is that Henry over there?

5 Would you mind telling me what you thought of the film?

6 Are we nearly home?

7 Can you tell me if this is the train to Manchester, please?

38 **Rewrite the questions using the verbs in brackets.**

0 How much does it cost? (know)
   Do you know how much it costs?

1 Can you tell me if the supermarket is open? (is)

2 Are these Toby's books? (tell)

3 Do you know when the term starts? (does)

4 What's this? (do)

5 What do they want to eat? (could)

6 Is Sally OK? (can)

7 Which room is the exam in? (do)

8 Could you tell me the answer to the question? (is)

1 Communication

Latest

EXAM STRATEGIES

- B2 FIRST: Reading, Speaking and Listening
- IGCSE: Reading, Speaking and Listening
- IELTS: Reading, Speaking and Listening

SPEAKING SKILLS

- Recounting a story

CHANGING LANGUAGE

- Narrative tenses

LIFE SKILLS

- Communication skills

Learning goals

Grammar

- Past tenses review
- Past simple v past perfect

Vocabulary

- Correspondence

LEAD IN

1 Look at the photos. What is breaking news? What kind of stories appear on breaking news?

2 ⏵ [1.11] Read, listen and watch. How have phones changed the way news is reported?

BREAKING NEWS

Has your TV show ever been interrupted by a special news report? Or perhaps you have received a notification on your phone that someone is broadcasting live. Since the
5 arrival of the internet, we have been able to receive the latest news as it happens.
Sixty years ago, most people either relied on a TV or radio news bulletin once or twice a day, or read a printed newspaper. Live TV
10 reports were only possible if the journalists and camera crew were in the right place at the right time. Newspapers were out of date even before they left the printing presses. It's very different these days. We
15 have 24-hour news channels constantly updating their information, and news is also communicated via social networks like Twitter and Facebook.
These days most people carry a mini-
20 computer, complete with a camera and microphone, in their pockets.

Now everyone can be an instant news reporter. For example, when a powerful earthquake struck central Italy in 2016, the news spread around the world in minutes. 25 Buildings were still shaking when the rescue effort started. While survivors were still appearing from the ruins, offers of help were flooding in. The latest technology undoubtedly saved lives. 30
However, is this new world of *rolling news* always a good thing? Some experts think it has harmed us. They say it has brought war and suffering into our living rooms and made it normal. They say we have lost our 35 sensitivity. Perhaps they are right.

PRACTICE

3 **[1.11]** **Read, listen and watch the video again. Choose the correct option.**

1 The text is mainly about:
   A technology.
   B reporting the news.
   C journalists.

2 The text mentions the Italian earthquake:
   A to show the value of smartphones.
   B to describe how people help each other.
   C to explain the power of earthquakes.

3 The writer:
   A supposes things were better 60 years ago.
   B believes things are better now.
   C does not express an opinion.

GRAMMAR GUIDE

Past tenses review

Past simple v past continuous

- Newspapers **were** out of date even before they **left** the printing presses.
- Buildings **were** still **shaking** <u>when</u> the rescue effort **started**.
- <u>While</u> survivors **were** still **appearing** from the ruins, offers of help **were flooding** in.

Past simple v present perfect

- Sixty years <u>ago</u>, most people **relied** on a news bulletin.
- <u>Since</u> the arrival of smartphones, Facebook, Twitter and web channels **have overtaken** TV.
- Many people **have not bought** a printed newspaper <u>for</u> years.

➡ See **GRAMMAR REFERENCE** Workbook page 116

4 **Complete the rules. Write** *past simple*, *past continuous* **or** *present perfect*. **Find examples in the text.**

1 The .... and the .... describe past events that are completed.

2 The .... describes past actions or events that still affect us now.

3 To measure a period of time from now back to a past event, we can use the .... with *for* + the length of time or *since* + a fixed time.

5 **Choose the correct option.**

1 An earthquake (*has struck*) / *struck* Japan early this morning, while most people *have slept* / *were sleeping*. So far we *have not received* / *didn't receive* any reports of serious injuries.

2 Where *have you bought* / *did you buy* that phone? I*'ve never seen* / *was never seeing* one like that. *Have you got* / *Did you get* it online?

3 I *haven't watched* / *didn't watch* the news last night. I *have written* / *was writing* an essay all evening and then I *fell* / *was falling* asleep on the sofa.

6 **Read and complete with the verbs in brackets. Use the past simple, past continuous or present perfect form.**

Mary **⁰** **Have you heard** ... (*you / hear*) the news? A big hole **¹** .... (*appear*) in the middle of the High Street. A car **²** .... (*fall*) into it. The police **³** .... (*just / arrive*). I'm watching from my window.

Di Wow! The same thing **⁴** .... (*happen*) a few weeks ago somewhere in Manchester, I think. I **⁵** .... (*see*) it on the news. A man **⁶** .... (*walk*) his dog when the pavement suddenly **⁷** .... (*open*) up. What's happening now?

Mary They **⁸** .... (*rescue*) the driver, and now they **⁹** .... (*start*) telling people to leave their houses. A lot of people are standing around. They **¹⁰** .... (*not / leave*) yet. One man **¹¹** .... (*obviously / have*) .... a bath when they **¹²** .... (*knock*) on his door – he's wearing a towel.

Di What about you? **¹³** .... (*they / knock*) on your door yet?

Mary No, they **¹⁴** .... (*have not*) yet. But I'd better get dressed.

7 **SPEAKING** **Practise the above conversation in pairs.**

READING SKILLS

LEAD IN

8 PAIRWORK Answer these questions. Then share your answers with the class.

1 How often do you look at blogs or vlogs?
2 Have you got a favourite?
3 Why do you (or don't you) like them?
4 Do you have your own blog or vlog?

PRACTICE

9 [1.12] Read and listen to the article. Which bloggers does it mention?

READING STRATEGY

Understand paragraphs

Paragraphs usually have clear themes. When you know what a paragraph is about, it is easier to understand the whole text.

- Read the first sentence of each paragraph.
- Try and predict what each paragraph is about.
- Then read the whole paragraph again carefully.

B2 FIRST | IGCSE | IELTS

10 Read the article again and match the paragraphs to the correct heading. There is one extra heading.

1 ☐ Blog your way to fame and fortune
2 ☐ Blogging takes off
3 ☐ Progress?
4 ☐ Screens v paper
5 ☐ Blogging for health and happiness
6 ☐ What's in a blog?

11 PAIRWORK Read the article again. Then answer the questions.

1 What is the blogosphere?
2 Why does the article say it exploded?
3 According to the article, what subjects are blogs usually about?
4 How long did it take Ryan Higa to attract 3 million followers? How old was he then?
5 What are *blooks* and why does the article mention them?
6 According to the article, what do today's parents have in common with parents of 60 years ago?

WELCOME TO THE BLOGOSPHERE!

A Blogging, when it first started, was not an overnight sensation. The first blog appeared on a website in 1994. Five years later, in 1999, the total number of blogs on the internet was only 23! However, by 2016 that figure had gone up to a staggering 150 million. Someone, somewhere in the world, was creating a new blog (or vlog) every half a second. The blogosphere had exploded! ⁵

B These days there are blogs about everything and anything – from cookery and lifestyle advice to social issues and politics. Many offer pure entertainment, with music, comedy, acting and dance. Some express intensely personal thoughts, others remain detached – the most popular ones are often a mixture of both. ¹⁵

C Most bloggers and vloggers do it for fun, not for a living. On the other hand, some have attracted armies of fans or followers. It has made them

12 Critical thinking Answer the questions and then share your ideas with the class.

1 Why do people produce blogs and vlogs?
2 Do you think blogs and vlogs are killing books? Why / Why not?

GRAMMAR GUIDE

Past simple v past perfect

past simple	past perfect
The first blog **appeared** on a website <u>in 1994</u>.	<u>By 2016</u> that figure **had gone up** to 150 million.

Look at these differences in the time sequence.

*We **got up** late, **had** breakfast and **went** out.* (The actions happened one after the other.)

*He **had read** all the Harry Potter books **by the time** he **was** 12.* (He read them before he was 12.)

 See **GRAMMAR REFERENCE** Workbook page 116

BLOG

extremely wealthy, and opened up a world of new opportunities. When he was 17, Ryan Higa started making short, funny videos of himself and his friends. He posted them on a web channel. Within four years his channel had gained 3 million subscribers. That was in 2010. Six years later, that number had multiplied by six. By then Ryan had become a successful actor as well as seriously rich. 20

D Are blogs and vlogs killing books and the love of reading? Some people believe that they are. Others point out that successful bloggers are skilled writers, and that they actually encourage reading. Moreover, some bloggers, and vloggers too, have started producing books (*blooks*). For example, the fashion vlogger Zoella published her first book, *Girl Online*, in 2014. It sold over 75,000 copies in its first week alone. 30

E The truth is, technology has always brought fears for the future. Sixty years ago, parents and teachers worried about the effect of TV on young people. When video games became popular, many adults expressed similar fears. These days some people say the same about the internet. What will today's teenagers say about tomorrow's world? Only time will tell! 35

13 Complete the rules. Write *past simple* or *past perfect*. Find examples in the text.

1 If we are simply describing single, completed past events we use the ....

2 If we want to show the sequence of events, we often use the two tenses close together. The .... describes the event that happened first.

14 Complete the sentences with the past simple or past perfect form of the verbs in brackets.

1 I .**d already read**.. (already / read) the book before we .... (study) it in class.

2 Stuart .... (go) to India last year. He .... (never / be) abroad before.

3 By the time we .... (arrive) at the theatre, the play .... (already / start).

4 Rick .... (move) to Germany when he .... (be) ten. When we met a year later, he .... (learn) the language.

5 How .... (you / know) all the answers? .... (you / see) the questions before we .... (take) the exam?

WRITING SKILLS

LEAD IN

15 Read the information and do the task. You are going to write part of a travel blog. It can be about a real or imaginary trip or holiday. It's the end of Day 1. Think about these questions and make notes.

1 Where are you? How are you feeling?

2 What was the journey like?

3 What have you done / seen so far?

PRACTICE

16 Tell your partner about your day. Use the questions above to ask and answer questions and add to or change your notes.

WRITING STRATEGY

Write a travel blog

A blog is a story or a diary of a journey or events in someone's life. It is usually online. The writer adds to it from day to day.

- A blog can become a vlog if it has videos with it.
- A blog has an informal style. It usually includes some personal feelings, thoughts and reactions.
- A blog also includes descriptions to give it colour and be attractive.
- A blog normally has a title, so that it attracts attention and followers.

 See **WRITING EXPANSION** page 124

VOCABULARY

Correspondence

17 PAIRWORK Which do you prefer? Discuss and then share with the class.

1 text or call?
2 email or instant message?
3 birthday card or e-card?
4 blog or vlog?

18 Read the text. What does *media bombardment* mean?

Teenager, Screenager

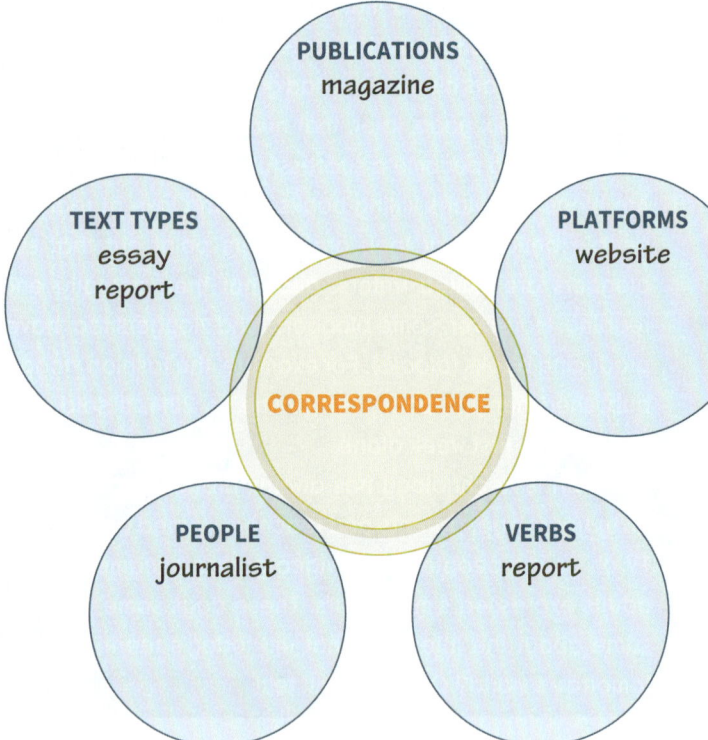

How much time do you spend every day in front of a screen? These days the average teenager spends at least four hours a day with screen media, and for many it is a lot more. Not only that, many teenagers are comfortable ⁵ with multitasking – e.g., doing their homework while watching TV, or chatting online while watching a film. Watching TV or videos is the most popular activity, followed ¹⁰ by playing video games and using social media. According to a recent survey, boys spend an average of 56 minutes a day playing video games, while the ¹⁵ average for girls is seven. On the other hand, girls spend more time on social media than boys.

Parents and teachers worry that multitasking affects concentration, ²⁰ although many teenagers insist that it does not. In particular, about 80% said that listening to music helps their work. Some even prefer studying in a noisy environment like a coffee shop ²⁵ rather than the calm of their bedrooms. Experts say that more research is needed. Meanwhile one thing is certain, *media bombardment* is not going away.

19 Critical thinking Discuss the questions in pairs.

1 Are you a *screenager*? Do you think the text is true of you and your friends?
2 Do you ever multitask? If so, what do you do?
3 Do you agree that music helps concentration? If so, what kind of music?

20 Put the words into the correct categories. What is special about the grey words?

blog ▪ blogger ▪ block ▪ call ▪ comic ▪ comment ▪ ~~essay~~ ▪ follow ▪ follower ▪ ~~journalist~~ ▪ leaflet ▪ ~~magazine~~ ▪ message ▪ ~~report~~ ▪ social media ▪ message board ▪ newspaper ▪ novelist ▪ post ▪ share ▪ text ▪ troll ▪ update ▪ ~~website~~

PUBLICATIONS
magazine

TEXT TYPES
essay
report

PLATFORMS
website

CORRESPONDENCE

PEOPLE
journalist

VERBS
report

21 Complete the sentences with the verbs below.

block ▪ comment ▪ follow ▪ give ▪ post ▪ share ▪ text ▪ update ▪ write

1 I have to .... a history essay tonight.
2 Next time you're in town, ... me a call.
3 I must .... my blog with the latest news.
4 If you .... an ad online, I'm sure you'll get some replies.
5 I'll .... this picture with my friends. They'll like it.
6 .... me when your train gets in. I'll come and meet you.
7 I'm going to .... on this article. I don't agree with it at all.
8 Do you .... many celebrities online?
9 Don't let trolls upset you – just .... them!

22 SPEAKING Look back at exercise 17. What other ways of correspondence are there?

 See **VOCABULARY EXTENSION** page 134

SPEAKING SKILLS

Recounting a story

23 PAIRWORK Discuss these questions.

1 When do you need to call emergency services (ambulance, police, fire brigade)?

2 Have you ever called emergency services? What happened?

24 ▶ ◀ [1.13] **Listen and watch the video. What did the firefighters do?**

key expressions	
recount a story	ask questions
☐ Guess what? ☐ Well, … ☐ First, then, after that ☐ In the end …	☐ What happened (next)? ☐ Who? ☐ Why? ☐ When? ☐ How? ☐ What happened in the end?

25 ▶ ◀ [1.13] **Listen and watch again and tick (✓) the key expressions you hear.**

SPEAKING STRATEGY

Ask for clarification

We ask for clarification to check that we understand what the other person is saying. Use these phrases:

☐ *No way! Really?*
☐ *What do you mean (by that)?*
☐ *Do you mean …?*
☐ *What was that again?*
☐ *Did you say …?*
☐ *… (is that) right?*

B2 FIRST | IGCSE | IELTS

26 ▶ ◀ [1.13] **Listen and watch again and tick (✓) the expressions from the strategy box you hear.**

27 PAIRWORK Think of another story. Use these questions and the key expressions to help you.

- Where were you?
- What did you first see / hear / think?
- What happened next?

CHANGING LANGUAGE

Narrative tenses

28 Match the past tenses to the correct timeline.

past continuous ▪
past simple ▪ past perfect

1 ....
8 am   9 am   10 am   now

2 ....
8 am   9 am   10 am   now

3 ....
8 am   9 am   10 am   now

past simple

29 ▶ **Watch the video and check your answers from exercise 28.**

CORPUS

The correct tenses to talk about past narratives are:
- past simple for finished activities
- past continuous for past activities in progress at a set time
- past perfect for past activities that happened before other past activities

However, native speakers sometimes use present tenses in spoken narratives to give a story more immediacy. But be careful – this is only used in informal spoken English and occasionally in written fiction.

LISTENING SKILLS

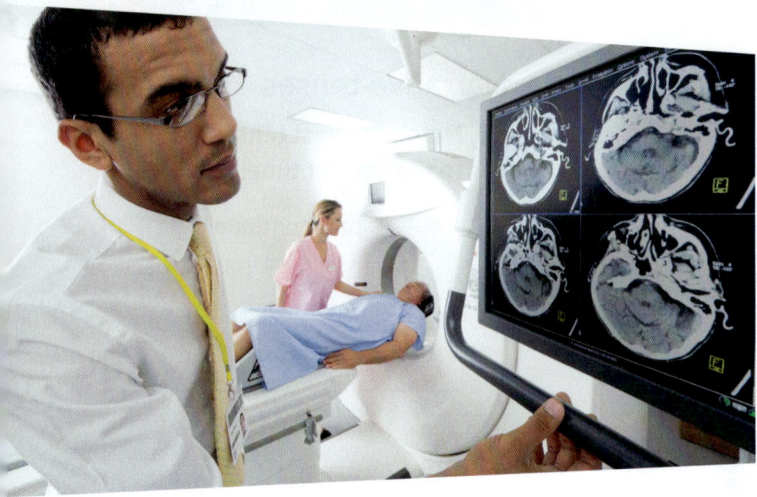

LEAD IN

30 PAIRWORK Look at the photos and discuss these questions.

1 What's happening in the photos?
2 How old were you when you started using digital devices?

PRACTICE

31 [1.14] Now read and listen to the first part of the talk. Underline the important words.

'Technology is changing the way we communicate with each other. That much we know. But is it changing *more* than just the way we communicate? Scientists believe that it is. They think that the use of social media in particular is actually changing our brains.'

LISTENING STRATEGY

Use context to understand unknown words

Use these strategies to help you with words you don't know:

- use keywords you know to help you understand the general gist of the text.
- the context around the words will help you guess what they mean.
- if the word resembles a word you already know or is similar to a word in your language, it will help you guess its meaning.

B2 FIRST | IGCSE | IELTS

32 PAIRWORK Look at the words below. Tick (✓) the ones you think you might hear.

- [ ] concentrate
- [ ] internet
- [ ] drugs
- [ ] brain
- [ ] health
- [ ] games
- [ ] relationship
- [ ] social media
- [ ] addict
- [ ] emoji
- [ ] emotion
- [ ] parents

33 [1.15] Listen to the complete talk. Guess the meaning of these words and expressions.

1 drug addiction: ....
2 brain scan: ....
3 mental health: ....
4 face-to-face: ....
5 dating site: ....
6 empathise: ....

34 [1.15] Listen again and complete the sentences.

1 Scientists think that the use of social media is ....
2 About .... of internet users are addicted to it.
3 The changes make it harder for us to make .... and control ....
4 ....% of what we put online is about ourselves.
5 Emoticons and emoji make us less able to ....
6 Couples who meet online have a .... chance of a successful relationship than other couples.

35 SPEAKING From your own experience, do you think the speaker is right?

Communication skills

Barriers to communication

If you've ever tried to talk to someone through a closed window, you know what a communication barrier is like. But physical barriers are not the only kind; there are also invisible barriers to communication. In some ways, these are more difficult to overcome because   5
we may not be aware of them.

Language barriers

There is obviously a barrier when two people don't speak the same language. But even if they do, they might not understand each other's version of it. If you are speaking to someone from a different background,   10
you need to adjust the way you speak to avoid the local slang you normally use. Similarly, if the other person does not share your specialist interest, you need to avoid using the jargon that goes with it.

Psychological barriers

Emotions may form a psychological barrier to   15
communication. It is difficult to reason with a very angry person, and someone who is stressed will find it difficult to pay attention. But there may be longer-term barriers. For example, a person with low self-esteem may feel that everything that people say to them has a hidden   20
negative meaning. We need to be aware of these psychological barriers in the people we speak to, but also in ourselves.

Listening barriers

Communication is a two-way process, and if one of the participants is not interested, that is obviously a serious   25
barrier. However, a listening barrier may be quite hard to detect – especially in yourself. Often, in conversation, we spend the time when we should be listening, planning what we are going to say next instead. This means we are not really listening. To be effective   30
communicators, we need to try to understand the other's point of view, rather than focusing only on our own concerns.

LEAD IN

36 PAIRWORK Discuss these questions.

1   You have something important to tell someone. What do you do?
2   A friend is sharing a problem with you. What do you do?

PRACTICE

37 PAIRWORK Look at the photos. Then read the article and answer the questions. Compare and discuss.

1   How do the photos relate to the content of the article?
2   Match each photo to a section of the article and explain how it relates to that section.

38 THINKING FURTHER Discuss these questions.

1   Do you think you have good communication skills? Why / Why not?
2   Read the tips below. What can you do to improve your communication skills?
3   How can you help to remove communication barriers in your daily life?

LIFE STRATEGY

Tips for communication skills

- Listen and try to understand the other person's point of view, rather than worrying about what you're going to say.
- Don't speak in anger. If you are in an emotional state, stay calm and count to ten before you reply.
- Don't go into a conversation with the attitude that you are right. Keep an open mind.
- Remember the world is not all about you. Don't look for hidden negative meanings about you in everything the other person says.
- Be aware of the limitations of different means of communication. An email that you think is brief and informative may seem rude to the other person.
- Pay attention to the other person's body language and be aware of your own.

39 TASK In groups look at the final tip in the strategy box, then read the situations and say what the body language means.

1   boy with his arms folded
2   girl yawning
3   girl holding her head in her hands

2 Advertising

EXAM STRATEGIES

- B2 FIRST: Reading, Writing, Speaking and Listening
- IGCSE: Reading, Speaking, Listening and Academic
- IELTS: Reading, Speaking and Listening

SPEAKING SKILLS

- Persuading

ACADEMIC SKILLS

- Note taking

Learning goals

Grammar

- Direct and reported speech
- Reported questions

Vocabulary

- Emotive words

LEAD IN

1 PAIRWORK Describe the photos and answer the questions.

1 What do you think connects the two pictures?
2 Which advertisements do you remember from when you were younger?

2 ▶ ◀[1.16] Read, listen and watch. What do you think the heading means?

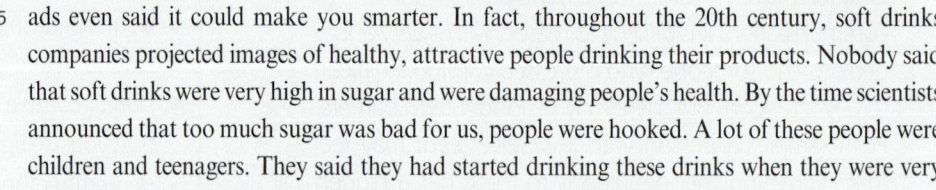

SUGAR IS NOT AS SWEET AS YOU THINK

Believe it or not, in the late nineteenth century, Coca-Cola syrup (the basis of the fizzy drink) was actually sold as a medicine. People were told it would get rid of fatigue and headaches. Later advertisements actually showed nurses drinking Coke and serving it to patients. Some
5 ads even said it could make you smarter. In fact, throughout the 20th century, soft drinks companies projected images of healthy, attractive people drinking their products. Nobody said that soft drinks were very high in sugar and were damaging people's health. By the time scientists announced that too much sugar was bad for us, people were hooked. A lot of these people were children and teenagers. They said they had started drinking these drinks when they were very
10 young. No one told them that the advertisers had been deliberately targeting them all along. Meanwhile, scientists researching health and nutrition said that they had found a link between sugar and serious illnesses, such as cancer and diabetes. As a result, governments in many countries pressured food companies and fast food restaurants to make their products healthier or stop advertising them altogether. Some countries went even further.
15 In Quebec, Canada, they passed a law which prohibited fast food marketing to children under 13. As result, Quebec has the lowest obesity rates in Canada. In France, authorities said that ads for products containing added fats, sweeteners, or sodium had to contain healthy eating advice. Product labels now told the public to eat fruit and vegetables daily. Then a decade ago, the UK banned television ads of foods high in fats, sugar, and salt to children under 16.
20 Government efforts and an increased awareness of the dangers of sugar have made large food and drinks companies produce less harmful products. Coca-Cola, for example, has recently announced that it is trying to reduce sugar levels in its products in Australia and New Zealand by 10 per cent. Although these changes are positive, we still all need to pay attention to what we're eating and not believe everything that the ads tell us!

PRACTICE

3 ▶ ◀ [1.16] **Read, listen and watch the video again. Then choose the correct statement.**

1 In the past …
   A soft drinks ads were not truthful.
   B people believed Coca-Cola could make them more intelligent.

2 By the time sugar was declared unhealthy, …
   A many young people had become addicted.
   B many ads had been banned.

3 *Research in health and nutrition* led to …
   A new laws.   B changes in public opinion.

4 **Look at the Grammar guide. Complete the gaps in the table with examples from the text.**

5 **Transform the sentences from direct speech to reported speech.**

0 'Sheen Shampoo will make your hair shine.'
   They told me …**(that) Sheen Shampoo would make my hair shine** .

1 'It's very expensive.' He said …

2 'We can't afford it.' She said …

3 'I don't like it very much.' He said …

4 'You must try it!' She told him …

5 'I won't spend much.' She said …

6 'I didn't buy anything.' He told us …

6 **Complete the reports.**

0 'Sugar is bad for you.'
   They were told **(that) sugar was bad for them.**

1 'The advertisements aren't telling the truth.'
   Scientists said that ....

2 'Soft drinks will give you energy.' The ads told them
   that ....

3 'Sugar has been causing illnesses for decades.'
   Scientists claimed ....

4 'Ads have to contain healthy eating advice.'
   Authorities in France said that ....
   ....

5 'Eat more green vegetables.' The nutritionist told
   me ....

7 **SPEAKING You recently bought a new phone, but you don't like it.**

1 Decide what is wrong with it.

2 Go to the shop to complain. Use reported speech.
   The ad said that … but …

GRAMMAR GUIDE

Direct and reported speech

direct speech	reported speech
Present simple 'Too much sugar **is** bad for you.'	**Past simple** Scientists said that too much sugar ^{0} ...**was**... bad for us.
Present continuous 'The soft drink **is damaging** your health.'	**Past continuous** Nobody said that ^{1} ....
Past simple 'We **started** drinking Coke when we were very young.'	**Past perfect** They said that ^{2} ....
Past continuous 'Advertisers **were targeting** us.'	**Past perfect continuous** No one told them that advertisers ^{3} ....
Present perfect 'We **have found** a link between sugar and serious illnesses.'	**Past perfect** Scientists said that they ^{4} ....
will 'It **will get rid of** fatigue and headaches.'	**would** People were told it ^{5} ....
can 'Coca-Cola **can** make you smarter.'	**could** The ad said ^{6} ....
must / have to 'Ads **have to contain** healthy eating advice.'	**had to** The government said that ^{7} ....

Look!: *tell* + direct object:

*They told **us** / **everyone** / **him** … (that) it was safe.*

Be careful with pronouns:

*Too much sugar is bad for **you**.*

→

*Scientists said that too much sugar was bad for **us**.*

➡ See **GRAMMAR REFERENCE** Workbook page 117

READING SKILLS

LEAD IN

8 PAIRWORK Discuss these questions.

1 Do you think you are influenced by advertisements?

2 Brainstorm some advertisements that you think are effective.

3 How do they work?

PRACTICE

9 **[1.17] Read and listen to the text. What is the best definition of a *glamping holiday*?**

1 A luxury camping holiday.

2 An outdoor sports holiday.

3 A glamorous, luxurious holiday.

> ### 🌐 READING STRATEGY
>
> **Read between the lines**
>
> Often what is *not* said is as important as what *is* said. Think about:
>
> - the purpose of the text
> - the vocabulary used
> - how much factual information is given
>
> B2 FIRST | IGCSE | IELTS

10 Read the first section of the text again. Find these emotive words and expressions and match them to their meanings.

1 ☐	the great outdoors	**a**	most comfortable
2 ☐	home comforts	**b**	with lots of furniture
3 ☐	a leisurely bike ride	**c**	outside
4 ☐	lavishly furnished	**d**	a short distance by bike
5 ☐	generously equipped	**e**	things you have at home
6 ☐	cosiest	**f**	with lots of equipment

11 These extracts from the text give us information without stating it. What do they tell us?

0 oil lamps, torches and candles provided

   there's no electricity

1 access to running water

2 outdoor cooking facilities including barbecue

3 luxury shower and toilet facilities on site

4 When did you last see the stars in a black sky? Or hear nothing but the crackle of a warm fire?

DREAMGLAMP
❄ Holidays with a difference

- ✔ fully equipped with bedding and towels
- ✔ oil lamps, torches and candles provided
- ✔ access to running water
- ✔ wood-burning stove (and plenty of wood!)
- 5 ✔ outdoor cooking facilities including barbecue
- ✔ luxury shower and toilet facilities on site
- ✔ woodland setting
- ✔ farm shop with delivery service
- ✔ cycle hire available

10 Do you love the great outdoors, but still need your home comforts?

Are you looking for an affordable holiday while dreaming of glamour and luxury?

Yes? Then here's the perfect solution – come glamping

15 with us!

Choose from our range of luxury yurts or state-of-the-art pods. Situated in extensive woodland, and a leisurely bike ride away from the beautiful Norfolk coast, they are all lavishly furnished and generously equipped with

20 everything you could possibly wish for. We even provide books and games for those rainy days.

Our wonderful yurts come in a range of sizes – the smallest (and cosiest) are perfect for two, and

25 the largest will accommodate up to eight people.

You'll find soft comfortable beds and colourful rugs and cushions. The wood-burning stove will

30 keep you warm and we provide

12 Read the text again. Decide if the sentences are true (T), false (F) or doesn't say (DS). Correct the false ones.

1	The site is near the sea.	T	F	DS
2	There are outdoor taps.	T	F	DS
3	You have to cook outside.	T	F	DS
4	*jacksmyname* didn't think it was comfortable.	T	F	DS
5	*dunglamping* had expected better facilities.	T	F	DS

everything you need to prepare your meal over an open fire.

35 Or perhaps you fancy staying in an eco pod. Suitable for couples or small family groups, our pods are the ultimate in stylish adventure.

40 They offer all the comforts of the yurts, with the addition of hard wooden floors and separate rooms for living and sleeping. When did you last see the stars in a black sky? Or hear nothing but the crackle of a warm fire? Now's your chance! Contact us now for

45 further details.

REVIEWS

jamie28 ★★★★★ Thank you for a fabulous weekend. We didn't really believe it would be as good as your description, but it was even better! We'll be back.

happycamper ★★★★
50 We had a great time, especially the kids. Just one thing – the advert said the yurts were warm, but actually ours was either freezing cold or boiling hot. Otherwise, all good.

gladtomeetyou ★★★ We were a bit disappointed. The brochure said that the yurt would be big enough for eight, but it wasn't. However, the setting is wonderful and it's true, the yurt was comfortable. Just not
55 spacious enough for our lively extended family!

jacksmyname ★★ Not a great experience – we won't be going again. The website is misleading. For example, we didn't take any food because it said that the farm shop would deliver, but when we got there it was closed. We had to drive for miles to find a supermarket. And there weren't enough
60 towels for a family of five. Luckily we'd brought some of our own. So be warned – check everything before you get there!

dunglamping ★ Oh dear! We didn't realise there wasn't any electricity in the yurts – or that you had to go to the farm shop to get a wi-fi signal. And worst of all – nobody told us the yurts didn't have
65 bathrooms. I don't call it luxury if you have to go outside to find a toilet in the middle of the night! Really horrible – never again!

13 Critical thinking Discuss these questions.

1 Do you think the ad was truthful? Why / Why not?

2 Do you think the problems the holidaymakers had were their fault (they didn't read the ads properly) or were the company's fault or no one's fault?

3 Can you think of an example of either something you bought or a place you went to that was very different from the ad?

WRITING SKILLS

LEAD IN

14 Most emails are informal, but some have to be formal. Tick (✓) the occasions when this is the case.

☐ applying for a job
☐ complaining
☐ requesting information
☐ describing an event
☐ reporting lost property

PRACTICE

15 Match the informal to the formal expressions.

1 ☐ Hi!
2 ☐ I'm writing …
3 ☐ I want …
4 ☐ Can you …
5 ☐ How much …?
6 ☐ Speak soon,
7 ☐ Love,

a I look forward to hearing from you,
b Dear …
c Could you …
d Yours sincerely,
e I would like …
f I am writing …
g I would like to know how much …

WRITING STRATEGY

Write a formal email

A formal email is an email that you write when you want to communicate to a company or an organisation. It contains:

- formal language (so no contractions or slang expressions)
- a very clear purpose, that is normally at the beginning
- a clear outcome, that is normally at the end

B2 FIRST

See **WRITING EXPANSION** page 125

VOCABULARY

Emotive words

16 Look at these headlines. Would you click on them? Why / Why not?

> **10 things you probably thought were good for you**

> **These kids are millionaires – you'll be amazed at how they did it** Click here!

17 **PAIRWORK** Choose one of the headlines and imagine what the story is.

18 Read the text. Find some examples of emotive words.

WORD OF THE WEEK: clickbait

What is clickbait?
Clickbait has only been a word since 2006. It's a catchy headline on a website that persuades you to click on it. Every click earns money for the website. **5**

Why? How? I'm confused.
If a website gets a lot of clicks, advertisers will pay to advertise with them. **10**

So clickbait is a kind of advertisement?
Exactly.

Can you give me some examples?
Sure. They all rely on emotive words to attract the reader, but there are several different styles. **15**
First, lists. You know, this kind of thing:
• 20 ways to look fabulous
• 10 photos that will amaze you
Second, a clue to the story and then a tempting comment: **20**
This dog has won a medal – but how?
Scientists have made a surprise discovery – and it's stunning!
Third, a dramatic word to attract the reader, and then **25**
a brief summary:
WOW! The Hollywood stars were out last night!
REVEALED: Supermarket Secrets

So now I know, I'll never click again.
I bet you do! **30**

19 Read the text again and answer the questions.

1 How is *clickbait* different from a normal headline?
2 Why do websites use them?
3 How do they persuade people to click on them?

20 **PAIRWORK** Look at the headlines, discuss what they mean, and then make them neutral.

0 Devastating defeat for United
United lost a match
1 Hooligans smash shop windows, causing chaos
2 Furious driver attacks elderly cyclist
3 Brave cops catch thieves after thrilling car chase

21 **PAIRWORK** Sort these words into positive and negative.

amazing · appalling · astonishing · awful · brilliant · delighted · disgraceful · disgusting · dreadful · extraordinary · fantastic · horrifying · magnificent · miraculous · ridiculous · scandalous · shocking · superior · terrified · wonderful

Positive: **amazing**, …
Negative: **appalling**, …

22 **PAIRWORK** Use the emotive words above to turn these neutral headlines into clickbait headlines.

1 15-year-old boy goes to university
....
2 car crash on motorway
....
3 man steals old lady's purse
....
4 a big storm is coming
....

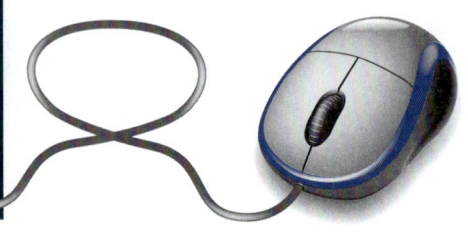

See **VOCABULARY EXTENSION** page 135

SPEAKING SKILLS

Persuading

23 PAIRWORK Discuss these questions.

1 Think of some examples of internet or telephone scams (frauds). How did they work and who did they target?

2 Have you ever been the victim of a scam?

3 How can you avoid scams?

24 **[1.18]** Listen and watch the video. What are they going to do?

key expressions		
persuading	agreeing	disagreeing
☐ Go on, have a look. ☐ Why not? ☐ We'll have to hurry up or we'll miss our chance.	☐ Oh, OK then … ☐ Well, OK, if you really want to.	☐ I can't believe that. ☐ I really don't think … ☐ I'm still not sure. ☐ I'm sorry, but … ☐ That's a ridiculous thing to say.

25 **[1.18]** Listen and watch again and tick (✓) the key expressions you hear.

SPEAKING STRATEGY

Agree in part

We often agree in part even when we disagree. This is to avoid sounding rude. Use these phrases.

☐ *Well, that's true, but …*   ☐ *Yes, I see what you mean, but …*

☐ *I know, but …*   ☐ *That's a good point, but …*

B2 FIRST   IGCSE   IELTS

26 **[1.18]** Listen and watch again and tick (✓) the expressions from the strategy box you hear.

27 PAIRWORK Read the instructions below, then practise the role play. Use the key expressions and the strategy box to help you.

1 You want to go to a party next weekend. You don't want to go on your own but your partner doesn't want to come.

2 You've seen an ad for an advanced maths course and you fancy trying it. Try to persuade your partner to come.

SOUNDS ENGLISH

The /ə/ sound

28 **[1.19]** **PAIRWORK** Listen to a British English speaker and a learner of English say the same sentence. Discuss the differences.

Would you like some bread?

SOUND STRATEGY

When pronouncing words that end in a consonant, learners often add the /ə/ sound.

This means they add an extra syllable, and change the sentence rhythm.

Try and notice the number of syllables in common words, and try not to add an extra one!

29 **[1.20]** Listen and circle the words you hear. Then practise saying them.

	No sound	/ə/
1	office	officer
2	corn	corner
3	farm	farmer
4	box	boxer
5	train	trainer

30 **[1.21]** **GAME** Read and listen. Repeat the sentences.

1 There's a farmer sowing corn on the farm.

2 I did some work in an office last summer.

3 What's the matter with the cat?

4 My sister's a dancer but I can't dance.

5 The man on the train was wearing trainers.

31 **[1.22]** **GAME** Now listen again and complete the sentences. Can you keep time?

LISTENING SKILLS

LEAD IN

32 Look at picture A. Answer these questions.

1 What is the shop advertising?
2 What do the words in red tell the customer?
3 Where do the clothes come from? Why is this important?

PRACTICE

33 Now look at the other two pictures. What do the words in red mean?

LISTENING STRATEGY

Understand inference

When you listen, it is important to identify who the speakers are, and what the context is. Use these questions to help you:

- Is the setting formal or informal?
- If there's one speaker, who is he / she addressing, and why?
- If there are several speakers, what is their relationship? Are they relaxed, happy …?

B2 FIRST   IGCSE   IELTS

34 [1.23] Listen to three recordings. Match them to the pictures A–C.

35 [1.23] Now listen again and answer these questions.

1 How many speakers are there in each extract?
2 One of the extracts is an advertisement. Which is it?
3 When there are two speakers, is the tone formal or informal? How do you know?
4 When there are two speakers, what is their relationship: are they friends or work colleagues? How do you know?

GRAMMAR GUIDE

Reported speech: Questions

	direct question	reported question
wh- questions	'When did you buy it?'	She asked (me) when I had bought it.
yes / no questions	'Do you have the receipt?'	She asked (me) if / whether I had the receipt.

➡ See **GRAMMAR REFERENCE** Workbook page 118

36 Complete the sentences.

0 'How much is it?'
   He asked how much it was ....
1 '.. .'
   I asked if there were any special offers.
2 'Can I try it on?'
   She ....
3 '.. .'
   They asked when the sale would start.
4 'Do I have to keep the receipt?'
   He asked ....
5 '.. .'
   She asked me where I'd bought it.

37 [1.24] The girl from dialogue 3 in exercise 34, Anna, returns to the shop. Complete the sentences below.

1 The assistant asked me when ....
2 And if ....
3 Then she asked why ....
4 I just said ....
5 I asked if I ....

38 Now write the actual questions the assistant asked Anna.

Note taking

LEAD IN

39 PAIRWORK Look at the title of the text and the three headings. Then discuss the statements below.

1 What's your answer to the question in the title?
2 Look at the headings. Think of current examples of each kind of ad.
3 Brainstorm the advantages of each of the three forms of advertising.

WHAT'S THE MOST EFFECTIVE WAY TO ADVERTISE?

RADIO

Radio advertising is relatively cheap, your audience are more constant: radio listeners don't flick between channels or fast forward through the ads. They are perfect targets for advertising.
5 A catchy ad with a memorable jingle will lodge in the listeners' memories. Then every time they repeat it they are passing on your message – it's effective and free! On the other hand, it probably isn't the best way to reach young people, who tend to stream their
10 music directly rather than listen to radio shows.

CINEMA

Think about it – the audience have nowhere else to go, and nothing else to do, except watch your ad. They tend to be young people with disposable income, or families with young children who often
15 exert pester power. So, if you're aiming at this kind of market, you shouldn't dismiss it. It's expensive because cinema audiences expect high quality.

BILLBOARDS AND POSTERS

This is possibly the oldest form of advertising – but a good ad can cheer up an otherwise
20 gloomy street, and even provide welcome entertainment for bored motorists and passengers. These ads are often comical and if an ad makes you laugh, you remember it. Of course, vandals can deface your ads with graffiti, so make sure you place
25 them out of reach! If you choose the right location, you will find that an eye-catching, interesting ad will pay for itself very fast.

ACADEMIC STRATEGY

Note taking is a way of summarising the main points of a text. It is important when you are learning key information for an exam.

- Read the text and underline the important points.
- Try and identify the key information.
- Rewrite the information in your own words, with headings and bullet points.

IGCSE

PRACTICE

40 Read the text. Look at the notes below. Underline the points they refer to in the text. Then complete them with key information from the text.

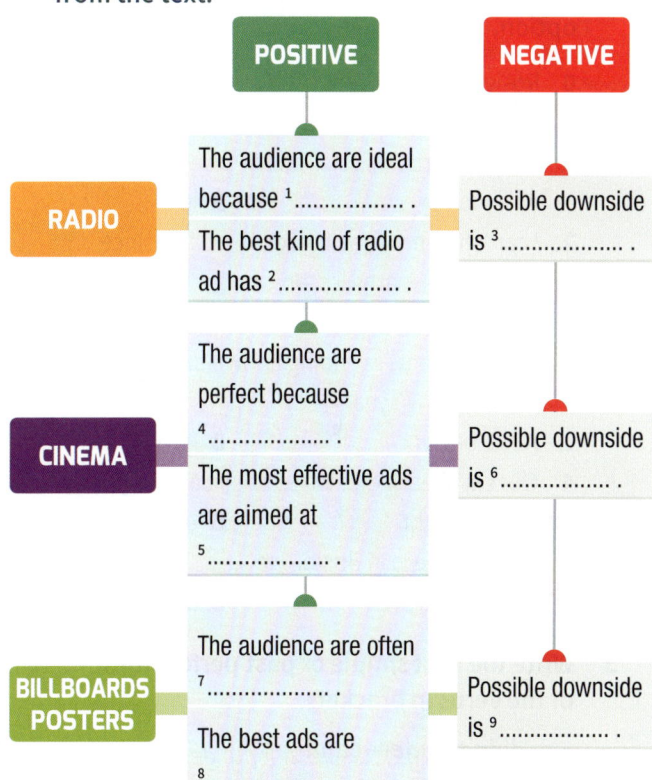

	POSITIVE	NEGATIVE
RADIO	The audience are ideal because [1]................ . The best kind of radio ad has [2].................. .	Possible downside is [3].................. .
CINEMA	The audience are perfect because [4].................. . The most effective ads are aimed at [5].................. .	Possible downside is [6]................ .
BILLBOARDS POSTERS	The audience are often [7].................. . The best ads are [8].................. .	Possible downside is [9]................ .

41 WRITING Now think of TV advertising.

1 Make a chart like the one above outlining the pros and cons of TV advertising.
2 Now write a paragraph on TV advertising.

REVISE AND ROUND UP

1 **Complete the dialogues. Write the past simple or past continuous form of the verbs in brackets.**

0 **A** What time **did you finish** (*you / finish*) your homework last night?

   B I'm not sure, but I know I .... (*still / work*) at 11.

1 **A** You're late! What .... (*happen*)?

   B Sorry. I .... (*leave*) my phone at home so I .... (*go*) back to get it.

2 **A** I .... (*see*) you in town yesterday, but you .... (*not / say*) hello. In fact, you .... (*walk*) straight past me!

   B Oh, sorry! I .... (*think*) about my exams, I expect.

2 **Read the sentences and choose the correct option.**

0 Rosie's at home. She .... school for a week.
   Ⓐ hasn't been to   **B** wasn't at

1 My arm hurts. I .... off my bike last night.
   A 've fallen   **B** fell

2 I can't find my pencil case. I .... it since yesterday's maths lesson.
   A haven't seen   **B** didn't see

3 It's my parents' wedding anniversary. They .... married for 20 years.
   A 've been   **B** got

4 Our car's really old. We .... it ages ago.
   A 've bought   **B** bought

5 Rick's home is in Bristol. He .... there.
   A 's always lived   **B** always lived

3 **Write the past simple or past perfect form of the verbs in brackets.**

0 I **didn't understand** (*not / understand*) the play because I **hadn't studied** (*not / study*) it first.

1 Last month we .... (*visit*) some friends in Scotland. We .... (*not / see*) them for ages.

2 We were surprised when it .... (*rain*) because we .... (*check*) the weather forecast before we .... (*set off*).

3 Jack was amazed and delighted when he .... (*hear*) his exam results. He .... (*not / expect*) to pass.

4 Somebody .... (*steal*) my bike last week. I .... (*forget*) to lock it.

5 We .... (*not / be*) on the train for very long before it .... (*break*) down.

4 **Write sentences using the prompts and the past simple, past continuous or past perfect form of the verbs.**

0 When Anna / be / 16, she / move / to London.
   When Anna was 16, she moved to London.

1 She / prepare / for school exams when she / change / schools. By then, she / already / live / in ten different places.

2 A loud noise / wake / me up. Something / hit / the window. I / look / outside. It / snow / heavily and some boys / throw / snowballs at the houses.

3 When we / go / into the concert hall, some people / sit / in our seats. We all / check / our tickets, and they / be / the same. Somebody in the box office / make / a mistake.

4 While she / travel / by train to York, Emily / start / talking to another passenger. Some time later she / be / very surprised to see they / be / in Scotland. She / miss / her station.

5 When I / see / Stuart, he / wear / a very smart suit. I think he / just / be / to a wedding.

5 **Complete the sentences. Use reported speech.**

0 'I can't go out on Saturday, because it's my grandmother's birthday and we've planned a party.'
   Maria said **she couldn't go out on Saturday because it was her grandmother's birthday and they'd planned a party** .

1 'There are a few more things I must do before we go on holiday.'
   Tom told me ....
   ....

2 'I hope everyone has a great time!'
   Clara said ....

3 'It'll be cold in the evenings so I'm going to pack some warm clothes.'
   Ted said ....
   ....

4 'I haven't finished my essay because I had a bad headache and went to bed early.'
   Stella told us ....
   ....

5 'Max has just texted me to say he's missed the bus so he'll be late.'
   Jack said ....
   ....

6 'I've been trying to fix my laptop but I can't work it out.'
   Jane told me ....

6 Complete the missing words.

0 Martin ....**told**........ me that he ......**would**...... lend me some money.

1 My parents .... that I ....
to be home by 11.

2 I didn't know .... today ....
Jamie's birthday.

3 Did Harry .... you he ....
passed his driving test?

4 Sorry, I didn't realise you .... still in bed,
I thought you always .... up early!

5 The website .... that my order
.... arrive today.

6 Jack said he .... working today
but Nathan told me he .... seen him
in town.

7 Report the dialogue.

Ticket
inspector Can I see your ticket, please?

Jack I don't have one.

Inspector Why don't you have one?

Jack The ticket office at my station was closed.

Inspector That's no excuse. Where did you start
your journey?

Jack I got on at Stratford.

Inspector There's a ticket machine at Stratford
station.

Jack I tried to use it but I didn't have the right
money.

Inspector Well, I'll have to take your details.
What's your name?

The ticket inspector asked if he could see
my ticket.

8 Read the text and choose the correct option.

At school we 0 *started* / *'ve started* a history
project and I 1 *was* / *'ve been* researching my family's
history. Last night while my grandparents 2 *were*
visiting / *visited* us, I asked them what life was like
when they 3 *were* / *have been* my age. Of course they
4 *haven't* / *hadn't* heard of the internet in 5 *these* / *those*
days, so when they 6 *wanted* / *have wanted* some
information they had to look in a book, or ask
someone. I said that sounded awful, but they
laughed and said life 7 *has* / *had* been much better in
those days.

TOWARDS B2 FIRST

Reading and Use of English

9 Complete the gaps with one word.

Smile!

A 0 ......**few**....... years ago a Chinese woman was
working in a mobile phone factory 1 ....
she accidentally became world famous.
How 2 .... this happen? 3 ....
she was working, one of her colleagues
4 .... a photo of her with one of the
phones he 5 .... testing. Sometime
6 ...., somebody in the UK was trying
out the phone 7 .... he had just bought,
when he found a photo of a beautiful young
woman. She was smiling and 8 .... a
peace sign. 9 .... colleague had forgotten
10 .... delete the photo.
The owner of the phone posted the photo
on a message board and within a few weeks the
worker 11 .... become quite famous.
She thought she 12 .... lose her job but
her boss told her that nobody 13 ....
angry. He said that 14 .... made mistakes
sometimes. In fact, she had 15 .... done
anything wrong, because they had 16 ....
testing the phone. 17 .... any case,
everybody loved the photo and wanted to know
18 .... the woman was. Some people
even 19 .... why every phone didn't
come with a photo of the person who
20 .... made it!

Writing

10 Write your story in about 140 and 190 words.

You have seen this announcement in an
English-language magazine for teenagers.

Short story competition! Your story must begin
with this sentence:
Grace opened the parcel but was disappointed when
she saw they had sent her the wrong thing.

Your story must include the words:
• advertisement   • blog

3

A better world

EXAM STRATEGIES

- B2 FIRST: Reading, Writing, Speaking and Listening
- IGCSE: Reading, Writing, Speaking and Listening
- IELTS: Reading, Writing, Speaking and Listening

SPEAKING SKILLS

- Expressing an opinion

CHANGING LANGUAGE

- Use of *like*

LIFE SKILLS

- Giving a presentation

Learning goals

Grammar

- Revision of comparative and superlative adjectives
- Comparative and superlative adverbs

Vocabulary

- World resources

LEAD IN

1 Look at the photos and read the title of the article. Can you guess what it is about?

2 ▶ ◀ [1.25] Read, listen and watch. Which photo matches the text best? Why?

THE POWER OF MONEY

More than one billion people use Facebook every day. The phenomenal success of his creation has made Mark Zuckerberg not only one of the youngest billionaires ever but also one of the wealthiest people in the world. He has far more money than most people dream of – but he isn't as interested in a celebrity lifestyle as you might think.

5 For example, he is famous for always wearing the same style of clothes – in order to spend a little less time choosing what to wear! He said he wanted to make as few decisions as possible so he could concentrate on serving his community. When his daughter Maxima was born, he and his wife Priscilla wrote a letter to her (and posted it on Facebook!). Max, the letter said, had changed the way they see the world.

10 They wanted to make it a better, more equal place. Because of that, they promised to give away 99% of their Facebook shares over their lifetimes. That means billions of dollars to help people much less fortunate than they are.

The Zuckerbergs are not alone. Bill Gates, the founder of Microsoft, is even richer (and more famous) than Zuckerberg. He is also one of the world's greatest philanthropists.

15 He and his wife Melinda run a wide range of charities across the world, particularly in the poorest countries. Their vaccination programmes alone have already saved millions of lives and will save many more in the future.

Zuckerberg and Gates have bigger incomes than some entire countries. They are also among the most generous people in the world. They use their extreme fortunes to help

20 the least fortunate. This is, most people agree, by far the best way to spend their money. However, some people think that this is not the way to tackle the world's problems.

25 They say that governments should do this. One thing is for sure, the world would be a worse place without this

30 kind of philanthropy.

PRACTICE

3 ▶ ◀ **[1.25]** **Read, listen and watch the video again. Then answer the questions.**

1 Why does the article mention Zuckerberg's clothes?
2 What happened to make him and his wife start thinking differently?
3 What have they promised to do?
4 How have Bill and Melinda Gates saved millions of lives?
5 Why do some people object to philanthropy?

GRAMMAR GUIDE

Revision of comparative and superlative adjectives

comparative	
much / a lot / far / even / a little / a (little) bit	young**er than** wealth**ier than** big**ger than**
	more / **less** fortunate **than** **more** / **less** generous **than**
	better than **worse than**
superlative	
by far	**the** young**est** **the** wealth**iest** **the** big**gest**
	the most / **least** fortunate **the most** / **least** generous
	the best **the worst**

➡ See **GRAMMAR REFERENCE** Workbook page 118

4 **Complete the rules. Write *comparative* or *superlative*. Then find examples in the text.**

1 We make .... adjectives stronger with *much, a lot, far, even,* and we make them weaker with *a little, a (little) bit.*
2 We make .... adjectives stronger by putting *by far* first.

GRAMMAR GUIDE

Comparatives and superlatives with nouns

comparative		
countable	many / a lot / far	**more** cars **fewer** cars
uncountable	much / a lot / far	**more** money **less** money
superlative		
countable	by far	**the most** cars **the fewest** cars
uncountable		**the most** money **the least** money

➡ See **GRAMMAR REFERENCE** Workbook page 118

5 **Write the sentences with the correct form of the adjectives.**

0 Who is / rich / person in the world?
  Who is the richest person in the world?
1 Health is / important / wealth.
2 We don't have much money but others have even / little.
3 Which makes us / happy / – money or love?
4 My aunt is one of / kind / people I've ever met.
5 Giving is often / enjoyable / receiving.
6 Not many people are millionaires and even / few / are billionaires.

6 **Rewrite the sentences so that they mean the same.**

0 These days living standards are much better than they were 50 years ago.
  Fifty years ago **living standards were much worse than they are these days** .
1 I don't give as much money to charity as I should.
  I should ....
2 Facebook has many more users than Twitter.
  Twitter ....
3 Mobile phones are far more popular than landlines these days.
  Landlines ....
4 A lot fewer people die of diseases like malaria than in the past.
  Not ....
5 Some people have a lot less food than us.
  Some people don't ....
6 Not many things are worse than hunger.
  There are ....

READING SKILLS

LEAD IN

7 PAIRWORK Discuss these questions.

1 What's in your fridge at home? Remember or guess.
2 Do you throw away a lot of food?
3 How would life be different without a fridge?

PRACTICE

8 [1.26] **Read and listen to the text. Which fridge do you think made the most difference?**

READING STRATEGY

Detect purpose and point of view

Each paragraph has a main purpose or point of view.

- Pay special attention to the first sentence of each paragraph.
- Look for keywords and expressions.
- Try to summarise each paragraph in a few words.

| B2 FIRST | IGCSE | IELTS |

9 PAIRWORK Read the text again. Say what the purpose of each paragraph is. Then write notes to summarise it.

Paragraph A – setting the scene:
the arrival of the two fridges

10 The text has five paragraphs, A–E. Which paragraph tells us about the following aspects of the story? Two letters can be used twice.

0 ....A.... The attitude of Santosh's neighbours
1 .... The wider benefits to two communities
2 .... The purpose of the British fridge
3 .... How Santosh acquired a fridge
4 .... The inspiration for the British project
5 .... Global inequality
6 .... How Santosh's family have benefited

11 PAIRWORK Look at exercise 10 again. Give examples of what the text tells us about each aspect.

0 The attitude of Santosh's neighbours.
They were curious and envious.

GRAMMAR GUIDE

too many / too much, too few / too little, (not) enough + nouns

Countable

- *too many / too few people*
  (not) enough people

Uncountable

- *too much / too little food*
  (not) enough food

➡ See **GRAMMAR REFERENCE** Workbook page 119

12 Complete the text with the words below.

a lot (x2) ▪ enough (x2) ▪ too many ▪ too much (x2)

Real Junk Food Café

The volunteers who run a café in Leeds, England, believe that there are far ⁰ ...*too many*... hungry people in the city, and that there is ¹ .... food waste.
At their café, the Real Junk Food Project, all the food comes from donations. For example, bakers often have ² .... bread at the end of the day, so they give it to the café. In the same way, supermarkets donate food that is getting close to its sell-by date. If restaurants have ³ .... of food, they often donate it too. The customers are often people who don't have ⁴ .... money. They only pay what they can afford.
Other customers, who have ⁵ .... money, sometimes pay ⁶ ....

13 **Critical thinking** Discuss the questions in pairs.

1 What kind of problems might Santosh's fridge cause? What about the community fridge in Frome?
2 Are there any projects like the community fridge or the Real Junk Food Café in your town?

A TALE OF TWO FRIDGES

A In 2015, a small Indian village saw the arrival of its first fridge. The proud new owner, Santosh Chowdery, had saved hard for ten years to pay the deposit on it. Villagers watched curiously and enviously when the fridge arrived (on a rickshaw). Santosh and his wife welcomed it with a religious ceremony. It was a life-changing moment. Meanwhile, in the same year but on the other side of the world, a far wealthier community also celebrated the arrival of a fridge. That fridge, too, was about to make a dramatic difference. 5

B For Santosh's family, the fridge was revolutionary. For one thing, they could for the first time ever enjoy cold water in the heat of the Indian summer. What's more, they could store food, including any leftovers from family meals. Because of this, they didn't need to go to the market every day, and Santosh's wife no longer had to cook every day, either. Now she had enough time to get a job, and so the family's income rose. 10

C Back in the UK, the small town of Frome in Somerset was using a fridge to solve a rather different problem. Nearly everybody there had a fridge, but some fridges had too much food in them, and some had too little. In other words, too many people were wasting food while others didn't have enough. A group of volunteers came up with a solution. Inspired by the example of *solidarity fridges* in Spain, they set up (and still run) a *community fridge*. People donate food that they don't need, and anybody can help themselves to anything, completely free. Volunteers supervise the project, and make sure all the food is safe to eat. 15 20

D Santosh and his family are not the only people in the village to benefit from his fridge. It has helped the whole village – for example, they are able to store food for their neighbours, who then have more free time to work. In Frome, too, the fridge has had positive knock-on effects. There is less food waste, and there are fewer hungry people. Perhaps most important of all, it has brought the whole community together, both rich and poor. 25

E As the world's population grows, the gap between the rich and poor widens – and the gap is much bigger than experts predicted just a few years ago. The richest 1% of the world's population now own 50% of the world's wealth, while the world's poorest people own 1%. This is not just a gap between rich and poor countries on opposite sides of the world – it's also between rich and poor people, who often live side by side. Both Santosh and the people of Frome have, with their fridges, taken small steps towards bridging the gap. 30 35

LEAD IN

14 An opinion essay requires you to consider different aspects of a topic and reach a conclusion. Which of the following are opinion essays?

- Cars should not be allowed in city centres. Do you agree?
- Write an essay describing an event you really enjoyed.
- What's the best way to stop air pollution?

PRACTICE

15 Complete the text with the words below.

linking ▪ opinion ▪ summarising ▪ paragraphs ▪ topic

In an opinion essay, you should give a general introduction to the 1......................... in the first paragraph. In the second and third 2........................., you should discuss different points of view. Use 3......................... words and phrases to order your points and prepare the reader for what is going to come next. Finally, in the last paragraph, conclude by 4......................... the main points and giving your own 5......................... .

WRITING STRATEGY

Write an opinion essay

An opinion essay includes different points of view. It can present two points of view (for and against). It can also present just one point of view with lots of reasons to justify it. It contains:

- one or multiple points of view
- clearly defined paragraphs

B2 FIRST | IGCSE | IELTS

See **WRITING EXPANSION** page 126

VOCABULARY

World resources

16 Look at the webpage and describe the pictures.

THE GREEN ZONE

A Don't throw it away

Think of your world! Remember to use the recycling bins and reduce our landfill sites.

B Keep it local!

Buy fresh produce grown on your doorstep! Support your farmers' market!

C Fair for everyone

A fair deal for workers in developing countries. And a great-tasting product for you!

17 Look at the groups of words below and match each group to the headings A, B or C in exercise 16. Use a dictionary to help you.

1 fair trade, working conditions, standard of living, minimum wage

2 bottle bank, greenhouse gases, climate change, waste disposal

3 seasonal food, locally produced, homegrown, vegetable patch

18 Complete the text with the words below.

minimum wage · landfill sites · working conditions · standard of living · seasonal food · greenhouse gases · climate change · bottle bank · farmers' market · vegetable patch · developing countries · homegrown

Fair trade means farmers and workers in [1].......................... receive fair pay for their products, so that they have better [2].......................... . They are paid a [3].......................... so they have a better [4].......................... at home, too. Waste disposal is important because the rubbish we put in [5].......................... contributes to [6].......................... because it produces [7].......................... . So always remember to recycle your glass in the [8].......................... ! Locally produced food doesn't travel very far – so it doesn't cause much pollution. In addition, [9].......................... is healthier than food that has travelled round the world to reach you. So buy fresh food from your local [10].........................., or even start your own [11].......................... in the garden and enjoy [12].......................... food!

19 **Critical thinking** Discuss in pairs. What do you think of these statements and opinions? Do you think these things matter? Why / Why not?

1 I don't buy that kind of chocolate. They treat their workers badly.

2 I don't care if these mangoes come from the other side of the world. They're delicious.

3 I want the apples but I don't want the packaging, thanks.

See **VOCABULARY EXTENSION** page 136

SPEAKING SKILLS

Expressing an opinion

20 Have you ever taken part in a sponsored event, for example a walk? Have you ever sponsored somebody? What was it in aid of?

21 ⏯ 🔴[1.27] Listen and watch the video. What are Luke's two ideas?

key expressions	
expressing an opinion	**responding to an opinion**
☐ I (don't) think … ☐ I reckon … ☐ If you ask me … ☐ To be honest … ☐ (Do) you mean …? ☐ In my opinion, … ☐ What I think is … ☐ You know what I mean.	☐ Well, not really. ☐ I don't think so. ☐ Maybe you're right.

22 ⏯ 🔴[1.27] Listen and watch again and tick (✓) the key expressions you hear.

🌐 SPEAKING STRATEGY

Support an argument

We often want to support an opinion with an example or by rephrasing it. We use phrases like these:

☐ *I mean, …*   ☐ *Listen, …*   ☐ *For a start …*
☐ *What I'm saying is, …*   ☐ *For example, …*   ☐ *For another thing …*
☐ *Look, …*

B2 FIRST   IGCSE   IELTS

23 ⏯ 🔴[1.27] Listen and watch again and tick (✓) the expressions from the strategy box you hear.

24 PAIRWORK Think about a charity you support. Look at these fundraising ideas. Then discuss what you're going to do to support your charity.

- sponsored events: extreme haircut, silence, go offline (*digital detox*), …
- other ideas: make and sell cakes, wash cars, sell your old clothes.

▶ CHANGING LANGUAGE

Use of *like*

25 Look at the sentences from the dialogue and circle examples of *like*. Is *like* always used as a verb?

1 I don't like the idea.
2 I mean, like, walking is something you do every day.
3 Your parents would, like, have a fit.

26 Look at the sentences in exercise 25 again. In each sentence is *like* used as:

- a verb?
- to make comparison?
- a filler?

27 ⏯ Watch the video. Have you heard *like* used as a filler before?

1 Has the use of *like* increased or decreased in the last 15 years?
2 Which age group most frequently uses the word *like*?
3 What is the most frequent use of *like*?

◉ CORPUS

Corpus data shows us that in spoken English the most frequent use of *like* is as a filler.

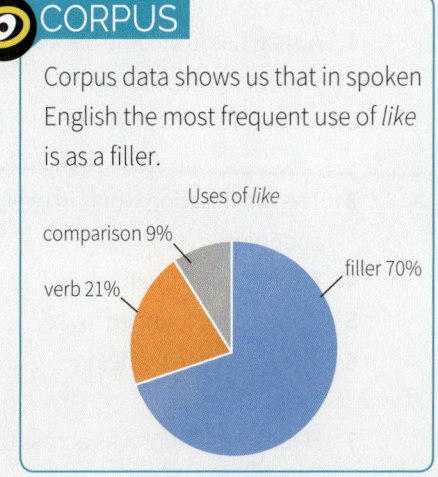

Uses of *like*

comparison 9%
verb 21%
filler 70%

LISTENING SKILLS

LEAD IN

28 **Describe what's happening in the photos. Then answer the questions.**

1   What do you think these people are doing?
2   Have you ever volunteered? Would you like to? Why / Why not?

LISTENING STRATEGY

Listen for more detailed content

In these tasks you are listening for specific information. This is usually names, numbers or details within sentences.

- Listen to the whole text and try and identify what it is about on a general level.
- Read the questions and ensure you know what they are asking for. Look for clues and predict the answers.
- Then listen again and do the task.

B2 FIRST | IGCSE | IELTS

PRACTICE

29 **[1.28] Listen and complete the sentences.**

1   Aishen has just come back from Chennai in ....
2   Habitat for Humanity helps low-income .... build affordable homes.
3   The organisation works in over .... countries.
4   Aishen was in Chennai for .... days.
5   Habitat was founded in ....
6   They renovate homes in .... areas.
7   Habitat also improves access to clean water and ....

GRAMMAR GUIDE

Comparative and superlative adverbs

comparative		
much / **a lot /** **far /** **even /** **a little /** **a (little) bit**	**regular adverbs** (quickly, slowly)	**irregular adverbs** (fast, well, badly)
	more / less quickly **than**	faster / better / worse **than**
	more / less slowly **than**	
superlative		
	regular adverbs (quickly, slowly)	**irregular adverbs** (fast, well, badly)
by far	**the most /** **the least** quickly	the fastest / the best / the worst
	the most / **the least** slowly	

➡ See **GRAMMAR REFERENCE** Workbook page 119

30 **Rewrite the sentences so that they mean the same.**

0   My sister is better than me at playing guitar. (*good, much*)
    My sister _plays guitar much better than me_ .
1   We don't shop as carefully as we should. (*less*)
    We ....
2   He is a far harder worker than me. (*hard, much*)
    He works ....
3   The person who sings better than everyone else wins a prize. (*the*)
    The person who ....
4   My new bike goes much faster than my old one. (*more*)
    My old bike goes ....

Giving a presentation

LEAD IN

31 PAIRWORK Answer these questions.

1 What is happening in the picture below?
2 How do you think this person feels? Why?
3 What advice would you give to someone
   in this situation?

PRACTICE

32 Read the article and complete the gaps in the text with the phrases in the list.

a practise in a safe environment
b start to see improvements
c the good news is that you can learn to deal with performance anxiety
d the very idea of this fills many people with anxiety
e rather than running away from a situation
f as well as parts which you want to change

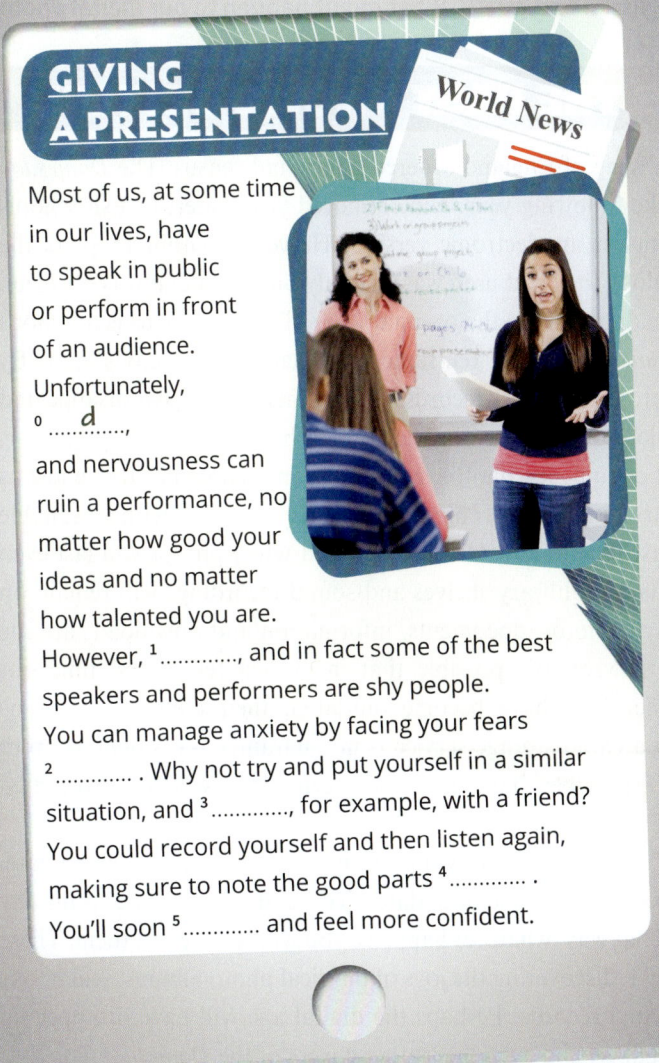

GIVING A PRESENTATION

World News

Most of us, at some time in our lives, have to speak in public or perform in front of an audience. Unfortunately,
0 *d* ....,
and nervousness can ruin a performance, no matter how good your ideas and no matter how talented you are.
However, [1] ...., and in fact some of the best speakers and performers are shy people. You can manage anxiety by facing your fears [2] .... Why not try and put yourself in a similar situation, and [3] ...., for example, with a friend? You could record yourself and then listen again, making sure to note the good parts [4] .... You'll soon [5] .... and feel more confident.

33 THINKING FURTHER Discuss the questions with your partner.

1 How do you normally feel when you have to do an exam or give a presentation in public?
2 Do you have any techniques for keeping calm?

⚙ LIFE STRATEGY

Tips for giving a presentation

- Don't worry about appearing nervous. It shows you are taking it seriously.
- Think positively: this will help replace negative thoughts with realistic and balanced thinking.
- Prepare! It's so much easier to stay calm if you know what you're going to do and what you're going to say:
  – make clear, ordered notes
  – practise – and time yourself (don't go on too long!)
  – visual aids will add interest to your presentation
- Stay calm. Use techniques to stay calm and relaxed:
  – take some deep breaths before you start
  – smile at the audience – make friends with them!
  – take your time – don't rush
- Be prepared to answer questions at the end. If you don't know the answer, promise to find out – and do it!

34 Read the tips for giving a presentation. Then answer the questions.

1 Which of the tips seem most useful?
2 Have you tried any of the tips before?

35 TASK You are going to give a presentation about your partner. Use the tips below to help prepare and give your presentation in pairs.

1 Interview your partner and find out about their:
   - early childhood
   - family
   - hobbies, likes and dislikes
   - ambitions and plans
2 Ask your partner to bring photos and other visual aids about their life.
3 Take turns to practise giving and watching your presentations.
4 Give your presentation to the class.

4 Our future

EXAM STRATEGIES

- B2 FIRST: Reading and Speaking
- IGCSE: Speaking
- IELTS: Listening

SPEAKING SKILLS

- Debating

ACADEMIC SKILLS

- Preparing a speech for a debate

Learning goals

Grammar

- Future predictions: *will* v *may* / *might*
- Future perfect
- Future continuous

Vocabulary

- Technology of the future

LEAD IN

1 Describe the photos and answer the questions.

1 How old do you think the book is?
2 When do you think the computer photo was taken?

2 ▶ ◀ [1.29] Read, listen and watch. What might happen to our digital photos?

SOMETIMES THE PAST KNOWS BETTER!

In about 1085, the King of England ordered a national census. The *Domesday Book* was ready the following year. Nine hundred years later, British schools helped collect data for an electronic version. However, within 15 years the *state-of-the-art* technology they had used was not only out of date, it was obsolete, and the data was unreadable (while the original was still intact!). This is a famous example of *digital obsolescence*. Will the same thing happen to today's data? By 2025, will all our photos, messages, records, music, memories have disappeared into a digital black hole? Unless we're careful, it might happen. [5]

Of course, non-digital documents, photos, recordings and data will survive just as they always have. Your grandparents' colour photos may fade, but with reasonable care the images will last indefinitely. Older, black-and-white photos will last even [10] better. Books will remain on library shelves and sound recordings will remain on vinyl. Ironically, today's photos, documents, information and downloads are the ones that might not survive. It's possible that in even a few years' time our smartphones and tablets will have become outdated; their contents won't be [15] accessible. Even using a cloud storage service is no guarantee – it's only as up to date as its servers. It's possible that tomorrow's technology will have forgotten today's information.

So, what can you do? First, make sure your storage system is always up to date. That way, you'll keep pace with system updates. To be absolutely safe, print any [20] extra-special photos. That way, whatever happens, you won't have lost them. These days people are already rediscovering the joys of physical photo albums, real books and – increasingly – vinyl records. Perhaps the digital age will have disappeared long before vinyl and paper, and even the leather covers of the *Domesday Book*!

PRACTICE

3 ▶ ◀ **[1.29]** **Read, listen and watch the video again. Answer these questions.**

1 How old is the *Domesday Book*?
2 Roughly how long did the modern version last?
3 According to the text, what will last longer than digital records?
4 The text makes two suggestions to help you protect your memories. What are they?
5 What does the title mean?

GRAMMAR GUIDE

Future predictions: *will* v *may | might*

- *Your grandparents' colour photos* **may fade**.
- *Unless we're careful, it* **might happen**.
- *… with reasonable care the images* **will last** *indefinitely.*
- *… their contents* **won't be** *accessible.*

➡ See **GRAMMAR REFERENCE** Workbook page 119

4 **Complete the rule. Write *certain* or *not certain*. Then find examples in the text.**

We use *will* or *won't* to express predictions when we are ...., and *may* or *might* (*not*) when we are ....

GRAMMAR GUIDE

Future perfect

+	Tomorrow's technology **will have forgotten** today's information.
−	That way, whatever happens, you **won't have lost** them.
?	In five or ten years' time, **will** our photos **have disappeared**?

➡ See **GRAMMAR REFERENCE** Workbook page 120

5 **Complete the rules. Write *future simple* or *future perfect*. Then find examples in the text.**

1 We use the .... to predict a future action or event.
2 We use the .... to say that an action or event will be finished before a time in the future.

6 **Write the future simple or future perfect of the verbs in brackets.**

0 How old are you? When ...**will you be**... (*you / be*) 18?
1 Hurry up. The film .... (*start*) by the time we get there.
2 I can't come out tonight. I .... (*not / finish*) my project in time.
3 It's a great story. What .... (*happen*) next?
4 .... (*scientists / discover*) a cure for cancer by 2030?
5 By this time next year, my sister .... (*leave*) school and .... (*go*) to university.
6 Please, wait for me. I .... (*not / be*) long.

7 **Write sentences with the future simple, *may | might* or the future perfect.**

0 The sun / rise / tomorrow
   The sun will rise tomorrow.
1 I'm not sure, but it / rain / next week.
2 We / definitely / land / on Mars in 100 years' time.
3 Sorry, but your order / not / be / ready until next month.
4 I / not / come / to the party. I don't know yet.
5 We / be / on the road all day by the time we arrive, so we / be / very tired.

8 **SPEAKING** **What will / won't you have done in ten years' time? Use the future perfect and the following ideas.**

- get married
- have a baby
- travel round the world
- learn to drive
- get a degree
- make a fortune
- become famous

READING SKILLS

LEAD IN

9 **PAIRWORK** Do you like shopping? Why / Why not? Which of these types of shop do you like best? Why?

- online
- supermarkets
- independent shops
- chain stores
- market stalls

PRACTICE

10 [1.30] Read and listen to the first part of the text (page 42). Do you like the idea of drones? Why / Why not?

11 Read the text again and decide if the sentences are true (T) or false (F). Correct the false ones.

1 The text is describing the pros and cons of drones.   T   F

2 The message of the text is drones are controversial.   T   F

3 According to the text, drones will definitely replace postmen.   T   F

READING STRATEGY

Complete a text

Choosing one word to insert in a text is a way of ensuring that you really understand the text and also testing your knowledge of English grammar.

- Read the whole text through for general meaning.
- Look at the words before and after each gap.
- Think what kind of word it is that you need (e.g., verb, noun, preposition, adverb, part of a phrasal verb, part of a collocation, etc.).
- Think about the form and tense.

B2 FIRST

12 [1.31] Read the rest of the text (page 43) and fill in the blanks. Then listen and check.

SHOP AND DROP

Imagine you've been shopping. What are you doing now? Are you struggling home with shopping bags, picking up packages at a collection point, or waiting at home for the post
5   to arrive? Soon, it seems, we won't be doing any of these things. Instead, we'll be checking the sky. Since the arrival of online shopping, delivery vans have become a familiar sight. We are used to next-day – even same-day – deliveries. However,
10   before long they might be a thing of the past. The next new big thing is coming soon – thirty-minute deliveries, *by drone*. These drones will fly distances of up to 16 kilometres and then land like a helicopter
15   and place your package on to a special mat, or possibly into a box. Critics predict all kinds of problems. For example, they say that these drones will be flying over us all the time, even our private gardens – so will they be spying on us?
20   They say that mid-air collisions and other accidents are inevitable. Moreover, they say it will be possible to hack them, with potentially disastrous consequences. Enthusiasts dismiss these fears and say they are obstacles to progress.

13 Look at the Grammar guide and find examples of future forms in the text.

GRAMMAR GUIDE

Revision of future

- *How **will** they **detect** shoplifters?* (We use *will* or *be going to* to make predictions.)
- *We're **going to miss** out on those friendly chats.* (We use *going to* when we can see evidence for our predictions.)
- *Others **are opening** soon.* (We use the *present continuous* to talk about arrangements.)

 See **GRAMMAR REFERENCE** Workbook page 120

Coming soon:
drone delivery

Drones are not ¹ .... only 25
change on the shopping
horizon. The first *walk out*
stores have opened in the USA,
² .... others are opening 30
soon. Customers will register
³ .... smartphones, then walk
into the store, help ⁴ .... to the goods, and leave. Again,
⁵ .... are plenty of possible problems – for a start, what
will people with ⁶ .... smartphones do? These 35
developments are examples ⁷ .... a trend towards less
and ⁸ .... personal interaction. Soon it's going to be
⁹ .... to buy everything without ever speaking to another
human being. No more friendly chats ¹⁰ .... shop
assistants. Experts say ¹¹ .... social interaction is vital 40
for our mental health. Do we really want to lose ¹² ....?
And will it really happen? We'll ¹³ .... out soon!

GRAMMAR GUIDE

Future continuous

+	We**'ll be checking** the sky.
–	We **won't be doing** any of these things.
?	**Will** they **be spying** on us?

We use the *future continuous* to talk about a continuous
action or event in the future.

→ See **GRAMMAR REFERENCE** Workbook page 121

14 Choose the correct option.

0 Don't run on the ice. You*'re falling* / ('ll fall) over.

1 This time tomorrow we*'ll lie* / *'ll be lying* on a beach!

2 I can't meet you this afternoon. I*'ll go* / *'m going* to the dentist's.

3 'I*'ll call* / *be calling* you at seven. OK?'
'No, sorry, we*'ll have* / *'ll be having* dinner then.'

4 I don't feel very well. I think I*'ll be* / *'m going to be* sick.

5 Everyone*'ll meet* / *'s meeting* at the cinema at half past six.

6 A red sky means it*'s being* / *'s going to be* fine tomorrow.

7 Don't text your brother this afternoon. He*'ll drive* / *'ll be driving*.

15 Critical thinking Discuss the question in pairs.

What advantages and disadvantages might drones and *walk out* shops
have?

WRITING SKILLS

LEAD IN

**16 Tick (✓) the situations when
an informal letter would
be appropriate.**

☐ A friend or relative is unwell.

☐ You want to congratulate
somebody on her / his success.

☐ You're applying for a summer job.

PRACTICE

**17 Complete the text with the words
below.**

contractions ▪ first name ▪
kisses ▪ address ▪ PS ▪ surname

In an informal letter, put your
¹ .... and the date at the
top. Start the letter with *Dear* and
then the person's ² ....
(or sometimes Mr / Mrs / Ms and
the ³ .... – it depends!).
Use informal language, so
⁴ .... and colloquial
expressions are fine. End the letter
in a friendly way, and if you want to,
you can add a few ⁵ ....,
like this: *xxx*. If you suddenly
remember something else to say,
you can add a ⁶ .... at the
bottom.

WRITING STRATEGY

Write an informal letter

You write informal letters
to someone you know.
They are much less common than
they used to be: however, they are
sometimes the best choice, and
they are always appreciated.

- Informal letters are usually short.
- They can contain informal
language and contractions.
- You usually include only
your first name at the end.

→ See **WRITING EXPANSION** page 127

VOCABULARY

Technology of the future

18 PAIRWORK Discuss these questions. Then share with the class.

1 Do you like science fiction? Why / Why not?
2 Brainstorm the names and plots of science fiction films, TV programmes or novels you have heard of. Make a note of their titles.

19 Match the words in the list to the definitions below. Use a dictionary to check any words you don't know.

1 ☐ astronaut
2 ☐ artificial intelligence (AI)
3 ☐ humanoids
4 ☐ robots
5 ☐ space colony
6 ☐ starship
7 ☐ virtual reality
8 ☐ aliens
9 ☐ galaxy
10 ☐ time machine
11 ☐ cyberspace
12 ☐ telepathy

a It travels through space.
b He or she travels through space.
c Something that looks like a human.
d A machine that performs tasks automatically.
e Computer-generated images and sensations that appear to be real.
f A star system.
g A community of people who live in space.
h Creatures from a different planet.
i Communication between minds.
j It can travel into the past and the future.
k A machine's ability to think like a human.
l The space in which computers communicate.

20 GROUPWORK Discuss in groups of four. Think of your list of sci-fi films again, then answer the questions.

1 Have you seen or read any of them?
  ▪ If yes: choose one but don't name it. Explain the plot to your group. Can they guess which one it is?
  ▪ If no: listen to the sci-fi plots and ask questions. Which one sounds the most interesting?
2 Which plots are the most credible?

21 Read the text about future technological predictions. Check the meaning of the words in bold.

What will our future be?

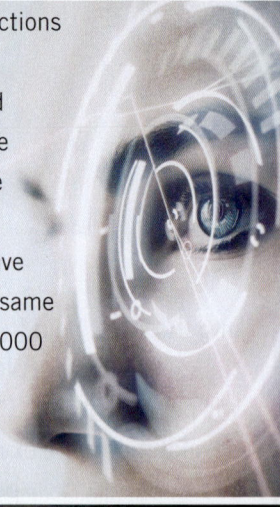

Futurologists have been making predictions about the future of **mankind** for many years. Some have already been proved correct – for example, Arthur C. Clarke predicted personal computers and the internet at least 30 years before they became a reality. Some, of course, have been proved wrong. For example, the same man also predicted that by the year 2000 there would no longer be any cities – and that one day we would be using trained monkeys as servants!

Other predictions include:
■ **driverless cars** fitted with sophisticated **sensors** will completely replace today's cars;
■ solar power will supply all of the Earth's energy;
■ **genetic engineering** will lead to the **eradication** of disease and the end of **ageing**;
■ **virtual reality** will make it possible to travel anywhere;
■ it will be possible to upload and store people's memories, and to enter other people's minds remotely;
■ robots will become **conscious**;
■ human and artificial minds will **merge**.

22 Critical thinking Discuss the questions in pairs.

1 Do you think these predictions will happen? If so, when?
2 Which of these developments would you welcome, and which (if any) would you fear? Why?

➡ See **VOCABULARY EXTENSION** page 137

SPEAKING SKILLS

Debating

23 PAIRWORK Read and discuss the questions.

1 Fifty years ago, people believed that they would have more free time in the future because computers would free them from work. Were they right?

2 Brainstorm examples of machines that have liberated us (for example, washing machines). What do we do with the extra time?

24 ▶ 🔊 [1.32] Listen and watch the video. Why is Grace worried?

key expressions	
presenting argument	asking questions
☐ The first thing we have to consider … ☐ I am convinced that … ☐ It is clear to me that … ☐ Anybody can see that … ☐ You can't deny that …	☐ Could you explain what you mean by …? ☐ Can you define …? ☐ Where did you get your information from?

25 ▶ 🔊 [1.32] Listen and watch again and tick (✓) the key expressions Grace uses to present her argument.

🌐 SPEAKING STRATEGY

Challenging information / facts

☐ *Oh, come on!*
☐ *You're exaggerating.*
☐ *Be reasonable!*
☐ *I doubt that very much.*

☐ *But surely … (+ counter-statement)*
☐ *I'm not so sure.*
☐ *That's not the point …*

B2 FIRST | IGCSE

26 ▶ 🔊 [1.32] Listen and watch again and tick (✓) the expressions from the strategy box you hear.

27 GROUPWORK Discuss in groups of four. Pair A: brainstorm reasons why the jobs below are in danger because of technology. Pair B: brainstorm reasons why the jobs will always exist.

- shop assistants
- farmers
- teachers
- firefighters
- nurses

SOUNDS ENGLISH

The /ɪ/ and /iː/ sounds

28 🔊 [1.33] **PAIRWORK** Listen to a British English speaker and a learner of English say the same sentence. Discuss the differences.

Do your new shoes fit your feet?

📢 SOUND STRATEGY

When pronouncing words that contain the short sound /ɪ/, learners of English often lengthen the sound and say /iː/. Practise each sound, and notice how the shape of your mouth changes.

29 🔊 [1.34] Listen and repeat. Then practise.

	A /ɪ/	B /iː/
1	sit	seat
2	hit	heat
3	fit	feet
4	did	deed
5	mill	meal
6	fill	feel

30 🔊 [1.35] **PAIRWORK** Listen, read and repeat. Then practise reading.

1 Please take a **seat** and **sit** down.
2 It was so hot that the **heat hit** us.
3 These shoes don't **fit** my **feet**.
4 When **did** you do the **deed**?
5 Let's have a **meal** at the **mill**.

31 🔊 [1.36] **GAME** Listen and repeat the sound you hear. Your partner guesses and shows you if it's short or long.

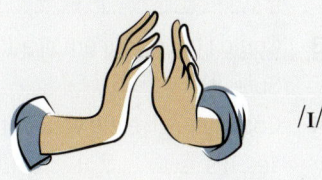

/ɪ/

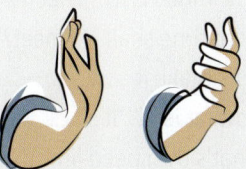

/iː/

LISTENING SKILLS

A

B

LEAD IN

32 PAIRWORK Describe the two photos. Then discuss these questions.

1 What are their similarities and differences?
2 Which one would you prefer to use?

LISTENING STRATEGY

Take notes and fill in tables and charts

In these tasks you are listening for detail. They are often numbers, times, dates and spellings.

- Read all the questions first, including the example.
- Watch out for *distractors* – e.g., when a speaker says something and then changes it, or when several possibilities are mentioned.
- Note down the answers as you listen.

IELTS

PRACTICE

33 [1.37] Look at the questions. What kind of detail are you listening for? Circle the most important words. Then listen and complete.

1 'What's your number?' 'It's ....'
2 'How do you spell your surname?'
'It's ....'
3 'Could I have your email address?'
'Sure. It's ....'
4 'Could you give me your date of birth?'
'Yes. It's ....'
5 'How much is it?' 'That'll be £............, please.'
6 'What time shall we meet?'
'Let's make it .... Is that OK?'
7 'How far is it?' 'It's ....'
8 'What's the speed limit?' 'It's ....'

34 [1.38] Before you listen, look at the cues and try and predict what you are going to hear. Then listen to the conversation and complete the notes.

- ◢ Destination   1 .... (place)
- ◢ Single or return?   2 ....
- ◢ Cheapest option   3 ....
- ◢ Last bus leaves at   4 ....
- ◢ Cheap train ticket costs 5 ....
- ◢ Train takes   6 .... minutes
- ◢ Train arrives at   7 .... station

35 [1.39] Look at photo B in exercise 32 again. Listen to the speaker and complete the notes.

1 name of system: ....
2 number of passengers per capsule: ....
3 speed: ....
4 capsules float above layer of ....
5 distance between San Francisco and Los Angeles:
....
6 cost of single ticket: ....
7 cost of project: ....

36 PAIRWORK Would you like to travel in this way? Why / Why not?

Preparing a speech for a debate

LEAD IN

37 Look at the photo of a class debate. Answer the questions.

1 What happens in a debate?
2 How is a debate different from a normal presentation?
3 Have you or your class ever had a debate?
4 What kind of topics do you think are good choices for a debate?

PRACTICE

38 Match the lists (1–6) to the headings (a–g).

0 [c] in fact, actually, don't forget …, certainly, definitely
1 [ ] that's why …, for this reason, therefore, consequently, so, because of this …, due to, as a result …
2 [ ] moreover, in addition, furthermore, what's more, that's not all …
3 [ ] however, although, on the other hand, in contrast, whereas, on the contrary …
4 [ ] for example, let me explain / give you an example, in other words, what I mean is …
5 [ ] first of all, let me begin by saying …, I'd like to say I support / am against this statement, because …
6 [ ] so, finally, as a conclusion, I want to conclude by saying …

a to make another point (on the same side)
b to contrast the opposing view
c to emphasise
d to explain further
e to describe reasons and consequences
f to conclude the reasons
g to start the presentation

ACADEMIC STRATEGY

In a debate, there are usually two speakers who present opposing views. Then the group discusses and asks questions.

- Before the debate note down the points you want to make and decide in which order to make them.
- Prepare a strong introduction which makes your position clear.
- Connect your points with linkers that give emphasis (for example, *instead of*, *moreover*, *that's not all* …).
- Finish with a memorable conclusion that echoes your introduction.

39 PAIRWORK Think about the topic below and add ideas to both columns. Put the ideas in order of importance, then use the expressions in exercise 38 to link some of the ideas.

Technology will make our lives better in the future.

■ FOR	■ AGAINST
• less work (driverless cars, robots) = more leisure time	• more unemployment – less money – increased poverty
• better medicine, nutrition – live longer – quality of life better	• no need to leave home – lazy, unfit – forget how to use brains – isolated
• instant entertainment – alone or with friends – virtual travel, games, movies – never bored	• smart devices replace newspapers, books – lose ability to think, judge, make decisions

First of all, I'd like to say I support this statement. There are many reasons for this. Firstly, there'll be less work for us because of new inventions like driverless cars and robots that do the housework and cooking. Consequently, we'll have more leisure time.

40 WRITING With a partner prepare a speech to present to the other pair in your group. Use the tips from Unit 3 Life Strategy to help you.

Group A (two students): You are *for* the topic. Prepare your opinions.

Group B (two students): You are *against* the topic. Prepare your opinions.

REVISE AND ROUND UP

1 Complete the sentences using the correct form of adjectives in brackets.

0   gold / silver / plastic (*valuable*)
   A Silver **is more valuable than** plastic.
   B Plastic is the ...**least valuable**... .
1   bikes / motorbikes / cars (*expensive*)
   A Bikes .... motorbikes.
   B Cars are the ....
2   100% / 80% / 50% (*good*)
   A 100% is .... mark.
   B 80% is .... 50%.
3   Italian summers / British summers (*hot*)
   A Italian summers .... British summers .
   B British summers .... as ....

2 Complete the sentences with the words below.

> a lot ▪ a little ▪ more ▪ most (x3) ▪
> people ▪ quicker ▪ than ▪ the (x2)

A recent survey of people in more than 140 countries
show that the ⁰......**most**...... generous nation on earth
is also one of ¹......................... poorest. The survey
showed that in Myanmar the people are ².........................
generous than anywhere else, including the USA
and the UK. People from countries like Nepal, Libya
and Iraq were also among the ³......................... generous
people in the world. In contrast, it showed that British
people give ⁴......................... bit less money
⁵......................... they used to. Even though there are
⁶......................... more ways to donate these days, fewer
⁷......................... actually use them. It seems that people
with ⁸......................... least money can be ⁹.........................
to help others than people with the ¹⁰......................... .

3 Complete with *too many, too much, too few, too little* or *enough*.

0   Yuk! I've put far ...**too much**... sugar in my coffee.
1   We haven't got .... money to go out
    tonight.
2   This website doesn't help at all. There's
    .... information.
3   Forty students in one class are ....
4   Is there .... bread for tomorrow's
    breakfast?
5   Sorry, we can't stop for lunch. There isn't
    .... time.
6   We need more doctors. .... young
    people are studying medicine.

4 Complete the sentences with the correct form of the adverbs in brackets and add any extra words if necessary.

0   These days, I have to get up **earlier than** I used
    to. (*early*)
1   Sometimes the people who work the ....
    are paid the .... (*hard / bad*)
2   Let's try that dance again! Try to move
    .... than the first time and not
    as .... (*careful / fast*)
3   I sing quite .... but my sister sings far
    .... me! (*good / good*)
4   The show started .... we were
    expecting, so we didn't get home as ....
    we promised. (*late / early*)
5   There will be a prize for the person who performs
    .... (*good*)

5 Rewrite the sentences so that they mean the same. Use the word given in brackets.

0   There are too few well-paid jobs. (*enough*)
    There ......**aren't enough well-paid jobs**...... .
1   Jamie can do mental arithmetic faster than me.
    (*fast*)
    I ....
2   I don't speak French as well as my brother. (*than*)
    My brother ....
3   Some people don't have enough food. (*little*)
    Some people ....
4   We didn't sell enough tickets. (*too*)
    We ....
5   Nobody works as hard as Tom. (*the*)
    Tom ....

6 Complete the sentences. Write *will, won't, might* or *might not*.

0   Jack is 17. His next birthday ....**will**......... be
    his 18th.
1   Perhaps I'll go shopping on Saturday, or I
    .... stay at home – I haven't decided.
2   I usually go running on Sundays, but I ....
    have time this week – I'm not sure yet.
3   The shop is closed for the weekend.
    It .... be open again until Monday.
4   Don't worry. I'm sure Pete .... call you
    soon.
5   I didn't like that café at all. I certainly ....
    go there again!

7 Complete with the future or future perfect form of the verbs in brackets.

0 David will be very tired when he gets off the plane and he **won't have slept** (not / sleep) properly for 24 hours.

1 Andy is travelling round the world. By the time he comes home he .... (visit) 20 countries.

2 I'm not really tired. I don't think I .... (go) to bed until later.

3 They're still building the new hospital. I'm sure they .... (not / complete) it by the end of the month.

4 Do you think people .... ever .... (live) on Mars?

5 If we aren't careful, in 20 years' time there will be office blocks everywhere and all our green spaces .... (disappear).

6 Hurry up! By the time we get there, the party .... (finish)!

8 Choose the correct option.

0 What .... tomorrow? Would you like to meet up for a coffee?
(A) are you doing   B will you do

1 This time tomorrow I .... my driving test. Wish me luck!
A will do   B will be doing

2 They .... a good film next week. Shall we go?
A 're showing   B will show

3 I'm excited about the party. We .... fun.
A 're having   B 're going to have

4 John's on his way to Paris. In a few hours' time, he .... along the Champs-Élysées!
A 's walking   B 'll be walking

5 Really, don't worry. You .... your exams.
A 'll pass   B 'll be passing

6 The weather forecast says it .... tomorrow.
A 's raining   B 's going to rain

9 Complete the text with the words below.

living ▪ be x 2 ▪ live ▪ might ▪ is

I believe that in thirty years' time life will **0** ....**be**........ much better than it **1** .... now. People will **2** .... longer and they will **3** .... happier and healthier. My friends and I **4** .... live to be a hundred. I'm certainly going to try! I also believe that people will soon be **5** .... on Mars.

Reading and Use of English

10 Choose the correct option.

Will robots change our lives?

In the **0** .... future, we will all have domestic robots in our homes. However, they won't **1** .... like the robots in *Star Wars* – no, they will be much **2** .... mechanical and a lot more human. Perhaps this sounds like sci-fi – but it is **3** .... going to happen (or so scientists say!). We'll have fewer **4** .... to perform around the home. **5** .... of doing housework and preparing meals, we'll be relaxing and socialising. Does all this **6** .... too good to be true? Well, perhaps it is. We can't be certain, but we might end **7** .... with too **8** .... free time – because robots will have **9** .... over many of our jobs! So, on the one hand, we'll be **10** .... less busy, but on the other hand, we **11** .... not have enough money to enjoy our new freedom. Only time will **12** ....

	A	B	C	D
0	close	far	(C) near	ready
1	see	look	watch	touch
2	less	not	little	least
3	surely	nearly	not	certainly
4	chores	work	duties	housework
5	Instead	Rather	Whereas	Alternatively
6	hear	tell	sound	mention
7	on	up	over	down
8	plenty	many	lots	much
9	got	taken	made	given
10	very	more	few	far
11	could	would	might	going
12	say	speak	tell	see

5 Law and order

LEAD IN

1 Describe the photos.

2 [▶] [🔴] [2.02] Read, listen and watch. In what ways is this prison successful?

PRISON PARADISE

Originally prisons were places where criminals stayed while they waited for their punishment. Around 200 years ago *going to prison* became an actual punishment. Since then, both our idea of prisons and the prison
5 buildings have not really changed. Prisons in Britain are old, dark, uncomfortable places.

Many people believe that prison is a place where bad people go, people whose crimes are serious, people who deserve to be locked up. The walls that surround them
10 should be high and the bars on the doors and windows strong – they should be, and usually are, miserable places.

However, there is growing evidence to suggest that this type of imprisonment doesn't work. People go to prison
15 and come out unchanged, ready to continue with their life of crime. As a result some countries are trying a different approach.

Bastøy is a small island off the southern coast of Norway, the kind of place which you might choose for a holiday. However, it is in fact a prison – but a prison like no other.
20 The prisoners, whose crimes include murder, live in wooden cottages and carry their own keys. They work, shop and socialise freely. There's a library, a health centre and a church. Prisoners can visit the beaches, where they sunbathe or swim. Some work on the farm, which produces fresh ingredients for the kitchen. Others help to keep the ferries running. All of them receive an education and training that will prepare them for
25 the outside world. The guards, who don't wear uniforms, socialise with the prisoners; often it's difficult to tell them apart. This is completely different from most prisons where offenders spend their days in small cells with very little to do. Many people argue that criminals do not deserve such a lifestyle. However, this system is mostly successful. Not many ex-prisoners reoffend – in fact some even return as visitors. No wonder, then,
30 that this innovative approach is attracting attention from countries all over the world.

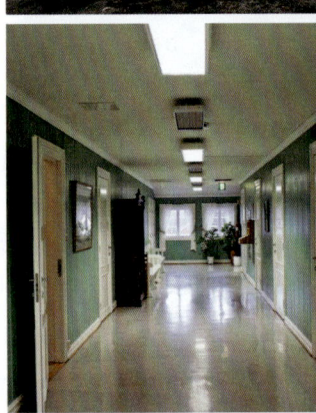

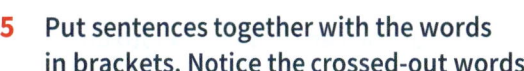

PRACTICE

3 ▶ ◄ [2.02] **Read, listen and watch the video again and answer the questions.**

1 What was the original purpose of prisons?
2 What is the main problem with traditional prisons?
3 Have any of the prisoners at Bastøy committed violent offences?
4 What kind of clothes do the guards wear?
5 What does the writer feel about prisons like Bastøy?

GRAMMAR GUIDE

Relative clauses

Defining relative clauses

- *Prison is a place **where** bad people go.*
- *They are for people **whose** crimes are serious.*
- *They are for people **who** / **that** deserve to be locked up.*
- *The walls **that** / **which** surround them should be high.*

When the relative pronoun is the object of a sentence, it can be omitted:

- *It's the kind of place (**which** / **that**) you might choose for a holiday.*

Non-defining relative clauses

- *The prisoners, **whose** crimes include murder, live in wooden cottages.*
- *They can visit the beaches, **where** they sunbathe or swim.*
- *Some work on the farm, **which** produces fresh ingredients for the kitchen.*
- *The guards, **who** don't wear uniforms, socialise with the prisoners.*

➡ See **GRAMMAR REFERENCE** Workbook page 121

4 **Look at the Grammar guide and complete the rules. Write *defining* or *non-defining*.**

1 A .... relative clause gives us information that is vital to the sentence.
2 A .... relative clause gives us extra information.
3 You could remove a .... relative clause and the most important part of the sentence would still be there.

5 **Put sentences together with the words in brackets. Notice the crossed-out words.**

0 A prison cell is a small room. Prisoners sleep ~~there~~. (*where*)
   A prison cell is a small room where prisoners sleep.
1 Guards are officers. ~~Their~~ job is to look after the prisoners. (*whose*)
2 Criminals often regret the crimes. They committed ~~them~~. (*which / that / -*)
3 A convict is someone. A court convicted ~~him~~. (*who / that / -*)

6 **Write sentences with relative clauses.**

0 Alcatraz is the name of a prison. Some of America's most dangerous criminals lived there.
   Alcatraz is the name of a prison where some of America's most dangerous criminals lived.
1 It's built on an island. The island lies about 2 km away from the Californian coast.
2 There were no successful escapes from Alcatraz. It had extremely high security.
3 There are stories and films about some of the prisoners. Their names include Al Capone and Machine Gun Kelly.
4 Al Capone was a criminal. He was famous for his violence.
5 Al Capone went to prison not for violent crime but for tax evasion. He died in 1947.
6 Machine Gun Kelly was another violent gangster. His most famous crime was the kidnapping of an oil magnate and businessman in 1933.
7 He collected $200,000 ransom for the man. He had kidnapped him.
8 The prison is now a tourist attraction. Thousands of people visit (it) every year.

7 **Critical thinking** **Do you think these people are criminals? Why / Why not? Discuss in pairs.**

1 People who steal food because they're hungry.
2 Environmental protesters who obstruct building work.
3 People who download films illegally.

READING SKILLS

LEAD IN

8 Describe what you can see in the photo on page 53. What do you think is happening?

PRACTICE

9 **[2.03]** Read and listen to the title and first paragraph of the text. Answer these questions.

1 What do you think you will read about in the rest of the story? Try to guess some words.

2 Is the story true? How do you know?

10 **[2.04]** Read and listen to the rest of the text. What was ironic about John's former job?

> ### 🌐 READING STRATEGY
>
> **Understand narrative texts**
>
> In some exams you need to answer open questions about a narrative text, using your own words. Questions may be about the story itself but might also ask about what you infer.
>
> - Read the whole text through to understand the sequence of events.
> - Read it again and notice the choice of vocabulary. Do some words have a different meaning from the obvious?
>
> IGCSE

11 **PAIRWORK** Answer these questions.

1 What was John's hobby?
2 What happened when Anne reported her husband missing?
3 What clues suggested that there had been an accident?
4 Where had John hidden?
5 Where did he go next?
6 How did the police find out that he was alive?
7 What happened to John and Anne?
8 Where do you think Anne used to go on her *frequent holidays*?

12 **PAIRWORK** Answer these questions.

1 What impression of Anne do we get from paragraphs 2 and 3?
2 How does paragraph 4 change this impression?
3 According to paragraph 5, what did John do to avoid detection, and how successful was he?

Stranger than fiction...

1 John Darwin and his wife Anne lived a quiet life in an English coastal town. There was nothing remarkable about them, or so it seemed. That all changed one spring day when John suddenly disappeared. And so began the strange story of the man who came back from the dead. 5

2 John liked canoeing. In March 2002 he paddled his boat out to sea, and failed to return. Anne reported him missing. A massive, but unsuccessful, search followed. A day or two later, the paddle and then the canoe 10 returned, but the man himself had disappeared.

3 Anne was unable to hold a funeral for her husband, but she threw flowers into the sea and mourned him. She and her two sons comforted each other. Life went on, and five years passed. Anne was rebuilding her life. She claimed 15 the insurance money, and enjoyed frequent holidays abroad. Then, suddenly, while she was away, her dead husband walked into the local police station, saying he had lost his memory.

4 What does paragraph 6 imply about John's motive for returning?
5 How did John manage to travel abroad? Where does the text tell us?

GRAMMAR GUIDE

Articles: *a / an*, *the*, no article

The indefinite article *a / an*
- *John Darwin lived **a** quiet life in **an** English coastal town.*
- *John had been **a** prison guard.*

The definite article *the*
- ***the** police*, ***the** cinema*, ***the** 1990s*, ***the** twentieth century*, *in **the** morning*
- ***the** Mediterranean*, ***the** Nile*, ***the** Dolomites*, ***the** Matterhorn*
- ***the** UK*, ***the** USA*, ***the** Netherlands*

No article
- *Mount Everest, Mont Blanc, Lake Geneva*
- *Russia, Italy, France*
- *go to / at sea, in hospital / prison / jail / court, on trial, at school / work / university, go to bed, have lunch*

the* or *a / an
The first time we mention something we use *a / an*. We use *the* when it is clear what we are referring to.
> *He lived in **a** flat. **The** flat had a connecting door.*

 See **GRAMMAR REFERENCE** Workbook page 121

the missing canoeist

4 Before the police could investigate this strange event, something even stranger happened. Darwin's face appeared all over the front pages of the nation's newspapers – and so did Anne's. They were together, smiling happily in a photo that someone had seen on Facebook … Where? In the central American country of Panama … When? The previous year. Darwin had faked his own death, and Anne had helped him.

5 The weird truth began to unravel. For much of the time Darwin had stayed out of sight in a flat. The flat had a connecting door to his own home. He'd grown a beard as a disguise and gone out for solitary walks. One of the most difficult moments had been when someone had said to him, 'Aren't you supposed to be dead?'. Then he had moved to Panama, where Anne was planning to join him.

6 Why, then, did he return to the UK? He said he was missing his sons, who had thought all this time that he was dead. It seems, however, that bureaucracy was catching up with him. The false identity which he had been using was under scrutiny. In any case, the Facebook photo gave the couple away. They both served sentences for fraud – particularly ironic for John, who had, in earlier, simpler times, been a prison guard.

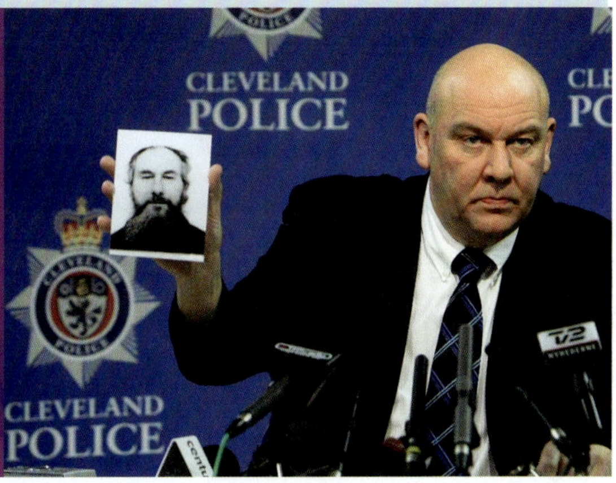

13 **Complete the sentences. Write *a* / *an*, *the* or –.**

Lord Lucan was [0]...an... English aristocrat who disappeared in [1]............ 1970s after [2]............ mysterious murder. [3]............ victim was his children's nanny ([4]............ nanny is someone who looks after [5]............ children). [6]............ police suspected Lord Lucan committed [7]............ murder but they have never proved it, and they have never found him. Some people say that he travelled to [8]............ South America, but nobody really knows [9]............ truth. Over [10]............ years, [11]............ story has become [12]............ legend. However, for [13]............ nanny's family it has always been [14]............ terrible tragedy.

14 **Critical thinking** **Discuss the questions in pairs.**

1 What do you think of John Darwin's crime?
2 Look at the statements below. Which do you agree with? Why?
- The worst thing they did was to deceive their sons.
- They were both really stupid as well as dishonest, and deserved to go to prison.
- They were clever, but unlucky at the end.

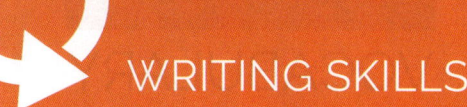

WRITING SKILLS

LEAD IN

15 **Tick (✓) the tasks where a news report would be appropriate.**

- ☐ your favourite place
- ☐ the results of a traffic survey
- ☐ a school committee meeting
- ☐ a person you admire
- ☐ a local election
- ☐ a childhood memory

PRACTICE

16 **PAIRWORK** **Look at two texts, A and B. Which is part of a newspaper article and which part of a news report? What are the differences?**

A Jennie Jackson is 18 and she's very angry. Why? A bicycle thief has just stolen her new bike. 'It was a birthday present,' said Jennie, 'and I can't afford a new one. It's such a mean thing to do.' Jennie's not the only one – the police say lots of people have reported the same thing in the last month. It looks like there's a gang of thieves at work.

B According to police records, there has been a sharp increase in the number of bicycle thefts over the last month.

WRITING STRATEGY

Write a news report

The aim of a news report is to present factual information as clearly as possible. It is a good summary of the main events. It contains:
- a list of the facts
- a clear sequence of events
- reported or direct quotations if appropriate
- formal language

See **WRITING EXPANSION** page 128

VOCABULARY

Crime and the justice system

1 SMILE! You're on TV!

2 BEWARE! Pickpockets operate in this area.

3 WARNING! DO NOT LEAVE VALUABLES IN YOUR CAR.

4  PRIVATE PROPERTY. KEEP OUT.

5 ▶ It is an offence to travel without a ticket.

6 NO SMOKING NO SMOKING

7 SHOPLIFTERS: We always prosecute.

8 KILL YOUR SPEED. NOT OUR WORKFORCE.

17 PAIRWORK Look at the signs and answer the questions.

1 Where might you see these signs? Think about:
- public transport
- shops
- car parks
- hospitals
- roads
- gates, fences or walls
- streets
- cinemas

2 What is their purpose?

3 Can you think of more examples of these kind of signs?

18 Use a dictionary to check the words in bold. Which are verbs and which are nouns? Put the sentences in the correct chronological order 1–5.

A

☐ The police **arrest** the **suspect**.

☐ The police **suspect** someone.

☐ The police **question** the **suspect** at a **police station**.

☐1 The police visit the **crime scene** and **investigate** the crime.

☐ The police **charge** or **release** the **suspect**.

B

☐ The **jury** decides on the **verdict** – they find the defendant **guilty** or **not guilty** (**innocent**).

☐ **Lawyers question witnesses**, who **give evidence**.

☐ The **defendant / accused** goes on **trial** in **court**, in front of a **judge**.

☐ **Witnesses swear** an **oath**.

☐ The **judge passes sentence** or **releases** the **defendant**.

19 PAIRWORK Use the words from exercise 18 to describe the photos. Think about these questions:

1 Who are the people?   2 Where are they?

3 What are they doing?   4 What will happen next?

20 Critical thinking Read the situations. Do you sympathise with any of these people? Which ones? Why / Why not?

1 Tom was driving his wife to hospital. She was in great pain. He broke the speed limit.

2 Grace cycled home in the dark with no lights on her bike.

3 Steve walked out of a bookshop without paying for the book he'd been looking at. It was a mistake, but he decided to keep it.

4 Molly said nothing when the girl at the supermarket checkout missed one of her items.

5 Dan knew his friend had been shoplifting, but kept quiet.

6 Chrissy had no money and was hungry. She stole a sandwich from a supermarket.

➡ See **VOCABULARY EXTENSION** page 138

SPEAKING SKILLS

Giving advice and warnings

21 PAIRWORK Read and discuss these questions.

1 When you go on holiday, how do you keep your money safe?
2 Do you feel nervous when you use a cash machine?

22 ▶ 🔴 [2.05] Listen and watch the video. Why does Grace think Joel is trying to scare her?

key expressions	
giving advice	asking for advice / responding to advice
☐ I'd be a bit careful …	☐ Do you think that's OK?
☐ The best thing to do is …	☐ What do you think is best?
☐ That's what I'd do.	☐ Yes, I suppose that's a good plan.
☐ It's a good idea to …	☐ OK, I'll follow your advice.
	☐ That's a good idea …

23 ▶ 🔴 [2.05] Listen and watch again and tick (✓) the key expressions you hear.

🌐 SPEAKING STRATEGY

Make suggestions

To make suggestions, we use phrases like this:

☐ *Why don't you …?*   ☐ *Have you thought of …-ing?*
☐ *You could (always) …*   ☐ *What about …-ing?*

B2 FIRST   IGCSE

24 ▶ 🔴 [2.05] Listen and watch again and tick (✓) the expressions from the strategy box you hear.

25 PAIRWORK Choose a town or city that you both know.

Student A: You are going to visit the city. Tell Student B what you're planning to do and where you're planning to go. Ask for advice about how to stay safe.

Student B: Give Student A some advice about visiting the city as a tourist.

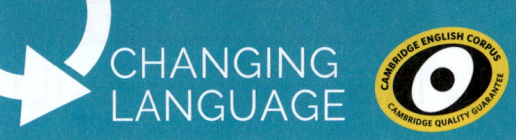

CHANGING LANGUAGE

Accents

26 Think back to the video in exercise 22. Which accent did Grace try to imitate?

27 Match the words to their phonetic transcript.

1 ☐ bath	a /njuːz/
2 ☐ bus	b /tʊər/
3 ☐ news	c /tɔːl/
4 ☐ tall	d /'tʃuː.nə/
5 ☐ tour	e /bʌs/
6 ☐ tuna	f /bɑːθ/

28 🔴 Watch the video. Which words from exercise 27 are associated with each accent?

1 Northern English ....,
   ....
2 Scottish ....
3 London ....
4 American ....,
   ....

29 PAIRWORK Discuss which accents you find the most difficult to understand.

◎ CORPUS

The Cambridge English Corpus is a multibillion-word collection of English language. Examples from the corpus are collected from all regions of the UK and provide insights into the way people use language in different places.

LISTENING SKILLS

LEAD IN

30 Look at the photo. What do you think you are going to hear about?

31 Check the meaning of the words below.

1 phishing: ....
2 scam: ....
3 virus: ....
4 Trojan: ....
5 hack / hacker: ....

PRACTICE

32 [2.06] **PAIRWORK** Listen to the conversation and answer the questions.

1 Whose laptop are Danny and May talking about?
2 What is Danny's brother called?
3 What happened when he clicked on a link?
4 What did the message say?
5 What did Danny's brother do?
6 What happened in the end?

LISTENING STRATEGY

Understand a point of view

In these tasks you are listening for opinions and attitudes.

- Read the questions, but if there are multiple options, do not read them yet (they will confuse you).
- Listen for the first time. Pay attention to the tone and mood of the speakers, e.g., are they enthusiastic? sad? disappointed? encouraging? critical? sympathetic?
- Read the complete questions and note down your answers. Then listen again to check.

B2 FIRST | IGCSE | IELTS

33 [2.06] **Listen again. Try to answer without looking at the options. Then look at the options and choose A, B or C.**

1 What is Danny's attitude to his brother's mistake?
   A He doesn't usually do things like that.
   B He was lucky to get away with it.
   C It was an easy mistake to make.

2 Who does May sympathise with?
   A Danny's father.
   B Danny.
   C Danny's brother.

3 How did Danny's father first react?
   A He was angry.
   B He was calm.
   C He was amused.

4 What does Danny hope?
   A His brother only uses his own laptop in future.
   B His brother has IT lessons.
   C His brother knows better now.

34 [2.07] **Listen to the next part. Try to complete the sentences without looking at the options. Then look at the options and choose A, B or C.**

1 May's mum had a message on her …
   A laptop.   B mobile.   C landline.

2 It said it was …
   A about her tax.   B from her office. C about a job.

3 At first she was …
   A worried.   B amused.   C annoyed.

4 May thinks the scam is …
   A stupid.   B funny.   C effective.

35 Critical thinking **Discuss the questions in pairs.**

1 Are some people more vulnerable to scams than others?
2 What is the best way to help them?

Being a responsible citizen

THE GOOD CITIZEN

We are all citizens of a country, and all citizens have rights. But we also have responsibilities – in particular, a normal citizen must obey the laws of his or her country. However, being a good citizen involves much more than not breaking the law.

A good citizen must respect others, participate in decision-making and contribute to the well-being of all. Consider these examples of bad, normal and good behaviour:

🙁 **THE BAD CITIZEN** crosses the road when the light's red;

😐 **THE NORMAL CITIZEN** crosses the road when the light's green;

🙂 **THE GOOD CITIZEN** helps a disabled person to cross the road.

LEAD IN

36 **Look at the title of the text. What do you think *citizen* means? Tick (✓) the phrases below (more than one is correct):**

☐ any adult who lives in your country / town
☐ any adult who has the right to vote
☐ anybody who was born in your country
☐ anybody who lives in your country (including children)

PRACTICE

37 **PAIRWORK** **Read the magazine article. What are the differences between a good citizen and a normal citizen?**

38 **THINKING FURTHER** **What about you? Discuss these questions.**

1 How often do you behave like a good citizen?
2 Look at the photos in the article and decide what a good citizen should do in these situations.

⚙ LIFE STRATEGY

Tips for being a responsible citizen

- Know or find out about the law and follow it.
- Report crimes. This will help protect others from possible future criminal activity.
- Learn about the differences between the political parties in your country and vote if you can.
- Get involved in charity work.
- Help keep your neighbourhood clean.
- Hand in lost property. If you find it, don't keep it for yourself.
- Try and find out about the different views and beliefs in your community and respect those differences.

39 **PAIRWORK** **Discuss these questions.**

1 Read the tips for being a responsible citizen. Which of them do you already do?
2 Do you agree that they are all necessary?
3 Are there any that you would find difficult to do?

40 **TASK** **Plan to help your community.**

1 In groups of four, look at the list below of ways you can help your community.
   - Pick up litter.
   - Recycle your rubbish.
   - Research a local charity and see if you can help out in any way (fundraising, helping in charity shops, etc.).
2 Decide which one you are going to do. Try and do that task for a month.
3 After one month, report back to your group and give a quick summary of what you did.
4 As a group, decide on the best activity. This person then presents their task to the class.
5 The class can then vote on the best activity.

6 World wonders

EXAM STRATEGIES

- B2 FIRST: Speaking and Listening
- IGCSE: Reading, Writing, Speaking and Listening
- IELTS: Listening and Academic

SPEAKING SKILLS

- Describing people and places

ACADEMIC SKILLS

- Interpreting a graph

Learning goals

Grammar

- The passive (all tenses)
- Passive with *can*, *could* and verbs with two objects
- Passive with *say*, *believe*, *know*, *think*

Vocabulary

- Buildings and materials

LEAD IN

1 **PAIRWORK** Describe what you can see in the photo above.

2 ▶ ◀ [2.08] Read, listen and watch the video.

Another Venice

Venice is sometimes called the eighth *wonder of the world*. It's not only famous for its beauty – the fact that it's there at all makes it an engineering miracle. Every year it's flooded, and every year it sinks a little more. The magnificent buildings that line the waterways are constantly eroded by both pollution and
5 water. The problem is made even worse by rising sea levels (which are caused by climate change). It's not helped by the crowds of tourists who go there every year. In addition, Italian cities like Venice have the ever-present threat of earthquakes too.

Action is being taken to defend Venice. It will not necessarily be submerged.
10 However, no such action was taken to protect the ancient Egyptian port of Thonis-Heracleion. Like Venice, this magnificent city was constructed on marshland, intersected by waterways, and located in an earthquake zone. Until recently, very little was known of this ancient wonder – except that it had been covered by the sea over 2,000 years ago. Then in 1933 a pilot noticed some
15 underwater ruins as he flew over the Mediterranean. That led to the extraordinary discovery of an ancient city called Canopus. Then, in 2001, and while Canopus was still being excavated, Thonis-Heracleion itself was located. Archaeologists were rewarded for years of research when divers found an enormous stone statue which had fallen into the sea during an earthquake. The pieces had lain on
20 the sea bed for centuries. Now they showed where the great city lay.

This sunken city, which is three times the size of Pompeii, is of enormous significance. So far only a small part has been excavated, but already important discoveries have been made. Many things have been perfectly preserved, including stone monuments covered with inscriptions, which are invaluable to historians.
25 These amazing cities have many things in common – but let's hope historians of the future won't be wondering what happened to the ancient city of Venice.

PRACTICE

3 ▶ ◀ [2.08] **PAIRWORK Read, listen and watch the video again and discuss these questions.**

1 The text mentions two reasons why Venice is a *wonder of the world*. What are they?
2 What are the main threats to Venice?
3 What led to the discovery of Canopus?
4 Which city did the statue guard?
5 What caused the statue to fall?
6 What are the main similarities and differences between Venice and Thonis-Heracleion?

GRAMMAR GUIDE

The passive: *be* + past participle

Present simple: *The waterways **are** constantly **eroded by** both pollution and water.*
Present continuous: *Action **is being taken** to defend Venice.*
Future simple: *It **will not be submerged**.*
Present perfect: *Many things **have been preserved**.*
Past continuous: *Canopus **was being excavated**.*
Past perfect: *It **had been covered by** the sea.*

questions
active When did they discover the city?
passive When **was** the city **discovered**?
active Who saw the ruins?
passive Who **were** the ruins **seen by**?
active Where do they display the discoveries?
passive Where **are** the discoveries **displayed**?

To indicate the person or thing doing the action we use **by**.

➡ See **GRAMMAR REFERENCE** Workbook page 122

4 **Look at the Grammar guide and complete the rules. Write *passive* or *active*. Then find examples in the text.**

1 In .... sentences, the subject of the verb performs the action. For example, *They discovered the statue.*
2 In .... sentences, the object becomes the subject. For example, *The statue was discovered.*
3 In a .... sentence, we don't always say who or what performed the action (the agent). If we want to name the agent, we use *by*. For example, *The statue was discovered by divers.*
4 We form the .... with the appropriate tense and form of *be* + past participle.

5 **Read the active sentences, and rewrite them in the passive.**

0 In the future the sea will cover some coastal towns.
   In the future some coastal towns will be covered by the sea.
1 They have built flood defences in Venice.
2 Pollution is destroying buildings.
3 Climate change causes some of the damage.
4 Before they found the cities, they were just legends.
5 People had described the lost cities in ancient books.
6 They didn't discover the ancient cities for thousands of years.
7 Sea creatures, sand and mud were slowly covering the ruins all that time.
8 They won't complete the excavation for many years.

6 **Write the questions in the passive.**

0 Have they found anything?
   Has .... **anything been found** .... ?
1 When will they publish the results?
   When will .... ?
2 Who built the city?
   Who was .... ?
3 Did an earthquake destroy it?
   Was it .... ?
4 Are they still discovering new things?
   Are .... ?
5 How do they pay for these projects?
   How are .... ?

7 **SPEAKING In pairs, brainstorm what you know about a famous ancient site in your country. Remember to say:**

- when it dates back to
- why it is important
- when it was discovered
- if it is at risk of being destroyed

One of the most famous ancient sites in my country is Troy. It dates back to the 4th century BCE and ...

READING SKILLS

LEAD IN

8 PAIRWORK Discuss these questions.

1 Look at the photo on page 61. How do you think it was taken? What does it show?

2 How many countries, cities and towns can you identify?

3 What else can this kind of photograph show us?

PRACTICE

9 ▶ **[2.09] Read and listen to the text. Choose the best heading.**

1 An app that uncovers the world

2 Archaeology in outer space

3 Archaeologist wins a million dollars

READING STRATEGY

Take notes from a text

In some exams you will need to make notes from a text to summarise the main points.

- Read the whole text through to understand the general meaning.
- Read it again and underline key pieces of information.
- Make notes of the key points – use bullet points.
- Read your notes again and make sure you can understand them.
- Read the whole text again to check you haven't missed any key points.

IGCSE

10 PAIRWORK Read the text again. Decide which the key facts are and underline them.

11 PAIRWORK Look at the notes. Cross out the two notes that are unnecessary.

♦ Sarah Parcak – won $1,000,000 in 2016

♦ space archaeologist

♦ doesn't dig up things in space

♦ latest satellite technology – identifies things we can't see

♦ can't see through solid ground

♦ spending prize money on massive research project – smartphone game exciting

♦ project will identify where looting (funds terrorism) happens + help stop it

♦ starting in Peru, at Machu Picchu (a wonder of the ancient world)

12 Match the notes in exercise 11 to these headings.

1 Who Sarah Parcak is, and what space archaeology means.

2 What she won, and how it will be spent.

3 Why it's important.

4 The start of the project.

GRAMMAR GUIDE

Passive with *can* / *can't* / *could* / *couldn't* and verbs with two objects

affirmative and negative	
can / *can't be* *could* / *couldn't be*	**past participle**
They **can be**	**identified** from space.
They **can't be**	**seen by** the human eye.
Steps **could be**	**taken** to stop it.
questions	
How **can** things in space **be dug up**?	

Verbs with two objects

(*award, show, send, give, offer*, etc.)

Active *They awarded a prize to her.*
They awarded her a prize.

Passive *A prize **was awarded** to her.*
*She **was awarded** a prize.*

➡ See **GRAMMAR REFERENCE** Workbook page 122

13 Rewrite the sentences so that they mean the same.

0 They can locate buried ruins using modern technology.
Buried <u>ruins can be located using modern technology</u>.

1 What can they see with infrared photography?
What .... ?

2 They could find every archaeological site in the world.
Every ....

3 They can't do the work without help from volunteers.
The ....

4 Volunteers will be offered training.
Training ....

5 Volunteers will be given photos.
Photos ....

6 They have already sent photos to some volunteers.
Some ....

14 **Critical thinking** Discuss the questions in pairs.

1 Is archaeology actually useful? If so, how?

2 Would you like to take part in a project like this? Why / Why not?

What would you do with $1,000,000? That was the prize which Sarah Parcak won in 2016. It was awarded to her for her pioneering work as a space archaeologist.

✳ How can things in space be dug up?
No, she doesn't dig in space! She doesn't look for things above us – she's interested in things that are buried below us on Earth! They can't be seen by the human eye, but they can be identified from space, with the use of the latest satellite technology.

✳ How? Is it now possible to see through solid ground?
No – that's still in the future! But infrared photography can show up patches of ground where chemical changes have occurred.

✳ I'm not sure why that's so exciting ...?
The changes are signs of human activity. They are mostly caused by building materials. In other words, they show where people used to live. Already whole cities have been discovered in this way.

✳ So that's how she's spending her prize money? On technology?
Well, yes and no ... She's using it to fund a massive research project, involving ordinary people all over the world. It's a kind of game, which can be played on a smartphone.

✳ Sounds weird. What's involved?
Volunteers will be sent photos of small areas of land. They'll be asked to study them and report any significant signs. The results will be analysed by Parcak's team, and promising information will be followed up. With enough volunteers, she says the whole world can be covered.

✳ Surely that's a bit overambitious?
She doesn't think so. The project is very exciting for historians – but there's another reason why it's important. Historic sites are frequently looted, especially in war zones, and highly valuable items are sold for huge sums of money, which often goes into the hands of terrorists. This study could identify places where this is happening, and then steps could be taken to stop it.

✳ So when does the project kick off?
It already has! They're starting in Peru and looking at the land around the ancient city of Machu Picchu. It's already one of the wonders of the ancient world, but there's a lot more waiting underground.

LEAD IN

15 Tick (✓) features that should appear in a summary.

- [ ] full sentences
- [ ] relevant information
- [ ] correct grammar
- [ ] the same style as the original text
- [ ] your own comments
- [ ] direct speech
- [ ] linkers
- [ ] reported speech

PRACTICE

16 Look at the notes about Yury Gagarin. Join them to make sentences.

0 first man in space – Yury Gagarin – Russian cosmonaut
The first man in space was Yury Gagarin, who was a Russian cosmonaut.

1 born 1934 – family poor – managed to attend secondary school
Gagarin was born in 1934, and although his family ....

2 joined army – 1955 – trained as pilot
He joined ....

3 very intelligent, fit, popular – chosen for space programme
Gagarin, who was ....

🌐 WRITING STRATEGY

Write a summary

The aim of a summary is to identify the key points in a text / article and present them clearly in a shorter text.

- It is based on notes taken from the original text.
- It includes only key points, to reflect the core message of the original text.
- It is written in full sentences and the style should match that of the original text.

IGCSE

 See **WRITING EXPANSION** page 129

VOCABULARY

Buildings and materials

17 PAIRWORK Discuss these questions.

1 The buildings in these photos are considered some of the most beautiful in the world. Do you agree? Which one is your favourite? Why?

2 Think of your own town or city. Which are your favourite and least favourite buildings? Why?

The Blue Mosque, Istanbul

The Shard, London

Garnier Opera House, Paris

Guggenheim Museum, Bilbao

Taj Mahal, India

18 Look at the list of materials. Use a dictionary to check their meanings. Think of some items that are made of these materials.

- brick
- concrete
- copper
- cotton
- glass
- gold
  (adj: golden)
- iron
- lead
- leather
- linen
- Lycra
- marble
- paper
- plastic
- polyester
- rubber
- silk
- silver
- steel
- wood
  (adj: wooden)
- wool
  (adj: woollen)

houses, made of brick

19 Look at the list in exercise 18 again and answer the questions.

1 Which ones are fabrics (textiles), which ones are metals and which ones are rocks?

2 Which fabrics are natural and which ones are synthetic?

Countables and uncountables

- Iron and steel are **metals**.
  Cars are made of **metal**.
- Cotton and silk are **fabrics**.
  Clothes are made of **fabric**.
- There are lots of **rocks / stones** in the road.
  The wall is made of **rock / stone**.
- How many **bricks** do you need?
  Houses are made of **brick**.

20 Read the information on raw materials. Then tick (✓) the raw materials.

Raw materials are the basic, natural materials used to create man-made things. For example, wood is the raw material for making paper.

- ☐ bone
- ☐ clay
- ☐ coal
- ☐ cotton (plant)
- ☐ diamonds
- ☐ glass
- ☐ grass
- ☐ mud
- ☐ nylon
- ☐ oil
- ☐ plastic
- ☐ rubber
- ☐ sand
- ☐ slate
- ☐ water
- ☐ wood
- ☐ wool

clay – bricks

21 Look again at the buildings in exercise 17. Which materials do you think were used to build them?

22 SPEAKING Discuss the questions in pairs.

1 Which raw materials do you think might run out soon? What can be done about it?

2 Some people object to the use of these materials. Why? Do you agree?
   - leather
   - fur
   - snake skin
   - wood from tropical forests
   - ivory

See **VOCABULARY EXTENSION** page 139

SPEAKING SKILLS

Describing people and places

23 **[2.10]** Listen and watch the video. Who are the people in the photo Joel and Anna are describing?

key expressions	
describing people	describing places
☐ The one with long hair?	☐ It's massive.
☐ He looks familiar.	☐ There is / are …
☐ He's got …	☐ It's got a swimming pool
☐ He's the one standing	in the grounds / basement.
next to …	
☐ He looks like a film star.	
☐ He's the one that / who …	

24 **[2.10]** Listen and watch again and tick (✓) the key expressions you hear.

SPEAKING STRATEGY

Check facts

☐ *Really?*　　　　　　　　☐ *Sorry, what was that?*
☐ *Is that really (his house)?*　☐ *What did you say (his name was)?*
☐ *Are you sure?*　　　　　☐ *(Do) You mean …?*
☐ *Can you say that again?*　☐ *What do you mean?*

Echo questions:
'It's got a swimming pool.' 'Has it?'
'He's the one that won The X Factor last year.' 'Is he?'

Question tags:
He's the lead singer in that band, isn't he?

B2 FIRST　IGCSE

25 **[2.10]** Listen and watch again and tick (✓) the expressions from the strategy box you hear.

26 Now choose a photo of a famous person or someone you like. Take turns to ask and answer about the photo. Make sure your partner is certain of the facts.

SOUNDS ENGLISH

The /ɪə/ and /eə/ sounds

27 **[2.11] PAIRWORK** Listen to a British speaker and a learner of English say the same sentence. Discuss the differences.

I fear the fare is very dear.

🔊 SOUND STRATEGY

Learners of English often confuse the /ɪə/ and /eə/ sounds. Practise making each sound, and notice how the shape of your mouth changes.

28 **[2.12] PAIRWORK** Listen and repeat. Then practise.

	A /ɪə/	B /eə/
1	ear	air
2	hear	hair
3	tear	tear
4	fear	fare, fair
5	clear	Clare
6	beer	bear, bare
7	dear, deer	dare
8	rear	rare
9	cheer	chair
10	steer	stare, stair
11	peer	pear, pair

29 **[2.13]** Listen and decide if the word you hear is in A or B.

30 **[2.14] GAME** With your partner listen and repeat. Then say the sentences very quickly. How fast can you say them?

1 Clear air is very rare.
2 Look here, a pair of deer.
3 It's rude to stare but you can peer.
4 Never fear, we're aware of the bear.

LISTENING SKILLS

LEAD IN

31 You are going to hear about a *human swan*. Check the meaning of the words below. Which words do you think you will hear?

- [ ] conservation, conservationist
- [ ] equipment
- [ ] habitat
- [ ] hunting
- [ ] migrate, migration
- [ ] motor
- [ ] parachute
- [ ] shooting
- [ ] swan
- [ ] temperature

PRACTICE

32 🔺 [2.15] **PAIRWORK** Listen to the talk and answer the questions.

1. What is Sacha Dench's job?
2. What was she studying? Why?
3. Where do the swans start and finish their journey?
4. What did Sacha do? How did she do it?
5. The speaker mentions two things that were necessary before she set off. What were they?

🌐 LISTENING STRATEGY

Listen and fill in sentences

In these tasks you are listening for details. It is essential to read the whole sentence and think about which word or expression could fill the gap. It will help you focus on what's important.

- Underline the keywords in each sentence.
- Anticipate the kind of answer you need, e.g., is it one word, more than one word, a number, a date?
- Listen and note down your answers.
- Then listen again and check.

B2 FIRST   IGCSE   IELTS

33 🔺 [2.15] **Read the text, then listen again and complete the gaps with a word, a short phrase or a number.**

In ¹........................ 2016, Sacha flew more than ²........................ km. The temperature was sometimes ³........................ °C. She was often cold while she was in the air because she ⁴........................ .
It took ⁵........................ for Sacha and her team to prepare for this adventure. In order to take off, she had to ⁶........................ . She landed every ⁷........................ .
The whole journey took ⁸........................ and in that time she crossed ⁹........................ . She met some school children who were ¹⁰........................ .
The worst part was when she ¹¹........................ and had to go to hospital.

GRAMMAR GUIDE

Passive with *say, believe, know, think*

- *It is* often **said that** birds are free.
- *Birds **are** often **said to be** free.*

- ***It is known that*** their numbers have declined.
- *Their numbers **are known to have declined**.*

- ***It is believed that*** birds face more threats now than in the past.
- *Birds **are believed to face** more threats now than in the past.*

➡ See **GRAMMAR REFERENCE** Workbook page 122

34 Rewrite the sentences so that they mean the same.

0. People think that climate change affects the birds.
   A. It is <u>thought that climate change affects the birds</u> .
   B. Climate change <u>is thought to affect the birds</u> .

1. We know that some birds are shot by hunters.
   A. It ....
   B. Some birds ....

2. They say that swans sing before they die.
   A. It ....
   B. Swans ....

3. People know that some birds die during storms.
   A. It ....
   B. Some birds ....

4. We believe Sacha Dench was the first person to fly with swans.
   A. It ....
   B. Sacha Dench ....

Interpreting a graph

LEAD IN

35 Read the information and discuss why this kind of information is important.

2011 EU CENSUS

In 2011 there was a census in every country across the European Union. Every household received a form with questions about the people who lived there. The aim of the census was not only to count the population. It was also to record the demographics (for example, age, sex, marital status) as well as race, religion, language, education, employment, etc.

PRACTICE

36 Look at the graph below carefully and answer the questions.

1 What is the purpose of the graph?
2 What does the vertical axis show?
3 What are the lowest and highest numbers shown?
4 What does the horizontal axis show?
5 What are the earliest and latest years shown?
6 What does the red line show?
7 What does the blue line show?

Projected populations of the UK and Italy

(based on statistics from the United Nations, 2016)

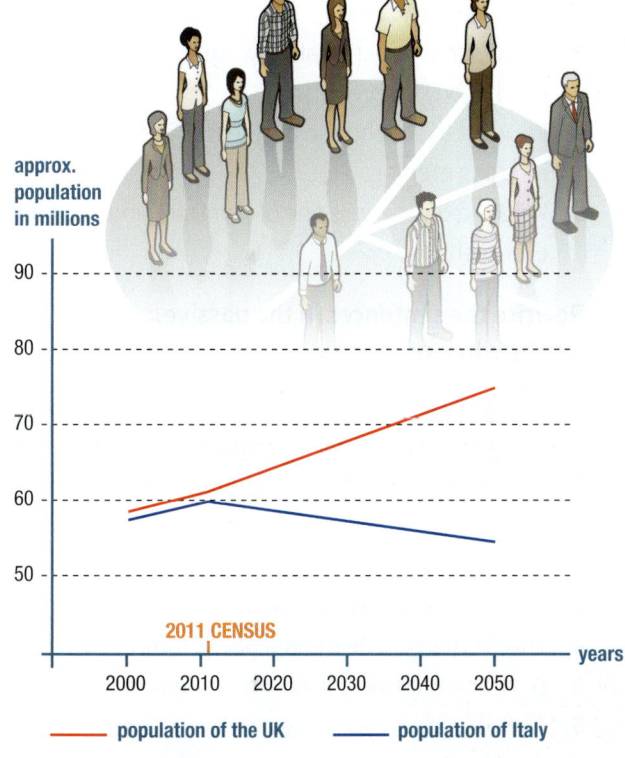

approx. population in millions

population of the UK — population of Italy

ACADEMIC STRATEGY

Graphs are a visual way of presenting information. You need to transform this information into words.

- Make sure you understand the purpose of the graph. That is also the purpose of your text.
- Use clear, formal language and only include relevant information.
- Read it again – could you draw a graph from your text?

IELTS

37 [2.16] Complete the summary of the graph in exercise 36 with the words below. Then listen and check.

approximately ▪ both ▪ contrast ▪ fallen ▪ in ▪ less ▪ rise ▪ slightly ▪ then

The population of the UK was [1].......................... 58.8 million in the year 2000, and that of Italy was [2].......................... less, at 57 million. [3].......................... 2011 there was a census in every European country. It showed that [4].......................... numbers had risen. The UK population was [5].......................... about 63 million and the population of Italy was about three million [6].......................... . According to the United Nations, the population of the UK will continue to [7].........................., and by 2050 it will be approximately 75 million; in [8].........................., by the same year, the population of Italy will have [9].......................... to about 56.5 million.

38 WRITING Now write a summary of the information in this graph. Use the model in exercise 37 to help you.

Projected populations of Germany and France

(based on statistics from the United Nations, 2016)

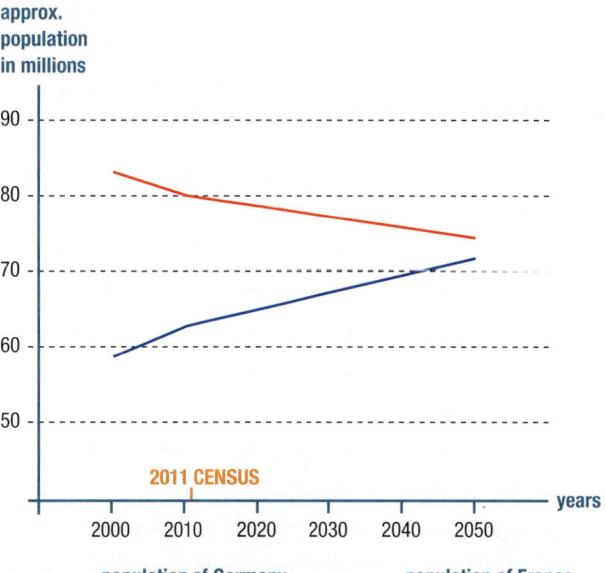

approx. population in millions

population of Germany — population of France

REVISE AND ROUND UP

1 Complete the sentences with *who, which, that, whose, when, where* or *–*. More than one answer in possible.

0 Did Jack like the present ...*which / that / –*... you gave him?

1 A university is a place .... young people continue their studies.

2 A vet is someone .... works with animals.

3 Is there a park .... we can go cycling?

4 I know someone .... father was an Olympic runner.

5 I've lost the notebook .... I write down ideas.

6 A widow is a woman .... husband has died.

7 Autumn is the season .... trees lose their leaves.

8 What's the music .... you're listening to?

2 Make one sentence with a non-defining relative clause.

0 David Bowie is a rock legend. He died in 2016.
   David Bowie, who died in 2016, is a rock legend.

1 About 22 million people live in Beijing. It's the capital of China.

2 Lady Gaga is a world-famous singer and performer. Her real name is Stefani Germanotta.

3 My brother is really interested in campanology. It means *bell ringing*.

4 Zoe has an exhibition in London soon. She's an exciting young artist.

5 Quebec City is a city in Canada. They speak French and English there.

3 Choose the correct option or options.

0 Is this the book (which) / *who* / (–) you were looking for?

1 There's a café near our school *that / which / where* I sometimes meet my friends.

2 I didn't understand the text *which / that / –* Luke sent.

3 Summer holidays are a time *when / that / –* you can relax.

4 My friend lives in Edinburgh, *that / which / who* is the capital of Scotland.

5 Do you know the name of the person *who / that / –* invented the World Wide Web?

4 Complete the relative clauses. More than one answer in possible.

0 A criminal is a person ....*who / that has committed a crime*....... .

1 Prisons are usually places ....

2 A *sentence*, ..., can be anything from a few days to life imprisonment.

3 The sentence depends on the crime ....

4 It also depends on the person's state of mind ....

5 Judges, ..., have to follow strict guidelines.

5 Read and choose the correct option.

In **0** *–* / (the) eighteenth and nineteenth centuries, British courts often sent criminals to **1** *a* / *–* new country on **2** *a* / *the* other side of **3** *a* / *the* world – **4** *–* / *the* Australia. Some of **5** *–* / *the* criminals were violent and dangerous but many of them were not. Most of them never returned to **6** *a* / *the* country where they were born.

6 Read the sentences and add articles where necessary.

0 Last summer we had *a* great holiday in *the* UK.

1 We visited London and went on trip down River Thames.

2 I took selfie of myself with guards outside Buckingham Palace.

3 It was summer but weather wasn't very good. I had to buy umbrella.

4 We went to see show in big theatre, and it was amazing evening.

5 We all said show was one of funniest things we had ever seen.

7 Rewrite the sentences in the passive. Use *by* when necessary.

0 They've just cut down a big tree in the park.
   A big tree in the park has just been cut down.

1 Will the Prime Minister present the awards?

2 The police are stopping motorists who are driving too fast.

3 They use wood to make paper.

4 They're going to deliver the parcel tomorrow.

5 Did they catch the person who stole your wallet?

6 They haven't recycled the paper.

8 Rewrite the sentences using the words in brackets so that they mean the same.

0 The manager was sent a complaint. (*to*)
A complaint ......*was sent to the manager*...... .

1 They couldn't prevent the floods. (*be*)
The floods ....

2 People say that your school days are the happiest days of your life. (*said*)
It ....

3 We weren't given the correct information. (*us*)
The ....

4 You can see the moon clearly at the moment. (*seen*)
The ....

5 They think the universe began with a Big Bang. (*thought*)
It ....

9 Correct the mistakes.

0 That's the shop which I bought my guitar. **where**

1 Cardiff, that is the capital of Wales, has an excellent university.

2 I don't like films which they frighten me.

3 I've already eaten the chocolate that I bought it this morning.

4 What's a best film you've ever seen?

5 The Netherlands is the country which has a monarch.

6 Have you ever visited USA or Canada?

7 The most famous river in the India is the Ganges.

8 The new supermarket will be open by a reality TV star.

9 I've been award a prize for my essay!

10 We hid behind the tree so that we can't be seen.

10 Complete the text with the words below.

> filmed · known · set · made · ~~directed~~ · called

Last night I watched an old film called *A Fistful of Dollars*, which was **0** ...*directed*... by Sergio Leone in 1964. It's **1** .... in Mexico, and it's about a stranger who is **2** .... as the Man with No Name. It's the film that made Clint Eastwood a star. Films like this, which were very popular in the '60s, are often **3** .... *spaghetti westerns* because firstly the people who made them were mostly Italian, and secondly, they were often **4** .... in Italy.

TOWARDS B2 FIRST

Reading and Use of English

11 Read the text. Use the words in capitals to form a word that fits the gaps.

HOLIDAY CRIMES

0 .....*Everyone*..... loves to bring home a souvenir of their holidays but you need to be **1** .... about what you choose. In some places, **2** .... are not allowed to take home sea shells or sand from the beach. If they do, they will have to pay a fine and leave their souvenirs behind. **3** ...., airport police arrested a tourist when they found a bag of objects he had collected on the beach. Be careful when you visit **4** .... buildings and archaeological sites. Visitors are **5** .... that writing their names on a wall or taking small pieces of stone is **6** .... This is called *heritage crime* and it is becoming **7** .... common. Minor damage to a place that has thousands of visitors is **8** ...., but people should realise that removing **9** .... – even a small piece of stone – is **10** ....

ONE
CAUTION
VISIT

RECENT

HISTORY

AWARE

LEGAL
INCREASE

AVOID

THING
THIEF

Writing

12 Write your essay in about 140 and 190 words.

In your English class you have been talking about school rules. Now your teacher has asked you to write an essay. Use all the notes and give reasons for your point of view.

School rules are not necessary.
Do you agree?

NOTES – Write about:

1 why schools need rules

2 what students can learn from school rules

3 (your own ideas)

7 Glorious food

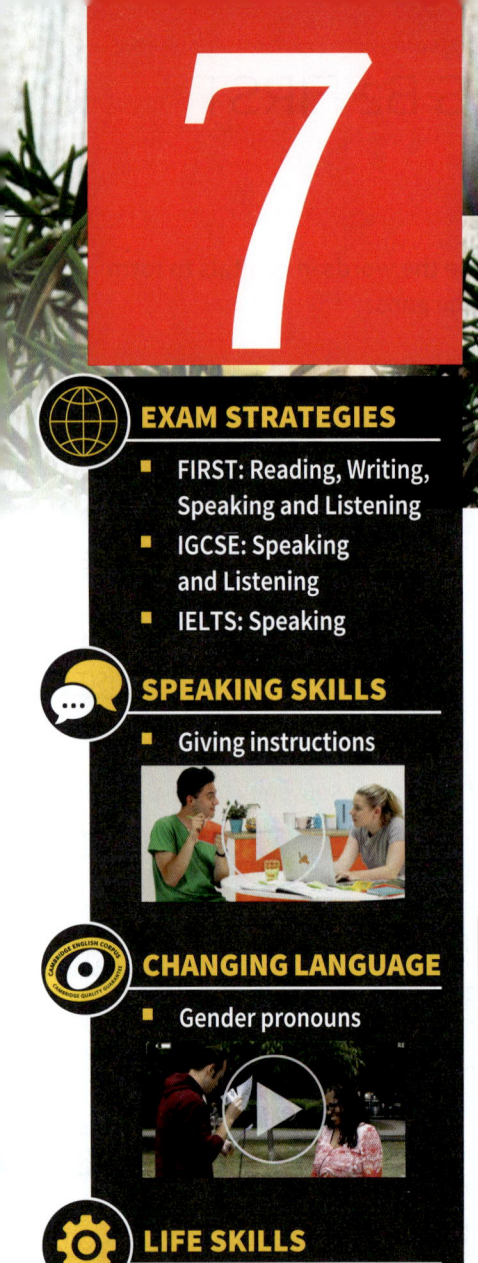

EXAM STRATEGIES

- FIRST: Reading, Writing, Speaking and Listening
- IGCSE: Speaking and Listening
- IELTS: Speaking

SPEAKING SKILLS

- Giving instructions

CHANGING LANGUAGE

- Gender pronouns

LIFE SKILLS

- Time management

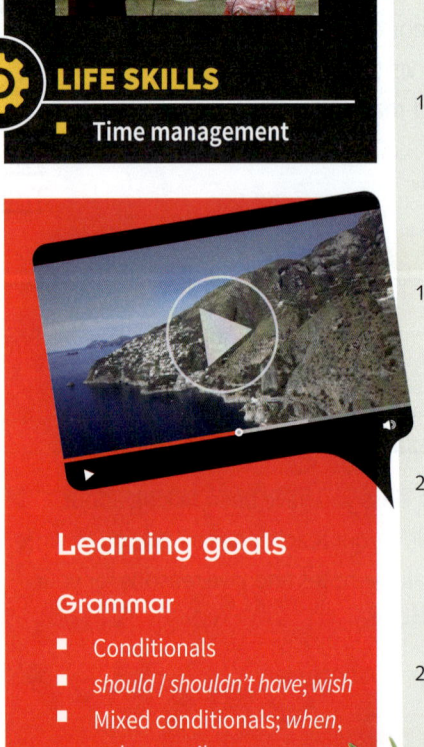

Learning goals

Grammar

- Conditionals
- *should / shouldn't have*; *wish*
- Mixed conditionals; *when, unless, until, as soon as*

Vocabulary

- Cooking

LEAD IN

1 PAIRWORK Look at the photo and answer the questions.

1 What food can you see in the picture?
2 Where does it come from?
3 What are its ingredients?
4 Do you think it's healthy?

2 [2.17] Read, listen and watch. What could be the simple secret?

The Secret of a Long Life?

What makes the small Italian town of Acciaroli one of the healthiest places in the world? Out of a population of around 2,000, a stunning 300 residents have reached, or passed, the age of 100. Why? How? There are a number of theories.

Genes Of course if we start life with good genes, we have the best possible
5 advantage. The centenarians of Acciaroli have inherited longevity genes. In other words, if they had grown up in a different place, they would probably still have lived long and healthy lives. But would they have lived as long as this? Probably not.

Geography This fishing port is famous for its clean water and unpolluted air. It's also near steep hills, which the inhabitants climb regularly. These factors
10 undoubtedly play a part. We would all be healthier and fitter if we breathed such clean air and took such frequent exercise. However, these things alone do not solve the mystery.

Lifestyle Surprisingly, despite their regular exercise, a lot of the elderly residents of Acciaroli are overweight and a lot smoke! So here's a question – how long would
15 they live if they were slimmer and if they didn't smoke?

Diet Their Mediterranean diet certainly helps. They eat plenty of fresh fish, fruit and vegetables as well as whole grains, nuts and olive oil. However, not all centenarians eat a similar diet – for example, in Iceland, where life expectancy is also high, they eat more milk products and meat. One thing in common is the lack of
20 processed food – perhaps if we cooked more from scratch, we would all benefit.

Rosemary The people of Acciaroli love this herb, and scientists think it might be the simple secret to their longevity. If their research proves this theory, rosemary will probably become the next superfood. If I were
25 you, I'd start eating it now!

PRACTICE

3 **[2.17] Read, listen and watch the video again and complete the sentences in your own words.**

0 About 300 residents of Acciaroli are __a hundred, or older__ .

1 It's an advantage if we inherit ....

2 The environment is healthy because ....
....

3 The region is hilly, so ....

4 Their lifestyle is not entirely healthy because ....
....

5 Neither the Mediterranean nor the Icelandic diet
....

6 The residents of Acciaroli often cook with ....
....

GRAMMAR GUIDE

Conditionals

zero *If we **start** life with good genes, we **have** the best possible advantage.*

first *If their research **proves** this theory, rosemary **will** probably **become** the next superfood.*

second *We **would** all **be** healthier and fitter **if** we **breathed** such clean air.*

third *If they **had grown up** in a different place, they **would** probably still **have lived** long and healthy lives.*

➡ See **GRAMMAR REFERENCE** Workbook page 123

4 Complete the rules. Write *zero*, *first*, *second* or *third*.

1 We use the .... conditional to talk about events or situations that always have the same consequences, e.g., *If you heat ice, it melts*.

2 We use the .... conditional to talk about possible future events or situations, e.g., *If it rains, I'll need an umbrella*.

3 We use the .... conditional to talk about imaginary or unlikely events or situations (in the present or future), e.g., *If I won the lottery, I'd buy a private jet*.

4 We use the .... conditional to talk about imaginary and impossible events or situations in the past, e.g., *If my parents hadn't met, I wouldn't have been born!*

5 Complete the sentences. Use the correct form of the verbs in brackets.

0 If we __hadn't eaten__ (not / eat) so many cakes, we __wouldn't have been__ (be) ill yesterday.

1 These days, Tom only .... (go) to restaurants if there .... (be) a vegetarian menu.

2 If someone offered you raw fish, ... (you / eat) it?

3 You'll get fat if you .... (have) too much junk food and .... (not / take) regular exercise.

4 If I .... (be) on holiday now, I'd be on the beach with an ice cream.

5 The biscuits .... (disappear) fast if I hadn't hidden them from the children.

6 If you .... (see) a pineapple in the supermarket, will you buy it, please?

7 I .... (cook) dinner last night if you .... (ask) me to – but you didn't.

8 If you .... (eat) too much sugar, it's bad for your teeth.

9 If I .... (be) you, I .... (not / eat) that cheese. It's green!

10 Wow! That pizza was really expensive! .... (you / order) it if you .... (notice) the price?

6 PAIRWORK Read the situations. How many conditional sentences can you make?

1 Frank missed school yesterday. He had an upset stomach.

2 Sarah wants to make a cake. She hasn't got any flour.

3 Amy wanted to cook from scratch but she didn't have time. She had a ready meal.

4 Nick dreams of becoming a chef. He hopes he'll get on a training course.

5 Mike is allergic to nuts. He needs to ask about the ingredients of a takeaway meal.

6 Kate isn't sure the supermarket will have all the vegetables she needs. There's a market a little further away.

7 SPEAKING In pairs, discuss the questions.

1 Would you want to live to be 100?

2 If you would, what would it depend on?

3 If you wouldn't, why not?

READING SKILLS

LEAD IN

8 PAIRWORK Discuss these questions.

1 Brainstorm the names of some popular TV cookery shows. What are they like?

2 Do you watch any of them? Why / Why not?

3 Why do you think people like them?

PRACTICE

9 Read the first part of the text. Use the words in capitals to form a word that fits the gaps.

READING STRATEGY

Insert the correct word for text completion

In some exams you will need to complete missing words in a text. This requires both reading skills and knowledge of grammar.

- Read the whole text to understand the general meaning.
- Look at each gap and think about what kind of word it could be (e.g., a verb, a noun, an adjective, an adverb). Remember to read the whole sentence before you decide.
- Use the stem word provided and change it so that it fits grammatically and makes sense.
- Always read the sentence again to check.

B2 FIRST

10 ▰ **[2.18]** Now read and listen to the whole text. Check your answers. Who enjoyed the competition?

11 Choose the correct option.

1 According to the text, British people often like cookery shows
   A and cooking.   **B** but not cooking.

2 The most popular shows feature
   A ordinary people.
   B celebrities and ordinary people.

3 The public enjoy them because they're
   A entertaining.   **B** educational.

4 Johnny didn't
   A have a good time.   **B** cook very well.

5 Kylie thinks
   A she deserved to win. **B** her friends were wrong.

6 Greg wishes
   A he hadn't gone on the show.
   B he'd cooked something different.

Reality Bites

Look at a British TV guide any day of the week, and you'll find a range of cookery programmes. They include
0 ...*demonstrations*......., contests and   **DEMONSTRATE**

5 documentaries, featuring a mix of celebrities and ordinary people. They cover every possible angle, from
1 .... to butchery, from   **BAKE**
budget meals to cordon bleu, and they
10 cater for every diet, from vegan to dedicated carnivore. Some are light-hearted, even 2 ....,   **FUN**
others are deadly serious. All this is despite the fact that the average British
15 person is not 3 .... keen   **PARTICULAR**
on cooking – at least not in practice. Reality shows are especially popular, and some become 'must-see' TV. Some are 4 .... in which   **COMPETE**
20 one contestant is eliminated each week. In others, the contestants themselves decide the 5 .... In one   **WIN**
such show, they take turns to host a dinner party, and award each other
25 marks out of ten. Part of the programme's appeal lies in our
6 .... curiosity – the   **NATURE**
cameras let us into private homes and kitchens. However, it's mainly popular
30 because of the 7 ....,   **AMUSE**
sarcastic comments made by the
8 .... Do the contestants   **NARRATE**
ever wish they hadn't taken part? We asked a few ...

GRAMMAR GUIDE

should / shouldn't have; wish

should / shouldn't have

   I *should have listened* to my friends.
   I *shouldn't have gone* on the show.

wish

About the present:
   I *wish* I *had* the chance to do it again.

About the past:
   Do the contestants ever *wish* they *hadn't taken* part?

 See **GRAMMAR REFERENCE** Workbook page 124

I'm not a very good cook so I shouldn't have gone on the show. I came last, but I don't regret it. It was fun and I met some really nice people. I also learnt quite a lot about cooking. Who knows, I might do it again one day! **Johnny Davis**

Well, I wish I could say I enjoyed it – but I didn't, to be honest. I felt really stupid cooking, and then eating, in front of a camera crew, and I didn't like the other people. I should have listened to my friends – they told me not to do it. Did I win? No, but I should have done! **Kylie Stewart**

I didn't win – in fact I made a terrible mess of it. I shouldn't have tried out a new recipe. It ended up in the bin – very embarrassing! I really think I would have won if I'd done something simpler. I wish I had the chance to do it again. **Greg Show**

12 Read the situations and write sentences using the verbs in brackets.

0 I went on the show but I regret it. (*wish*)
I wish I hadn't gone on the show.

1 We didn't make a shopping list – what a mistake! (*should*)

2 Jack would like to know how to cook. (*wish*)

3 You did the washing-up, although I asked you not to. (*shouldn't*)

4 Oh dear, Sam didn't wash the salad before he served it. (*should*)

5 What a pity. There aren't many people here. (*wish*)

6 I didn't use a recipe when I made the soup. It wasn't very nice. (*should*)

13 **Critical thinking** Discuss the questions in pairs.

1 Why do you think people go on these shows?

2 Would you ever do it? Why / Why not?

3 Is it OK for programmes to make fun of the people who appear on them?

WRITING SKILLS

LEAD IN

14 Imagine you're reading online restaurant reviews. Which of these points would influence you?

☐ The food is delicious.
☐ It's always busy – you have to book.
☐ The service is slow.
☐ The waiters are very friendly.
☐ It's cheap.
☐ The reviewer didn't like the decor.
☐ It serves local specialities.
☐ It's expensive but special.

PRACTICE

15 Complete the text with the words below.

criticise ▪ grammar ▪ informal ▪ positive ▪ short ▪ spelling

When you write an online review, use an ¹......................... style. Anybody can read it, so make sure your ²......................... and ³......................... are accurate. Keep it ⁴......................... and to the point – and remember, reviews don't always have to ⁵......................... – they can be ⁶......................... too.

🌐 WRITING STRATEGY

Write an online review

An online review contains positive and / or negative opinions, for example of a restaurant or a hotel, based on first-hand experience. These reviews are important to businesses because they can influence future customers.

▪ Online reviews are usually short.
▪ They use informal language and contractions.
▪ They can be positive, negative or both, but should include examples or reasons.

B2 FIRST

 See **WRITING EXPANSION** page 130

VOCABULARY

Cooking

16 PAIRWORK Answer these questions.

1 Do you like cooking?
2 Who usually does the cooking at home?
3 What's your favourite food / dish?
4 Do you know any recipes? If yes, which ones?

17 Look at the photo and guess the meaning
of the words in bold. Then use a dictionary to check.

Apple Crumble

This traditional British
dessert consists
of cooked, **sweetened**
apples with a
buttery, **crumbly** topping.
It's the perfect
comfort food,
and easy to make.

18 Check the meaning of the words below.
Then read and complete the recipe.

breadcrumbs · cores · fork · handful ·
mixture · ovenproof · pinch · raisins

Ingredients

- 3 large cooking apples
- 140 g sugar
- 175 g flour
- 110 g butter
- ¹ .... of salt
- (optional) ² ....
  of fruit, e.g., ³ ....
  (about 60 g)

Method

1 **Preheat** the oven to 190 °C.
2 **Peel** the apples, remove the ⁴ ....,
  and **slice** them.
3 Put the apples and raisins (if used) in a deep
  ⁵ .... dish and **add** about 30 g sugar.
  Mix it all up.
4 Put the flour, salt and the rest of the sugar
  into a bowl. **Cut** the butter into pieces.
5 Use your hands to **rub** the butter into the flour
  and sugar, until it looks like ⁶ ....
6 **Pour** the flour ⁷ .... over the apples
  and **spread** it out evenly with a ⁸ ....
7 **Bake** for 35–40 minutes, until the top looks
  golden brown.
8 Allow to **cool** for ten minutes. **Serve** with cream.

19 Match the verbs in blue in the recipe
to the correct pictures.

a ....

g ....

b ....

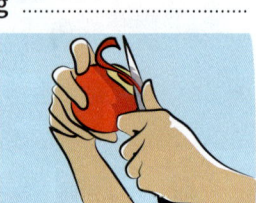

h ....

c ....

i ....

d ....

j ....

e ....

k ....

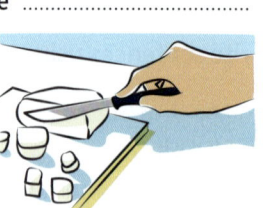

f ....

l ....

20 Match the food words below to the verbs.
Which words could match more than one verb?

bread · broccoli · carrots · cheese · eggs ·
fish · meat · onions · pasta · potatoes ·
soup · tomatoes · water

1 fry   2 stir   3 chop   4 boil   5 roast
6 steam 7 grill   8 toast   9 whisk 10 grate

➡ See **VOCABULARY EXTENSION** page 140

SPEAKING SKILLS

Giving instructions

21 **Which of these questions and requests could you help with? Which ones would you need to ask?**

1 How do you make a chocolate cake?
2 Do you know how to call the UK from your country?
3 Can you show me how to check in online for a flight?
4 How do you use a washing machine?
5 Can you help? My laptop's got a virus on it.

22  [2.19] **Listen and watch the video. How does Grace's attitude to Luke change?**

key expressions	
giving instructions	checking for items
1 Look	**5** Do you usually .... eggs and milk at home?
2 Make .... and serve	**6** What about .... ?
3 First, ... and break	**7** Oh, yes, good plan.
4 Then add	

23  [2.19] **Listen and watch again and complete the key expressions.**

SPEAKING STRATEGY

Check information

☐ ..., was it?
☐ Is that OK?
☐ Would ... be all right?
☐ Could you just talk me through it.
☐ Sorry, could you just say that again?

☐ Did you say ...?
☐ Hang on, ...?
☐ Is that what you said?
☐ What was that again?

B2 FIRST **IGCSE** **IELTS**

24  [2.19] **Listen and watch again and tick (✓) the expressions from the strategy box you hear.**

25 **PAIRWORK** **Imagine the rest of the conversation. Then practise the role play.**
Student A: You are Grace. Finish explaining how to prepare the meal.
Student B: You are Luke. Note down and check what Grace tells you to do.

CHANGING LANGUAGE

Gender pronouns

26 **Look at the adjectives and decide if they are positive or negative.**

funny ▪ weird ▪ lovely ▪ good ▪ bad ▪ nice ▪ stupid ▪ cool ▪ crazy

27 **Do you think the adjectives from exercise 26 are associated more with men or women or both?**

28  **Watch the video and check your answers from exercise 27.**

29  **Watch again and answer the questions.**

1 What do the top three adjectives associated with the word *woman* have in common?
2 Which words associated with men are negative?
3 What do some universities in the UK now consider unacceptable?
4 Why has the pronoun *they* become more common?

CORPUS

They is now commonly used as a gender-neutral third person singular pronoun. It replaces *he* as the default pronoun when talking about a person of unspecified gender.

▪ *The reader registers online, then* **they** *download the app.*

In recent years corpus data shows a marked increase in the use of the pronoun *they*.

LISTENING SKILLS

LEAD IN

30 **Discuss these questions.**

1 Do you follow a particular kind of diet (e.g., vegetarian, vegan)?

2 Brainstorm different kinds of diet you have heard of. Why do people follow them?

PRACTICE

31 **[2.20]** **PAIRWORK** **Listen to five speakers and answer the questions. Each question is related to one of the speakers.**

1 What change has she made to her diet?

2 What does she dislike?

3 What kind of food does he love?

4 Does she enjoy her diet?

5 Is his diet effective?

LISTENING STRATEGY

Link speakers to summaries

In these tasks you hear five different speakers talking about the same topic. You are listening for gist, attitude, opinion, purpose, feeling, main points and detail.

- Read all the options carefully.
- Listen for the general gist of what each speaker says.
- Be careful of distractors – words that might trick you into choosing the wrong answer.
- Note down initial ideas but keep an open mind.
- Then listen again and check.

B2 FIRST | IGCSE

32 **[2.20]** **Listen again and do the task.**

Each person (1–5) is talking about the kind of food they eat. Choose from the list the reasons (a–h) for each person's choice of food. There are three extra letters which you do not need to use.

a ☐ a specific health problem

b ☐ ethical reasons

c ☐ negative stories about food

d ☐ medical advice

e ☐ worried about their weight

f ☐ pressure from parents

g ☐ pressure from friends

h ☐ wants to be stronger

GRAMMAR GUIDE

Mixed conditionals

We can mix third and second conditionals to show how a different past would have created a different present.

past condition	present result
If I'd stopped completely,	**I'd feel** better by now.

 See **GRAMMAR REFERENCE** Workbook page 124

GRAMMAR GUIDE

Time clauses with *when, unless, until, as soon as*

- I **won't eat** them **unless** I **know** they're from happy hens.
- I **won't eat** any more **until** I **get** into those jeans.
- **When** I **stop** the training, I**'ll need** to be careful.
- **As soon as** my jeans fit, I**'ll stop**!

Remember: *unless = if not*

See **GRAMMAR REFERENCE** Workbook page 124

33 **Complete the sentences with the correct form of the verbs in brackets.**

0 If you **hadn't eaten** (*not / eat*) all that chocolate this morning, you **wouldn't be** (*not / be*) ill now.

1 Go and do your homework. I .... (*call*) you as soon as dinner .... (*be*) ready.

2 Thank you for the sandwich. I .... (*be*) very hungry by now if you .... (*not / share*) your lunch.

3 We .... (*not / have*) enough to eat tonight unless somebody .... (*go*) shopping soon.

4 Tom is in the coffee shop. I expect he .... (*stay*) there until it .... (*close*).

5 The cake .... (*be*) ready soon – when it .... (*look*) golden brown.

6 My mum .... (*not / know*) how to cook if Grandma .... (*not / teach*) her.

Time management

1	I have a very tidy bedroom.	1	2	3	4	5	
2	I always make a to-do list.	1	2	3	4	5	
3	I'm always punctual.	1	2	3	4	5	
4	I use a planner to organise my time.	1	2	3	4	5	
5	I never leave revision until the week before the exam.	1	2	3	4	5	
6	I always complete my homework on time.	1	2	3	4	5	
7	I never forget anything and I never lose anything.	1	2	3	4	5	
8	I always get enough sleep.	1	2	3	4	5	
9	I always do my homework and chores before I relax.	1	2	3	4	5	
10	I never run out of time.	1	2	3	4	5	

1 = No, I completely disagree.; **2** = Hmmm. I mostly disagree.; **3** = I partly agree.; **4** = Well, I mostly agree.; **5** = Yes. I agree completely.

Assessments

50–45	You're perfect! Are you actually real?
44–35	Impressive! You know how to manage your time. Don't forget to have fun, though.
34–25	You're pretty normal! There's room for improvement, but you have a reasonable work-life balance.
24–15	Hmmm. Maybe you should start organising your time a little better.
14–10	OK, you need to start planning right now!

LEAD IN

34 PAIRWORK Answer these questions.

1 Do you usually remember everything you have to do, or do you need help?
2 Do you use any of these things to organise your time? If so, could you manage without them?
  - a smartphone with a planner app
  - a wall planner
  - a diary
  - a notepad
  - an alarm clock
  - a homework timetable

PRACTICE

35 PAIRWORK Do the time management quiz. Compare your answers and assessment with your partner. Do you agree?

36 THINKING FURTHER Read the tips. Now answer the questions.

1 Which of these things do you already do?
2 What other tips could you add?
3 Which of the tips seem most useful?

37 TASK With your partner, look at the tips again. Then do the following:

1 Make a list of everything you have to do today and for the next three days (e.g., school work, homework, activities, home events). Compare ideas, but your lists should be individual.
2 Number the tasks according to how important they are (prioritise them).
3 Design a planner for the next three days.
  - Day 1: today – divide the rest of the day into hours until you go to bed.
  - Days 2, 3 and 4: divide each day into hours, from when you get up until when you go to bed.
  - Put in things that are fixed or already arranged (e.g., school times, after-school activities, etc.).
  - Decide where to fit in the tasks on your list – how much time will you need for each one?
  - Look at your partner's planner and make suggestions.
4 Use your planner for the next three days. Then report back to the class on the following points:
  1 Was it realistic? Did you allocate enough time for tasks, or too much time?
  2 Did it help you manage your time?
  3 Would you use it again? Why / Why not?

8 All in the mind

EXAM STRATEGIES

- B2 FIRST: Reading, Writing, Speaking, Listening and Academic
- IGCSE: Writing, Speaking, Listening and Academic
- IELTS: Reading, Speaking, Listening and Academic

SPEAKING SKILLS

- Talking about habits

ACADEMIC SKILLS

- Proofreading your work

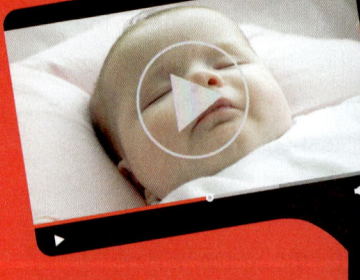

Learning goals

Grammar

- *used to* / *would* + infinitive without *to*
- *be* / *get used to* + something / *-ing*
- Gerunds and infinitives (1)

Vocabulary

- The mind

LEAD IN

1 **PAIRWORK** Describe the photos. What do you think you are going to read about? Guess some of the words you will see in the text.

2 ⏵ [2.21] Read, listen and watch. What is a *sleep cycle*?

ARE YOU SLEEP DEPRIVED?

You get up for school and already you're tired. You struggle to stay awake all morning and concentrate on your lessons. Then by the evening you think you're fine. You do your homework, watch TV and hang out online. By the time you fall asleep it's pretty late, and the next thing you know … there goes the alarm. Repeat, day after day. 5

If you're used to a sleep cycle like this, then you're probably suffering from sleep deprivation. You're not alone! Researchers believe that about 50% of British teenagers don't get enough sleep. This is a serious problem. It not only affects mood and concentration but also physical and mental health.

But how much sleep is enough? It changes with age. When you were a baby 10 you would spend more time asleep than awake (although your parents may remember this differently!). Your need for sleep declines over time, but teenagers still need about nine hours' sleep a night – about an hour more than adults. Doctors used to believe that older people need less sleep, although recent research questions this. 15

The official record for staying awake was set by a 17-year-old American student who, in 1964, stayed awake for about 11 days. After a few days he became moody and emotional, then he started to hallucinate. If he'd stayed awake much longer, he could have died. It was such a dangerous experiment that the Guinness Book of Records no longer includes the category. 20

Although none of us is likely to follow that example, many of us are sleep deprived. The problem is, we gradually get used to sleeping less. We think we're OK, and we're used to feeling sleepy – but we're damaging ourselves. The good news is, if we sleep a little longer every night, we will eventually revert to a healthy 25 sleep cycle. Perhaps it's time to ditch those devices and get to bed a bit earlier!

PRACTICE

3 **[2.21] PAIRWORK** Read, listen and watch the video again and discuss the questions.

1 What are the signs of sleep deprivation?
2 How does our need for sleep change with age?
3 What made a 17-year-old American famous in 1964?
4 How did sleep deprivation affect him?
5 Why wouldn't you find his name in the *Guinness Book of Records*?
6 How can we restore a healthy sleep cycle?

GRAMMAR GUIDE

used to / would + **infinitive without** *to*

+	You **used to / would spend** more time asleep than awake.
–	I **didn't use to sleep** through the whole night.
?	**Did** you **use to sleep** in the afternoon?

We use *used to* or *would* to talk about past habits.

We use *used to* to describe past states:

Doctors used to believe …

➡ See **GRAMMAR REFERENCE** Workbook page 125

4 Make sentences with *used to* or *would*. There may be two correct answers.

0 At my first school we .....**used to / would sing**..... (*sing*) a song every morning.

1 I .... (*believe*) in superstitions, but I don't now.

2 Before I started school, I .... (*go*) to my grandmother's house every day.

3 What .... (*people / do*) before mobile phones? I use mine all the time!

4 .... (*you / like*) classical music when you were younger? I .... (*hate*) it, but I love it now.

5 We .... (*play*) in the street when we were little. There .... (*not / be*) much traffic.

6 My grandparents .... (*not / live*) in London, but they do now.

GRAMMAR GUIDE

be / get used to + **something / -ing**

+	If you**'re used to** a sleep cycle like this … We **are used to** feel**ing** sleepy … *(We are accustomed to it, it is normal for us.)*
	We **get used to** sleep**ing** less. *(It's something we are learning to live with, we are becoming accustomed to this.)*
–	I**'m not used to** (hear**ing**) traffic outside.
?	**Are** you **used to** (hear**ing**) traffic outside?

With *get used to* we often use *can't / couldn't* or *never*:

*I **can't / couldn't get used to** (hear**ing**) traffic outside.*

*I **never got used to** (hear**ing**) traffic outside.*

➡ See **GRAMMAR REFERENCE** Workbook page 125

5 Complete the sentences. Use *be* or *get used to* and the verbs in brackets.

0 My sister has just had a baby. She ..**can't get**.... ..**used to waking up**.. (*can't / wake up*) in the night, and she's always tired.

1 Tomas has just moved to the UK. He's trying to .... the rain!

2 Amy is hiking with some friends. Her feet hurt. She .... (*not / wear*) hiking boots.

3 When we went to India I .... (*couldn't*) the heat.

4 Tom's starting a new job in a restaurant next week. The dining room is upstairs. He must .... (*run*) up and down stairs.

5 We had dinner at ten last night. I couldn't sleep. I .... (*not / eat*) so late.

6 **SPEAKING** In pairs, read the situation. Then make sentences using *be* or *get used to*. Use ideas from the list and / or your own ideas.

- language
- wear school uniform
- go home for lunch
- spicy food

Anna is from London. Her school day usually starts at 8:45 and ends at 3:30 pm. She has lunch at school and she wears a school uniform. At the moment she's on an exchange visit, staying with a family in your town, and going to school every day. She's been there for three weeks now.

READING SKILLS

LEAD IN

7 PAIRWORK Discuss these questions.

1 What's the best way to learn a language?
2 Why are some languages easier to learn than others?
3 Do you know anyone who is multilingual? What is his / her background?

8 Look at the headline. What do you think the text is about?

The Daily News

60 Pages, 7 Sections ••• 50 cents

Volume 260, No. 74

'We couldn't understand a word he was saying!'

Couple's shock as son wakes up from coma. Strange but true – teen becomes bilingual overnight!

PRACTICE

9 [2.22] Read and listen to the text. Then choose the best heading.

1 What's going on inside our heads?
2 New phenomenon puzzles doctors
3 Breakthrough in language learning

READING STRATEGY

Deal with four-option multiple choice

In some exams you will need to choose the correct answer from a list of options. Questions may focus on detail, opinion, tone, purpose, main idea, implication or attitude.

- The questions will cover the whole text, not each section separately, so make sure you read the whole text through carefully.
- Read all the options carefully, even if you think you know the answer. Remember there will be distractors.
- Read the whole text through again and check your answers.

B2 FIRST | IELTS

10 Read the text again and choose the correct option.

1 Immediately after his accident, Reuben Nsemoh
   A could understand English but couldn't speak it.
   B couldn't speak or understand English.
   C could understand Spanish but couldn't speak it.
   D couldn't speak or understand Spanish.
2 Before his accident, Ben McMahon
   A had not been to China.
   B had studied Mandarin in China.
   C knew only a little Mandarin.
   D had a Chinese girlfriend.
3 Alun Morgan
   A had never been able to speak Welsh before.
   B was fluent in Welsh and English for a few days.
   C interpreted for his Welsh-speaking wife.
   D remained a Welsh speaker.
4 Why is Ben McMahon different from the other two?
   A He was a young man.
   B He had been exposed to the new language before.
   C He recovered his English skills.
   D He kept his new skills.
5 The writer concludes that
   A learning a foreign language is easier than we thought.
   B brain damage is not always a bad thing.
   C we know more than we realise.
   D scientists don't know everything.

11 Critical thinking Discuss the questions in pairs.

1 Do you think it could be true that the brain remembers and stores everything?
2 Do you like the idea? Why / Why not?
3 What are your earliest memories? Why do you think we can't remember our first few years?
4 If a hypnotist offered to take you back to your past, would you accept? Why / Why not?

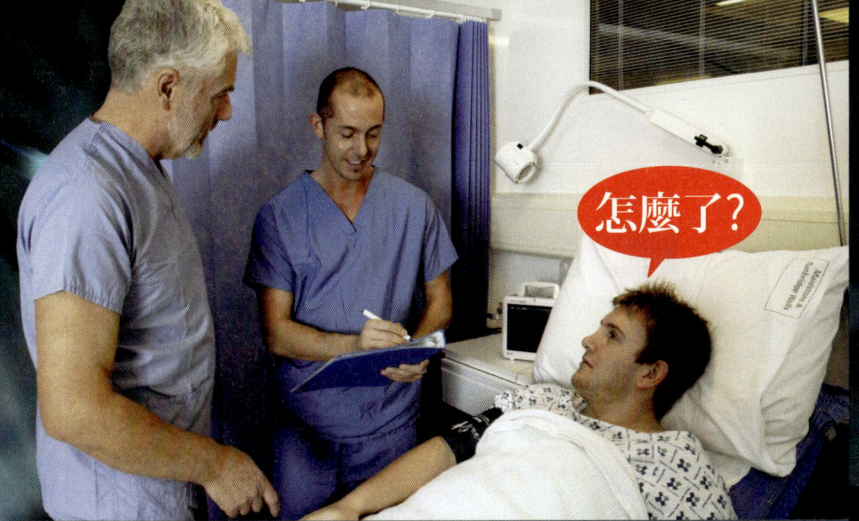

怎麼了？

Imagine this: you wake up one morning and suddenly you can speak a foreign language, but you've forgotten your own language completely! That's what happened to a 16-year-old American boy in 2016. During a game of football, Reuben Nsemoh suffered a head injury which
5 nearly killed him. However, after a three-day coma he regained consciousness and found that he could only speak and understand Spanish, which he had never studied. Within a few weeks, he was able to speak English again. At the same time, his fluency in Spanish was diminishing.

10 Australian Ben McMahon had a similar experience. After a serious car crash, he woke from a coma speaking Mandarin. Even more astonishingly – he could also read and write it! Like Reuben, Ben recovered his English skills, but unlike Reuben he didn't lose his ability to speak Mandarin. He went on to study at Shanghai University,
15 and also worked as a presenter on Chinese TV; he even appeared on a Chinese dating show and met a Chinese girlfriend.

Reuben and Ben were (and still are) young men. In contrast, Englishman Alun Morgan was 81 when he woke up in hospital able to speak only Welsh – the language of Wales, where he had not been
20 for 70 years. For a few days, he needed an interpreter (fortunately, that was his wife!) until his English came back to him, while his Welsh gradually faded.

These cases were all the result of some kind of brain damage, but they have more in common than that. Each person had been exposed
25 to the language they suddenly acquired. Reuben had friends who spoke Spanish in his presence. Ben had attended Mandarin classes at school, although he wasn't very good at it, and had been on a trip to Beijing – but only for a short time. As for Alun, as a child he had been sent to live with grandparents in Wales for a few years.
30 He heard Welsh all around him, but he had never spoken the language himself.

Scientists cannot explain this phenomenon fully. However, it seems that our brains absorb far more than we realise, and store it away. If one part of the
35 brain is damaged, another part is activated and takes over while the damage is repaired. In short, it's increasingly clear that our brains are capable of far, far more than we ever used to imagine.

WRITING SKILLS

LEAD IN

12 PAIRWORK Answer these questions.

1 What kind of stories do you like and dislike? Why?
2 What's the last story you read?
3 Did you have a favourite story when you were little? What was it?
4 Retell a fairy story from your childhood. Use past tenses.

PRACTICE

13 PAIRWORK Complete the text with the words below. Then compare your answers.

scene ▪ climax ▪ consequences ▪ story ▪ ending ▪ main characters

When you are writing a ¹........................ or a narrative, in the first paragraph you should set the ²........................ and introduce the ³........................ .
In the second paragraph, you should give details and write about the main events leading up to the
⁴........................ . And in the last paragraph, you should write your ⁵........................ and explain the ⁶........................ .

🌐 WRITING STRATEGY

Write a story

A story is a narrative, usually about the past, told in a way that will interest the reader. The sequence of events must be clear and logical. There is no rule for style, although most stories are fairly informal.

▪ A good story has an interesting opening, to *bring the reader in*.
▪ A story should contain intriguing details.
▪ The end of a story should be memorable.

B2 FIRST   IGCSE

See **WRITING EXPANSION** page 131

VOCABULARY

The mind

14 PAIRWORK Discuss these questions.

What do you do when you're feeling low? For example, do you …

- meet up with friends?
- get some exercise?
- read a book?
- play games, listen to music or watch TV?
- go to an app on your phone?

15 Read the text and check you understand the words and expressions in bold. Use a dictionary to help you.

16 Read the text and answer the questions.

1 Describe the three techniques that the apps use.
2 What are the main aims of the apps?

Feeling appy!

These days if you **feel low**, there's a wide choice of apps that can help. Some of them are simple games designed to train your mind. For example, you have to find one smiling face out of rows of **depressed** or unfriendly-looking people, or pick out **cheerful** words from lists that move across your screen. Others send 5 regular **encouraging** messages, or reminders to take time out, or even just smiley emoticons. The theory is that apps like this reinforce **positive** mind habits, encourage **optimism** and reduce **anxiety**. They aim to raise **self-esteem**, so that we have more **self-confidence** and are less affected by **peer** 10 **pressure**. Other apps offer ways to **reduce stress**, such as **relaxation techniques** like **meditation** or soothing sound effects. Do any of them actually work? Can a simple app really **alter** our **moods** and improve our **mental health**? The answer seems to be yes, a little, although they are 15 never a substitute for proper professional **counselling**.

17 Complete the table with words from the text.

noun	verb	adjective
[0] anxiety	-	anxious
[1]	-	confident
depression	depress	depressing / [2] ....
encouragement	encourage	[3] ....
[4]	meditate	-
[5]	-	moody
[6]	-	optimistic
[7]	relax	relaxing / relaxed
[8]	stress	stressful / stressed

18 Complete the sentences with words from the table above.

1 Shy people sometimes lack self-.................. .
2 John's cheerful one minute and low the next – he's very .... !
3 Alison always thinks positively and expects good things – she's a very .... person.
4 Parents sometimes have to .... their children to eat healthily.
5 My heart was beating very fast during the interview – it was very .... !
6 By the end of the film we were really miserable – it was such a .... story.
7 My dog hates fireworks. Sudden loud noises .... him.
8 After a warm bath my little sister was .... and sleepy and ready for bed.
9 It's normal to feel a bit .... and .... before your driving test – but if you fail, don't get .... You can try again!

19 Replace the underlined words with words from the text so that the sentences have the opposite meaning.

0 Liam seems <u>low</u> today. **cheerful**
1 Does <u>negative</u> thinking affect our luck?
2 Relaxation is important for our <u>physical</u> health.
3 Social media can sometimes <u>lower</u> self-esteem.
4 Does background noise <u>increase</u> stress?
5 My exam results are very <u>discouraging</u>.

➤ See **VOCABULARY EXTENSION** page 141

SPEAKING SKILLS

Talking about habits

20 PAIRWORK Discuss these questions.

1 How much have you changed in the past five years?
2 Think about things you used to do that you never do now, and vice versa!

21  **[2.23]** Listen and watch the video. What have Grace and Luke decided to do?

key expressions	
talking about habits in the present	**talking about habits in the past**
☐ You never do anything remotely sporty.	☐ I used to be quite sporty.
☐ I sometimes cycle to school.	☐ I used to go cycling with a club two to three times a week,
☐ It's always too crowded.	and I was in a football
☐ People get in your way all the time.	team, too.
☐ Don't tell me you go swimming first thing in the morning?	☐ But I used to have a swimming lesson every week. I'd go before school.

22 **[2.23]** Listen and watch again. Listen for the key expressions. Who says them: Grace (G) or Luke (L)?

SPEAKING STRATEGY

Generalise information

☐ *mostly*   ☐ *never*   ☐ *generally speaking*
☐ *most of the time* ☐ *on the whole*   ☐ *in general*
☐ *always*   ☐ *as a rule*   ☐ *generally*

B2 FIRST   IGCSE   IELTS

23 **[2.23]** Listen and watch again and tick (✓) the expressions from the strategy box you hear.

24 PAIRWORK Read the situation and do the task.

Think of your life five years ago: what you were like and what you did and liked. Use these headings: *Sport, Food you liked, Appearance.*

I used to play football when I was at middle school. Now...

The /e/ and /eɪ/ sounds

25 **[2.24]** **PAIRWORK** Listen to a British speaker and a learner of English say the same sentence. Discuss the differences.

Tell me again the tale of the men who sailed west to chase the whale.

📢 SOUND STRATEGY

Learners of English often confuse these two sounds. Practise making each sound, and notice when your mouth changes shape.

- *tell* /e/ your mouth doesn't change shape
- *tale* /eɪ/ your mouth changes shape

26 **[2.25]** **PAIRWORK** Listen and repeat. Then practise.

	A /e/	B /eɪ/
1	let	late
2	shed	shade
3	wet	wait, weight
4	sell	sail, sale
5	rest	raced
6	well	whale
7	men	main
8	chess	chase
9	tell	tail, tale
10	west	waste, waist

27 **[2.26]** **GAME** Listen and repeat. Then practise saying the sentences as fast as possible.

1 Ten men will wait by the main red gate.
2 If I'm late, tell Ted to stay in the shade.
3 Don't wait in the rain and get wet.

LISTENING SKILLS

LEAD IN

28 PAIRWORK Discuss these questions.

1 Do you think it's a good idea to sleep for a few hours (take a nap) during the day?
2 Have you ever done this? How did you feel after?

PRACTICE

29 [2.27] Listen to the information about sleeping in the daytime. Does the speaker recommend it?

LISTENING STRATEGY

Choose the correct option

In some exams, you have to choose the correct answer from a selection of options. This involves detailed listening and a very solid understanding of the information. To help improve these skills:

- read all questions and the options carefully (in some cases the options are part of the question).
- listen for the general gist.
- be careful of distractors – words that might trick you into choosing the wrong answer.
- remember the questions are about what you have heard, not general knowledge.
- choose your answer.
- then listen again and check.

B2 FIRST IGCSE IELTS

30 [2.27] Listen again and choose the correct option.

1 People in hot countries
   A take afternoon naps when they can.
   B don't need afternoon naps as much as they used to.
   C need air conditioning to help them sleep.

2 Many British people think
   A they shouldn't take naps.
   B naps will make them age faster.
   C naps are quite natural.

3 Which statement is correct?
   A A 30 minutes' nap is better than a 45.
   B A nap that is longer than 45 minutes is a bad idea.
   C The best length of time for a nap is 45 minutes.

4 A nap that lasts longer than an hour
   A will make you even sleepier.
   B will refresh you the most.
   C is a waste of time.

5 Which statement is correct?
   A We should go to bed early and get up early.
   B If you wake up late, you should stay awake until night time.
   C The best time for a nap varies.

GRAMMAR GUIDE

Gerunds and infinitives (1)

Gerunds

- **Sleeping** *in the afternoon is often seen as laziness.* (as subject of a sentence)
- *If you* **like taking** *a nap …* (after certain verbs, e.g., *enjoy, like*, etc.)
- *If you're worried* **about losing** *concentration …* (after certain prepositions)

Infinitives

- *People do it* **to avoid** *the heat.* (to describe purpose)
- *You'll be* **ready to face** *anything.* (after some adjectives)
- *If you'***d like to focus** *a bit better …* (after certain verbs, e.g., *would like, want, decide*)

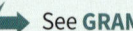 See **GRAMMAR REFERENCE** Workbook page 125

31 Look at the Grammar guide. Then choose the correct option.

Is **⁰** *to get* / getting to sleep a problem? Sometimes it's hard **¹** *to switch / switching* off. Try to avoid electronic devices for an hour before bed. **²** *To look at / Looking at* screens stops us from **³** *to get / getting* sleepy. So if you want **⁴** *to have / having* a better night's sleep, leave your phone well away from your bed.
⁵ *To clear / Clearing* your mind, read a book instead of **⁶** *to stare / staring* at a screen – and if you keep **⁷** *to get up / getting up* to find your phone, maybe think about **⁸** *to change / changing* your relationship with it!

Proofreading your work

LEAD IN

32 PAIRWORK What do you do when you've completed a piece of written work? Read the statements and choose A or B.

I …

1 A immediately read it again to check it.
   B have a break and then check it.

2 A check it on screen.
   B print it out.

3 A use a spell check.
   B use a dictionary.

4 A check everything, sentence by sentence.
   B check it systematically. First the spelling, then the grammar, etc.

5 A read it quietly.
   B read it out loud.

6 A only check it myself.
   B ask someone else to check it too.

ACADEMIC STRATEGY

Proofreading is all about accuracy. It's important because mistakes and errors affect how well the reader understands the meaning. They also give a bad impression.

If possible, …

- wait a little while before you start proofreading. You're more likely to spot mistakes.
- print it out – after you've done a spell check (but don't completely trust it – always double-check with a dictionary).
- read it out loud.
- check things one at a time. These are the areas you should focus on:
  - spelling: a good tip is to read the line backwards so you see each word in isolation.
  - grammar, especially: tenses and verb forms, linkers, word order.
  - punctuation, especially: capital letters, commas, speech marks and full stops, apostrophes.
  - numbers, names and other factual details.
  - style: Is it appropriate? Is it consistent?
- and finally, ask someone else to proofread for you (but do it yourself too!).

B2 FIRST | IGCSE | IELTS

PRACTICE

33 PAIRWORK Find and correct the mistakes in these sentences.

1 Sigmund Freud who died in 1939 was one of the worlds most famous psyciatrists.

2 He was born on Austria and lived most of his life in Vienna, moreover he has died in London.

3 It is said that his work are still very influential today, but actually I've got no idea if that's right or not.

34 PAIRWORK Read the text. Find and correct 14 mistakes. Then check with a partner.

A dream I'll never forget

have
When I was little, I used to ~~having~~ the same bad dream regular. I was siting on a bus and everything were fine, but then suddenly I realised I didnt know where was I going. I would look at the others passengers. They were all talking and laghing. Id try to ask for help but I couldn't speak at that point I'd get up.
I haven't had that dream since ages but I'll never forget it. The dream was horrible, and on the other hand it was lovely feeling when I woke up and realised it isn't true!

35 WRITING Now write a short text (about 100 words) with the same title. Then …

1 proofread your text
2 exchange with a partner
3 proofread your partner's text
4 check both texts together

REVISE AND ROUND UP

1 Complete the sentences with the correct form of the verbs in brackets.

0 Joe ....**will be**...... very surprised if he
.......**wins**........ the competition next week. (*be / win*)

1 I .... last night if I .... you
were asleep. (*not / phone / know*)

2 If plants .... enough sunlight, they
always ....! (*not / get / die*)

3 Take my advice. I .... that top
with those jeans if I .... you. (*not / wear / be*)

4 We .... the party last night if the music
.... better. (*enjoy / be*)

2 Complete the questions and answers.

1 **A** If you could live anywhere, where
would you live. (*you / live*)?

   B I .... (*stay*) right here.

2 **A** What happens if you .... (*heat*)
chocolate?

   B It .... (*melt*), of course.

3 **A** What would you do if you .... (*lose*)
your phone?

   B I .... (*panic*)!

4 **A** If a friend .... (*ask*) you to lend him
some money, would you agree?

   B Yes, but only if he .... (*be*) a close
friend!

5 **A** If the film had had better reviews, ...
(*you / watch*) it last night?

   B Yes, I probably ....

**3 Read the situations, then complete
the sentences using the prompts in brackets.**

0 I'm very tired today.
I wish ....**I hadn't gone to bed late last night**. .
(*go to bed late*)
I should ....**have gone to bed earlier**........... .
(*go to bed earlier*)

1 I'm hungry.
I wish ....
(*miss breakfast*)
I should ....
(*have breakfast*)

2 I'm cold.
I wish ....
(*have a warmer jumper*)
I should ....
(*forget my scarf*)

4 Choose the correct option.

0 (If) / When the weather is fine, we have / ('ll have)
a picnic tomorrow.

1 You won't catch the bus *until / unless* you *hurry /
'll hurry*.

2 I'll go shopping *if / when* school *'ll finish / finishes*.

3 You'd understand your homework *if / when* you
took / 'd taken some notes in the lesson yesterday.

4 *If / Unless* you *didn't join / hadn't joined* the gym
last year, you wouldn't be so fit now.

5 Text me *as soon as / until* your train *will get / gets*
in, and I'll meet you.

6 We'll wait at the bus stop *if / until* the bus *arrives /
will arrive*.

5 Choose the correct option.

0 In the past, people .... believe the world was flat.
   A would   (**B**) used to

1 I haven't got used to .... up early yet.
   A getting   **B** get

2 Where did your parents .... to go to school?
   A used   **B** use

3 We're all .... to looking for information online.
   A use   **B** used

4 My sister and I .... often buy sweets on the way
home from school.
   A used   **B** would

5 It was a shock when my brother was born – I wasn't
used to .... a baby in the house.
   A have   **B** having

6 Complete the missing words.

0 Toby has left school now, but we ....**used**........
to cycle to school together.

1 Jack's drunk three cups of coffee, and now he can't
relax. He .... not used to ....
coffee.

2 Which school did you .... to go to when
you were six?

3 I've got a new phone, and it's still a bit strange.
I'm getting .... to it.

4 In Scandinavian countries, the people
.... used .... extremely cold
winters.

5 In the past, I met my friends in the park every
Saturday. We .... to play football
and sometimes we .... climb trees.

7 Write the correct form of the verbs in brackets.

1 John is nervous about [0] ......taking...... (take) his exams. He keeps [1] .... (worry). I'm sure [2] .... (relax) would be better than [3] .... (read) his notes for the hundredth time!

2 Mandy has decided [4] .... (join) a gym [5] .... (get) ready for her summer holidays. She'd like [6] .... (be) fitter, although she doesn't need [7] .... (lose) any weight.

3 [8] .... (run) is a great form of exercise. Or, if you want [9] .... (avoid) [10] .... (breathe) in lots of traffic fumes, and if you don't mind [11] .... (get) wet, what about [12] .... (swim)?

8 Correct the mistakes.

0 My sister is interested ~~on~~ history and she enjoys visiting museums.
...........in...........

1 I used to collecting postcards, and I'd decorate my bedroom walls with them.
....

2 Are you ready go out yet, or would you like to stay here a bit longer?
....

3 Sightseeing is fun but it can be very tiring unless you used to it.
....

4 I want to get a new case protecting my new phone.
....

5 I can't stop my sister from borrow all my stuff.
....

9 Choose the correct option.

I went to Japan last summer to stay with some friends (they [0] (used to)/ would live near us in London). I had a great time, but I [1] did / made some mistakes. For example, I [2] should / should have taken off my shoes before I went into the house (I soon got [3] used / use to doing that!). And I wish [4] I took / I'd taken more presents with me. Giving small presents is very important in Japan. I [5] would pack / would have packed some English souvenirs if I'd known. Never mind – when I go again, I'll know!

TOWARDS B2 FIRST

Reading and Use of English

10 Complete the gaps with one word.

Got a problem? We're ready to help.

I've [0] ....just........ moved to a new town and I really can't [1] .... living here. I used to have [2] .... of friends and we [3] .... hang out at weekends – but so far I [4] .... not managed to make [5] .... friends here. [6] .... wants to talk to me. I didn't [7] .... to be shy but, honestly, starting a conversation with strangers [8] .... really hard. I'm not used to feeling [9] .... this. I wish we [10] .... not moved – in fact, I should [11] .... refused to leave my last school. Help!

Oh dear, you certainly sound miserable. If I [12] .... you, I'd talk to someone about this. Perhaps you don't want to tell your parents [13] .... you feel – but how [14] .... phoning one of your old school friends? Sharing problems helps! I'm sure that [15] .... you do that, things won't seem so bad. [16] .... used to a new school is always difficult – but give [17] .... time. [18] .... friends never happens instantly. But it [19] .... happen and when it [20] ...., you won't look back.

Writing

11 Write your review in about 140 and 190 words.

You read this announcement in an English-language website for young people.

Reviews wanted! STREET FOOD

Street food has become very popular all around the world. Tell us about a street food stall in your town that sells great food. Why would you recommend it? We'll publish the best reviews on our website.

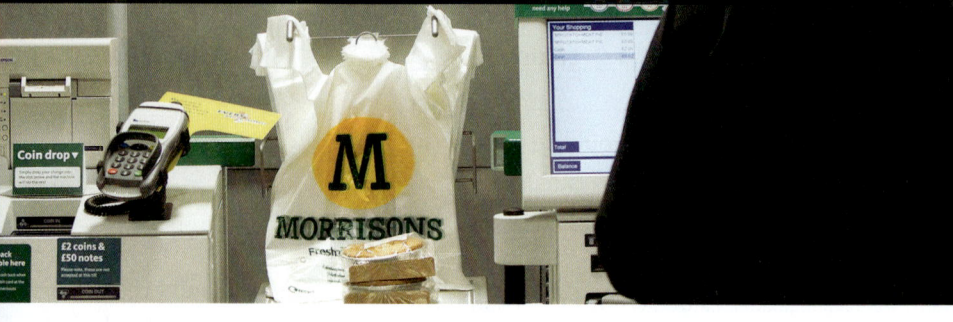

9 Business rules

EXAM STRATEGIES

- B2 FIRST: Reading, Writing and Speaking
- IGCSE: Reading and Speaking
- IELTS: Speaking

SPEAKING SKILLS

- Interviewing

CHANGING LANGUAGE

- New words

LIFE SKILLS

- Non-verbal communication

Learning goals

Grammar
- Reporting verbs
- Gerunds and infinitives (2)
- *have / get something done*

Vocabulary
- Money and business

LEAD IN

1 PAIRWORK Discuss these questions.

1 What do you think is the most common way of paying for things in your country — cash, card or cheque?

2 Do you think this is changing? In what way?

2 ▶ 🔊 [2.28] **Read, listen and watch. Guess the meaning of *bartering* and *haggling*. What is the difference between them?**

Fair exchange, or robbery?

As the English proverb says, 'Fair exchange is no robbery' – but what is a fair exchange? Who decides? Long before money was invented, goods were exchanged by **bartering**. Instead of buying and selling, items of similar value were exchanged. Usually, one side would ask (or tell!) the other to pay more, and they would continue to haggle until they were both satisfied. 5

Haggling still goes on today, although it's more common in some countries than in others. In British markets, people often ask stall holders to reduce their prices (with mixed success). However, not many people try to get a discount in ordinary shops. Bartering, on the other hand, had almost died out, although it's coming back in some parts of the UK. Some local groups have stopped using money for certain transactions, 10 and started bartering instead. In this scheme, group members decide on the value of goods and services, so nobody regrets paying too much or selling for too little. For example, you might exchange an evening's babysitting for a haircut, or a homemade cake for a music lesson. This system encourages a sense of community, and is useful for people on low incomes, as no money changes hands. 15

Of course, these days we're much more likely to conduct our transactions electronically. Whether we do it at home or in the high street, we don't really need to handle money any more. It doesn't matter if you forget to go to the cash machine, as long as you've remembered to bring your smartphone. It's ironic that the ancient practice of bartering and the very latest technology are both moving us in the same direction – 20 towards a cash-free society. However, along the way, haggling is in danger of disappearing. When we use our cards, do we ever stop to wonder who set the price, and whether it's fair?

One thing is certain: soon, we'll laugh when we look back and remember using 25 cash – how very old-fashioned!

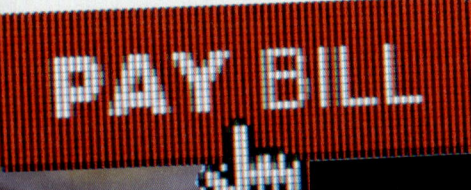

PRACTICE

3 ▶ ◀[2.28] **PAIRWORK** Read, listen and watch the video again and answer the questions.

1 How did people buy and sell things before they used money?
2 In the UK, who are most willing to give customers a discount?
3 How does *fair exchange* work in the bartering groups?
4 Why does the system benefit the poor?

GRAMMAR GUIDE

Gerunds and infinitives (2)

Some verbs take both the gerund and the infinitive.

- For some verbs the meaning stays the same: *continue, start, begin, prefer, like, love, hate.*
  *Some local groups have **started bartering** / **to barter**.*

- For other verbs the meaning changes: *remember, forget, regret, try, stop.*
  *Some local groups have **stopped using** money.*
  (The activity is finished permanently.)
  *Do we ever **stop to wonder**?*
  (We stop one activity in order to do another one.)

➡ See **GRAMMAR REFERENCE** Workbook page 125

4 Complete the text with the correct form of the verbs in brackets. There may be two correct answers.

I regret ⁰ ..buying.. (buy) my new phone. First, it started
1 .... (make) a funny noise, then it began
2 .... (get) hot, and finally it stopped
3 .... (work) altogether.
I tried 4 .... (get) my money back from
the shop but I'd forgotten 5 .... (keep)
the receipt so they refused. Next time I'll remember
6 .... (go) somewhere else!

GRAMMAR GUIDE

Reporting verbs

Reporting verbs, e.g., *tell, ask, order, command, warn, persuade, remind* follow this pattern:

verb + direct object + infinitive with *to*

*Usually, one side would **ask** (or **tell**!) the other*
***to pay** more.*

➡ See **GRAMMAR REFERENCE** Workbook page 126

5 Identify the sentences. Match them to the reporting verbs. Then complete.

1 [c] 'Oh come on, Amy, let's go out.' 'Oh, OK then!'
2 [ ] 'Could you give me a lift, Tom, please?'
3 [ ] 'Remember to bring your sports kit, Sam!'
4 [ ] 'Open your suitcase, Mr Smith.'
5 [ ] 'Be careful. Don't give your password to anybody.'
6 [ ] 'Sit, Fido! Sit! Good dog!'
7 [ ] 'Good morning. Open your books at page 10.'

a Rick reminded ....
b The Customs officer ordered ....
c They persuaded ....
d Joe's father warned ....
e The dog trainer commanded ....
f The teacher told ....
g I asked ....

6 **PAIRWORK** Read the situations, then complete the sentences. Use the prompts below.

forget + buy ▪ start + take ▪ try + not / touch ▪ persuade + change ▪ regret + inform ▪ try + do ▪ remember + not / make ▪ stop + eat ▪ try + call ▪ warn + not / walk

0 The baby's asleep. Please **remember not to make** a noise.
1 The London train will be late. We .... you of a 30-minute delay.
2 Jack isn't answering text messages. Maybe we should .... him.
3 I don't feel very healthy. I'm going to .... junk food and .... more exercise.
4 It's my friend's 18th birthday soon. I mustn't .... a present.
5 I didn't want to go out. However, my friends .... my mind.
6 I've just painted the door. Please .... it.
7 The path is icy. We should .... people .... on it.
8 That crossword was impossible! I didn't even .... it!

7 **SPEAKING** In pairs, take turns to talk about …

- a place you'll never forget visiting.
- something you regret doing.
- a person you'll always remember meeting.
- something difficult you've tried to do.

READING SKILLS

LEAD IN

8 PAIRWORK Discuss these questions.

1 Would you like to become an entrepreneur?
2 If you could start a business, what do you think it would be?
3 What do you think would be the most difficult part?

PRACTICE

9 **Read and listen to the text. Which business idea do you like best?**

10 Read the text again and decide if the sentences are true (T) or false (F). Correct the false ones.

1 The dragons didn't back any of the products in the text. T F
2 The suitcases can be pulled along. T F
3 The swim fin is a toy. T F
4 Shaun Pulfrey's time on the show was a waste of time. T F
5 Rachel Lowe's idea was inspired by her job. T F

READING STRATEGY

Match questions to multiple texts

In some exams you will need to match questions to different parts of a text. Questions may focus on specific information, detail, opinion and attitude.

- Read the questions first. Underline keywords and phrases.
- The questions will not necessarily follow the order of the text, so read the whole text carefully.
- Read each part again, and look for questions that could match them. Look out for synonyms – for example, if the text says 'He wasn't happy', the question might ask 'Who was miserable?'
- Look out for distractors – make sure the question doesn't trick you.
- Read the whole text through again and check your answers.

B2 FIRST **IGCSE**

11 Answer these questions by choosing from the products A–D. They may be chosen more than once.

Which product in the text

1 ☐ was invented by a student?
2 ☐ was faulty at first?
3 ☐ helps to keep people safe?
4 ☐ had a lot of competition?
5 ☐ was laughed at?
6 ☐ was rejected after an unfortunate mistake?
7 ☐ was not originally a business idea?
8 ☐ received some verbal encouragement from the dragons?

GRAMMAR GUIDE

have / get something done

We use *have / get something done* to talk about something that somebody does for us.

- *Buyers can **have** them specially **made**.*
- *Rachel managed to **get** her game **advertised**.*
- *The inventor **had** his product **mocked** by the dragons.*

➡ See **GRAMMAR REFERENCE** Workbook page 126

12 Rewrite the sentences. Use the correct form of the verbs in brackets, and *by …* if necessary.

0 I'll pay someone to clean my jacket. (*get*)
   I'll **get my jacket cleaned.**
1 We'll ask someone to remove the rubbish. (*have*)
   We ....
2 A football broke my window. (*have*)
   I ....
3 The dentist will check Sam's teeth. (*get*)
   Sam ....
4 The police took Tom's fingerprints. (*have*)
   Tom ....
5 The magazine published my story. (*get*)
   I ....

13 Critical thinking Discuss the question in pairs. What do you think a successful business person needs? Consider the ideas below and your own ideas.

- intelligence
- determination
- luck
- self-confidence
- money
- encouragement

Into the DRAGONS' DEN!

Dragons' Den is a popular British reality TV show. The dragons are five wealthy business people looking for investment opportunities. The contestants are aspiring entrepreneurs hoping to get their projects **backed** by a dragon. The dragons ask searching questions and frequently refuse to invest. However, rejected businesses don't always fail in the world.

A TRUNKI

This company makes suitcases for young children. The cases are on wheels and are specially built so that their young owners can sit and ride on them. The cases are designed to look like animals, or buyers can have them specially made to their own designs.

The original pitch failed after one of the dragons broke the strap on a demonstration case. However, the cases can now be seen in airports all over the world, and the dragons probably regret not investing!

B SWIM FIN

This child's swimming aid started as a bit of fun, but it was soon a serious, and massive, business. The idea is simple – instead of wearing inflatable arm bands, the child wears a shark's fin on his or her back. It keeps the swimmer afloat and also in the correct position (and it's still fun!).

The inventor had his product mocked by the dragons, who said it was unsafe and silly. Despite this setback, he borrowed money from the bank, continued with the business and achieved international success.

C TANGLE TEEZER

The man who invented this special pain-free hairbrush was told by the dragons that it was a waste of time. He is now a multimillionaire. Shaun Pulfrey had designed a hairbrush that doesn't get stuck in tangled hair. Unfortunately, he offended one of the dragons by (wrongly) saying she'd had her hair coloured. Although nobody invested in his idea, the dragons gave him some business advice, which he followed.

D DESTINATION LONDON

Single parent Rachel Lowe was working as a taxi driver while she studied for a law degree. She developed the idea for a board game in which players drive taxis around London. The dragons rejected her business plan and told her there were far too many other board games on the market.

Leaving the show with no help or encouragement, Rachel managed to get her game advertised in London's biggest toy shop. After a few years, her game had become a market leader.

WRITING SKILLS

LEAD IN

14 PAIRWORK Answer these questions.

1 What topics are you interested in reading about?
2 Where are you most likely to read an article? (online? newspaper?)

PRACTICE

15 PAIRWORK Complete the text with the words below. Then compare your answers.

comment ▪ conclusion ▪ details ▪ tenses ▪ sequence ▪ paragraph ▪ scene

The purpose of the first
¹......................... is to capture the reader's attention, and to set the ²........................., so start in an interesting way. Give the main information and ³......................... in the next paragraph(s). Use different ⁴......................... and linkers to show the ⁵......................... of events. The final paragraph is the ⁶......................... – for example, it could contain your opinion, or a ⁷......................... .

WRITING STRATEGY

Write an article

An article is an account of something factual (but you can include your own thoughts, feelings and opinions) written in a way that will engage the reader. It contains:

▪ a title that catches the reader's attention
▪ an opening paragraph on the main events
▪ a clear sequence of events
▪ a clear structure: introduction, middle, conclusion

B2 FIRST

See **WRITING EXPANSION** page 132

VOCABULARY

Money and business

16 PAIRWORK Discuss these questions.

1 Do you think it's a good idea for teenagers to have part-time jobs? Why / Why not?

2 Do you ever do paid work? If you do, what do you do? Do you enjoy it?

3 If not, would you like to? What would you do?

17 Read the text and check the meanings of the words in bold.

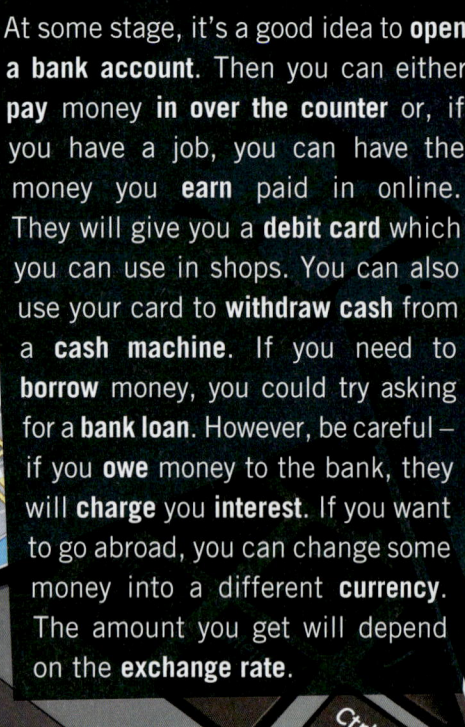

At some stage, it's a good idea to **open a bank account**. Then you can either **pay** money **in over the counter** or, if you have a job, you can have the money you **earn** paid in online. They will give you a **debit card** which you can use in shops. You can also use your card to **withdraw cash** from a **cash machine**. If you need to **borrow** money, you could try asking for a **bank loan**. However, be careful – if you **owe** money to the bank, they will **charge** you **interest**. If you want to go abroad, you can change some money into a different **currency**. The amount you get will depend on the **exchange rate**.

18 Read the text again. Then complete the sentences with words from the text.

1 It's a physical object between you and the bank clerk. It's the ....

2 It's made of plastic and you use it to pay for things. It's a ....

3 It's money that you can hold (coins and bank notes). It's ....

4 It's a machine that holds money. It's a
....

5 It's a system of money used in a country. It's a
....

6 It's the value of your money compared with a different country's money.
It's the ....

19 PAIRWORK What are the people doing in each photo? Use words from exercise 17 and your own ideas.

20 Choose the correct option. Use a dictionary to help you.

1 I need some money. Can you *lend / borrow / owe* me some?

2 Frank has *earned / gained / won* some money in a competition.

3 There's a £10 membership *expense / charge / cost* at our library.

4 The supermarket has recently *expanded / raised / lifted* its prices.

5 Nearly everyone who wants one now has a mobile phone, so the market is *reducing / falling / shrinking*.

21 Complete with the unused words from each sentence in exercise 20.

1 A I'd like to pay my bill. How much do I .... you?

   B My dad had to .... some money from the bank when he started his business.

2 A Since Jack started his new job, he's .... enough to buy a car.

   B Since we went on social media, we've .... a lot of followers.

3 A The .... of living is too high these days.

   B Buying a new computer is a big ....

4 A The school has .... the ban on mobile phones – they're allowed now.

   B The business is so successful, it recently ....

5 A Demand for sugary drinks is .... because people don't drink them so often these days.

   B My mum is worried about her banking job because they're .... the number of teachers.

➜ See **VOCABULARY EXTENSION** page 142

SPEAKING SKILLS

Interviewing

22 PAIRWORK Discuss these questions.

1 Have you ever had an interview? If you have, what was it for?

2 Imagine how you would feel during an interview. What would you do if you didn't know what to say?

23 ▶ 🔴 [2.30] **Listen and watch the video. What kind of job would Anna like to do?**

key expressions	
☐ Can / Could you tell me?	☐ What do you think about … ?
☐ What shall I call you?	☐ Have you ever … ?
☐ How can I address you?	☐ Can you describe … to me?
☐ Tell me about …	☐ Why do / did you … ?

24 ▶ 🔴 [2.30] **Listen and watch again and tick (✓) the key expressions you hear.**

🌐 SPEAKING STRATEGY

Use fillers

☐ *Well, …*	☐ *Oh, …*
☐ *Let me see, …*	☐ *Right …*
☐ *I think, actually, …*	☐ *Look, …*
☐ *Let's start with that.*	☐ *So, …*
☐ *That's an interesting question!*	☐ *The thing is, …*
☐ *I'm not sure, to be honest.*	☐ *I mean, …*
☐ *(Sorry) could you repeat that, please?*	☐ *How can I put it?*

B2 FIRST | **IGCSE** | **IELTS**

25 ▶ 🔴 [2.30] **Listen and watch again and tick (✓) the expressions from the strategy box you hear.**

26 PAIRWORK Interview each other. Look at the topics and think of questions and answers. Use the key expressions and the strategy box.

- school
- favourite holiday destination
- travel
- future job
- town or city where you live
- family / friends

New words

27 Look at the list of words. Can you guess which two words have been combined to make the new words?

- Brexit
- guestimate
- chillax
- webinar

28 Now look at the words below and match them to words in exercise 27.

chill ▪ Britain ▪ web ▪ exit ▪ guess ▪ relax ▪ estimate ▪ seminar

29 ⏺ Watch the video. Which words from exercise 27 are now in the Cambridge English Dictionary?

30 ⏺ Watch again and answer the question.

What two words are the following words made from?

- podcast
- edutainment

◉ CORPUS

Every year lexicographers use tools like the Cambridge English Corpus to study language use. A new word is added to the dictionary when it is used in many different contexts over a period of time. You can go to *https://dictionaryblog.cambridge.org* and vote for words which you think should go into the dictionary too!

LISTENING SKILLS

LEAD IN

31 PAIRWORK Look at the photo and discuss the questions.

1 What can you see in the photo?
2 You are going to hear about a scheme called *Young Enterprise*. Can you guess what kind of scheme it is?

PRACTICE

32 ◤[2.31] Listen to the information about the *Young Enterprise* scheme. Were your ideas in exercise 31 correct?

33 ◤[2.31] **PAIRWORK** Read the questions, then listen again and answer.

1 Who is eligible for the programme described by the speaker?
2 What two examples of businesses does the speaker give?
3 What do the groups need to do first?
4 What example is given of what a proper business does?
5 Who can the groups ask for advice?
6 What happens every year?

LISTENING STRATEGY

Listen for detail: true / false questions

To decide if a statement is true or false you need to listen for detail. To help improve this skill:
- read each statement carefully.
- look out for distractors – for example, you might see a word you have heard (or a synonym), but the statement could still be false.
- remember that you are answering according to what the speaker says, not general knowledge.
- listen again and check.

34 ◤[2.31] Now listen again and decide if the sentences are true (T) or false (F). Correct the false ones.

1 *Young Enterprise* offers programmes for people of all ages. ☐T ☐F
2 The speaker is describing a programme for school students. ☐T ☐F
3 Participants try to create and run a successful business. ☐T ☐F
4 Family and friends invest money in the businesses. ☐T ☐F
5 Most of the groups make a profit. ☐T ☐F
6 Local businesses help the groups by advertising them. ☐T ☐F
7 Individual group members compete against each other. ☐T ☐F
8 *Young Enterprise* offers careers advice to young people. ☐T ☐F

35 What helped you decide if a statement was true or false? Make notes for each question in exercise 34.

36 SPEAKING Imagine you are applying for a job. What is important to you about this job / company? Read the topics below and discuss in pairs.

what work you are doing

the kind of people you work with – your colleagues

the amount you earn

how much you enjoy what you do

how hard you have to work

how much profit the company makes

if the company is green

what you are producing or selling

Non-verbal communication

LEAD IN

37 PAIRWORK **Compare the photos of interviews and answer the questions.**

1 Who do you think are the interviewers?
2 Who do you think are the candidates?
3 How do you think the candidates are feeling?

PRACTICE

38 PAIRWORK **Read the text and guess the meaning of the words and phrases in bold. Check in a dictionary.**

Going for a job interview

In a survey of 2,000 employers, **33%** claimed that they know within the first 90 seconds of an interview whether they will offer someone a job. In the same survey, the worst mistakes made at a job interview were:

47% having little or no knowledge of the company
67% lack of eye contact
38% lack of smile
33% bad posture
21% crossing arms over chest
9% too many hand gestures
26% weak handshake
33% fidgeting too much
21% playing with hair or touching face

Statistics show that when meeting new people the impact is:
7% from what we actually say
38% the quality of our voice, grammar and overall confidence
55% the way we dress, act and walk through the door

Statistics show that bright colours are a turn-off and:
70% of employers claim that they don't want applicants to be fashionable or **trendy**
65% of bosses said clothes could be the **deciding factor** between two similar candidates

39 PAIRWORK **Answer these questions.**

1 According to the text, what are the worst things you can do at a job interview?
2 Does any of this information surprise you? If so, which parts?

⚙ LIFE STRATEGY

Tips for a non-verbal communication
Do …

- Eye contact is really important. It shows someone you are listening to them. When you are speaking, it shows you are sincere about what you are saying.
- Think about what you are wearing. Clothes are a big statement of your personality.
- Make it obvious you are listening to someone by nodding or saying 'Hmm' from time to time.
- Try to smile, but make it sincere and don't overdo it!
- Think about your posture: be relaxed but if you look too relaxed, you might seem bored.

Don't …

- Yawn – if you are tired, try and hide it.
- Fidget, or play with your hair – you will look nervous.
- Fold your arms across your chest – this can look aggressive.
- Wave your arms around too much – this can look as if you are excitable and not calm.
- Stare round the room – this will look as if you are bored or not interested in what the person is saying.

40 THINKING FURTHER **Read the tips. Answer the questions.**

1 Which of the tips seem most useful?
2 Which ones did you guess?
3 What other tips could you add?

41 TASK **In pairs, look at the Life strategy again and the infographic. Then do the task.**

1 Prepare two interview role plays. In each one, the candidate makes three non-verbal mistakes. Decide what the mistakes will be and note them down.
2 Then practise the role plays. (The questions can be very simple – e.g., *What's your name; address; date of birth*, etc.).
3 Act out your two role plays to another pair. They identify and note down the six mistakes. Then compare notes! Did you agree what the mistakes were?

10 Conflict

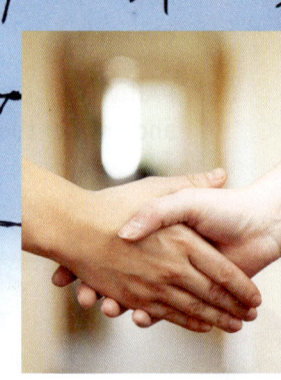

EXAM STRATEGIES

- B2 FIRST: Reading, Listening and Academic
- IGCSE: Listening and Academic
- IELTS: Academic

SPEAKING SKILLS

- Expressing annoyance

ACADEMIC SKILLS

- Writing a conclusion

Learning goals

Grammar

- Revision of modals
- Modals of deduction (past and present)
- Permission and obligation: *can / can't, be allowed to, let, be supposed to*

Vocabulary

- War and conflict

Glossary

crane : a tall bird with long, thin legs and a long neck

LEAD IN

1 Describe the three photos above. What do they all have in common? Can you think of any other images that represent the same idea?

2 ▶ ■ [3.02] Read, listen and watch the video. What do the photos at the bottom of the text show?

Symbols of peace

The statue below, which is in Hiroshima, Japan, is a symbol of peace.
There is a statue of the same girl in the Seattle Peace Park, in the USA. Her story must surely be one of the saddest war stories ever.
Her name was Sadako Sasaki and she was born during the Second World War.
5 When she was two, a nuclear bomb was dropped on her city, Hiroshima. The little girl was thrown right out of her house by the explosion. We can't imagine what it was like to experience such a thing, but it must have been completely terrifying.

Sadako could have died, of course, and tens of thousands of people did, but she survived, along with her brother and parents. She seemed a normal, healthy child and
10 they can't have known what was going to happen. Then, about ten years later, she became ill as a result of exposure to radiation. A school friend visited her in hospital and brought a piece of golden paper, which she folded into a crane. According to a Japanese legend, if you fold a thousand paper cranes, your wish will come true. Sadako decided to do just that, and started folding. Her wish was to live. She didn't have a lot
15 of paper, so she had to use old scraps which other patients gave her. She must have been a very determined child, because she actually managed to fold more than a thousand cranes before she finally died at the age of 12.

Although Sadako's wish to live wasn't granted, her story has inspired people all over the world, and
20 paper cranes have become a symbol of peace and hope. Sadako's brother, who was two years older than her, has worked hard to keep her memory alive. He travels around Japan and overseas, telling people what happened. It can't be easy for him to
25 talk about such terrible events, but he believes we should learn from them. He hopes that in this way we'll be able to build a safer, more peaceful future.

PRACTICE

3 **[3.02] PAIRWORK** Read, listen and watch the video again and answer the questions.

1 Where did Sadako live?
2 What caused her illness?
3 Where was she when she started making paper cranes?
4 Why did she do it?
5 There is something positive from this story. What is it?

GRAMMAR GUIDE

Revision of modals

Ability

- We **can / can't** imagine what it was like.
- We **could / couldn't** remember what happened.
- They **were / weren't able to** save her.
- We **will / won't be able to** build a safer, better world.

Obligation and necessity

- We **must / have to** remember what happened.
- We **mustn't** forget.
- You **don't have to** remind me – I already know.
- She **had to / didn't have to** use scraps of paper.
- You **will / won't have to** fold paper cranes if you want a wish to come true.
- We **should / shouldn't** learn from these events.
- The war **should / shouldn't** have happened.

See **GRAMMAR REFERENCE** Workbook page 126

4 Complete the sentences with a modal verb and the correct form of the verbs in brackets.

0 Where's Jack? **Can you see** (you / see) him?
1 We .... (pay) for the concert last week. It was free.
2 Sarah's just got a bike so she .... (walk) to school any more.
3 I haven't finished my homework, so I .... (do) it tomorrow.
4 My bike has just been fixed, so I .... (ride) it tomorrow.
5 I'm sorry, I .... (take) your book without asking. It was wrong of me.
6 I gave up watching the film. I .... (understand) it.
7 Sam's accident was serious but fortunately the doctors .... (save) him.

GRAMMAR GUIDE

Modals of deduction

Present

100% sure *must / can't + be*

50% sure *may / might / could + be*
may / might + not be

It **can't be** easy for him.

Past

100% sure *must / can't + have + past participle*

50% sure *may / might / could + have + past participle*
may / might + not have + past participle

It **must have been** terrifying.

 See **GRAMMAR REFERENCE** Workbook page 127

5 Choose the correct option.

0 John's lived in Valencia for 20 years. Surely he (must) / can't speak Spanish by now!
1 Suzie isn't at school today. She *must / could* be at the dentist's, or maybe she's ill.
2 I saw Tom in the supermarket this morning. He *might not / can't* be in Australia!
3 Anna's finger is bleeding. She *must / can't* have cut herself.
4 Luke didn't say much about the film. He *must / may* have enjoyed it – I have no idea.
5 Kate walked right into a glass door. She *might not / can't* have seen it.

6 Read the situations. Decide if you need the present or the past. Then write deductions.

✓ = sure it's true
✗ = sure it isn't true
?✓ = maybe it's true
?✗ = maybe it isn't true

0 Emma has a broken leg. (✓ have an accident)
She must have had an accident.
1 I can't find my keys. (?✓ drop them)
2 The baby's crying. We've just fed her. (✗ be hungry)
3 I texted Emma but she hasn't replied. (?✗ get it)
4 The film is sold out – there aren't any tickets left. (✓ be a good film)
5 Rob's just got his exam results. He looks very upset. (✗ pass)
6 My friend went to Las Vegas last month. (✓ be amazing)

READING SKILLS

LEAD IN

7 **Look at the photo and answer the questions.**

1 What's happening?
2 How could we avoid situations like this?

PRACTICE

8 **Read the gapped text. What does *agree to disagree* mean?**

9 **Read the text again and decide if the sentences are true (T) or false (F). Correct the false ones.**

According to the article,

1 arguments are usually caused
  by both sides.   T F
2 confident people are more likely to worry
  about other people's feelings.   T F
3 aggressive behaviour always hurts people. T F
4 it's best to avoid disagreements.   T F
5 assertive people don't mind being rude.   T F

READING STRATEGY

Insert sentences into the text

In some exams you will need to complete a text with missing sentences. This tests your ability to understand the structure and development of a text.

- Read the gapped text through first, for the general meaning.
- Read it again, until the end of the sentence *after* the first gap.
- Look through all the options. Look out for linking words and pronouns that might connect the sentences before and after the gap. Identify any sentences you think might fit the gap.
- Continue in this way with the rest of the text. Remember there will be one option you don't need. As usual, look out for distractors.
- Try reading it through with your chosen options. Does it make sense? Adjust your answers if necessary.
- Read the whole text through again and check your answers.

B2 FIRST

Disagree?

Have you ever disagreed with someone and ended up having a big argument? **1** .... Could you have handled it better, or would it have happened anyway? When friends fall out, there are usually faults on both sides – but it's always a shame when it happens. **2** .... [5]

Of course, it's important to stick up for yourself and state your own opinion. If you don't, it's probably because you lack self-confidence, and you're too afraid of hurting other people's feelings – you'd rather hurt your own! **3** .... [10]

The opposite extreme is to behave aggressively. That doesn't necessarily mean you hit anyone – but it does mean that you intimidate the other person in some way, perhaps by interrupting them, or by shouting. **4** .... This kind of behaviour never ends happily – if both people are aggressive, it could even develop into an actual fight, but even if it doesn't, someone gets hurt. [15] [20]

10 [3.03] **Read the text again and put sentences a–f in the correct gaps 1–5. There is one extra sentence. Then listen and check.**

a In many cases, if one or both sides had behaved differently, the whole thing could have been avoided.

b But be careful – it's easy to think you're being assertive when actually you're becoming aggressive – especially if you're angry.

c On the other hand, if they're obviously upset or out of control, would it be better to avoid an argument and walk away?

d Did you lose your temper and say things you shouldn't have said?

e This is known as passive behaviour, and it doesn't usually do you any good.

f You don't listen to other points of view, and you don't really care about how the other person feels.

Do it agreeably!

So how should we behave? The best way is to be assertive – in other words, to say what you think, but also to listen to the other side, respect the other person even if you disagree with what they say – and stay calm. [5] .... Here are some assertiveness tips:

▸ Speak in a normal, conversational voice – not too quietly, not too loudly.
▸ Make eye contact – but don't glare or stare!
▸ Watch your body language. Try to relax, and look friendly and interested.
▸ Listen to the other person and consider their points.
▸ Respect the other person's feelings, and their right to their own opinions.
▸ Remember it's OK to say *no* – it's possible to say it without being rude. It's fine *to agree to disagree*.

25

30

35

11 `Critical thinking` **Discuss the questions in pairs.**

1 Is it ever OK to show anger? If so, when, why and how? If not, how can we avoid it?
2 Do you think boys are more aggressive than girls? Are they more assertive?
3 Do you think assertiveness is important? Why / Why not?

WRITING SKILLS

LEAD IN

12 PAIRWORK **Answer the questions.**

1 Do you ever read and / or write comments *below the line*?
2 Think of some more examples of interaction between the media and the public.
3 Do you think this kind of interaction is valuable? Why / Why not?

PRACTICE

13 Read comments below two online articles. What were the articles about?

thread A What an interesting review. I wouldn't normally think of going to a photograph exhibition, especially not on the theme of war. However, I've now decided to get some tickets, and I'm looking forward to seeing it for myself. Thank you!

thread B I'm afraid I don't agree that toy guns are *just a bit of fun*. Just because children *play fight* doesn't mean we should encourage it, and we certainly shouldn't let them think that killing people is fun.

🌐 WRITING STRATEGY

Comment online

People often write their own comments after they've read online articles or reviews. Comments might agree or disagree with the main text, or continue the discussion. A sequence of comments that form a conversation is called *a thread*.

▪ Keep your comments short.
▪ Style is informal.
▪ Remember that anyone can read your post. So be assertive but not rude.
▪ Do not write in capital letters.

 See **WRITING EXPANSION** page 133

VOCABULARY

War and conflict

According to the classics, in ancient history, war **broke out** between the city of Troy (which is in modern Turkey) and King Menelaus of Sparta (which is in Greece). Menelaus and his **allies** surrounded Troy's walls, but in spite of the **siege**, the city did not **surrender**. After ten years, the Greeks pretended to **withdraw** their **army**. Before they left, they placed a gift outside the gates of Troy – it was the famous wooden horse. We all know what happened next. The Trojans brought the horse inside the city. They didn't know that there were Greek **soldiers** hiding inside the horse. The soldiers emerged and **attacked** the Trojans, who were **defeated** after a short **battle**. That's how the Greeks **invaded** and **conquered** the city of Troy.

14 PAIRWORK Look at the photo and answer the questions.

1 What does it show? Describe it.
2 What do you remember about the story?

15 Read the text and check the meaning of the words in bold.

16 Replace the underlined words and phrases with words in bold from the text.

1 It's important to have people who support you.
2 A blockade prevented people from leaving or entering the city.
3 A fight started after the football match.
4 In 1066 a French duke (William the Conqueror) forced his way into England.
5 The other side were better than us, and they beat us 5–0.
6 Waving a white flag shows that you accept you have lost.

17 Check the meaning of the words below, and place them in the correct category.

attacker ▪ beat ▪ blow up ▪ bomb ▪ bomber ▪ capture ▪ casualty ▪ civilian ▪ defend ▪ fight ▪ fighter ▪ injure ▪ injured ▪ innocent ▪ invade ▪ peaceful ▪ refugee ▪ shoot ▪ survivor ▪ terrified ▪ terrorise ▪ terrorist ▪ victim ▪ victorious ▪ wounded

People (noun): attacker, …

Acts (verbs): beat, …

Adjectives: injured, …

18 Complete the sentences with words from exercise 17.

1 Non-military people are known as ....
2 A person who has escaped from war is a ....
3 Aeroplanes are sent to war zones to .... the enemy forces.
4 If you have done nothing wrong, you are ....
5 A person who has been hurt is a ....
6 If you have won the war, you are ....

See **VOCABULARY EXTENSION** page 143

SPEAKING SKILLS

Expressing annoyance

19 PAIRWORK Discuss these questions.

1 What kind of things annoy you?
2 When someone annoys you, do you usually tell them?
3 Do you think *you* are ever annoying?
4 Do you ever moan about people *behind their backs*?

20 ▶ ◀[3.04] Listen and watch the video.
Who are Luke and Grace complaining about?

key expressions	
☐ She keeps borrowing …	☐ Just because …
☐ He's always coming …	doesn't mean …
☐ I wish he would / wouldn't …	☐ And another thing, …
☐ You should see / hear …	☐ It's just not on.
☐ It drives me mad.	☐ How come …?

21 ▶ ◀[3.04] Listen and watch again and tick (✓) the key
expressions you hear.

🌐 SPEAKING STRATEGY

Sympathise and agree

☐ *Oh, tell me about it!*	☐ *Too right!*
☐ *I know!*	☐ *That's true.*
☐ *Same here.*	☐ *That's harsh / awful / not fair.*
☐ *Hard luck!*	☐ *Poor you.*

22 ▶ ◀[3.04] Listen and watch again and tick (✓) the expressions
from the strategy box you hear.

23 PAIRWORK Choose one of the situations below. Imagine you
and your partner have a similar problem, and practise a role
play. Use some of the expressions from this lesson.

Your neighbours …

- play loud music late at night.
- have a baby that cries all the time.
- are always shouting at each other.
- have an unfriendly dog.
- are very noisy.
- are rude.

SOUNDS ENGLISH

The /ʃ/ and /tʃ/ sounds

24 ◀[3.05] **PAIRWORK** Listen to
a British speaker and a learner
of English say the same sentence.
Discuss the differences.

Watch the sheep chew the cheap shoe.

🔊 SOUND STRATEGY

Learners of English often confuse
these two sounds. Practise making
each sound, and notice the flow
of air through your teeth.

/ʃ/ the air flows out for a long
   time, so you can control the
   length of the sound (sh! shh!
   shhh!)

/tʃ/ the air flow is short, so
   the sound stops quickly

25 ◀[3.06] **PAIRWORK** Listen
and repeat. Then practise.

	A /ʃ/	B /tʃ/
1	wash	watch
2	ship	chip
3	sheep	cheap
4	wish	which, witch
5	share	chair
6	shoe	chew
7	shop	chop
8	sheet	cheat
9	cash	catch
10	shore, sure	chore

26 ◀[3.07] Listen and decide
if the word you hear is in A or B.

27 GAME Play a game in two teams.

1 Use two pieces of paper. Draw a
   symbol on each piece: /ʃ/ and /tʃ/.
2 One person from Team A says a
   word from exercise 25.
3 Everyone in Team B holds up
   the correct symbol at the same
   time.
4 Then swap round. Go as fast
   as you can.
5 The team that gets the most right
   in the fastest time wins.

LISTENING SKILLS

 A
 B
 C
 D

LEAD IN

28 PAIRWORK Look at the pictures and describe where the people are and what they are doing. Guess what they're saying.

PRACTICE

29 [3.08] Listen to four short recordings. Match them to the correct pictures from exercise 28.

LISTENING STRATEGY

Listen for detail

In some exams, you hear several short recordings and then answer open questions about them. This involves listening for detail. To help improve this skill:

- read each question carefully.
- underline keywords, for example *how*, *why*, *when*. They will help you focus on what to listen for.
- remember, you will hear some unnecessary information – don't be distracted.
- listen out for numbers and spellings.
- don't answer in sentences – just a few words (no more than three).
- try to answer each pair of questions in the pauses between recordings. Then listen again and check.

B2 FIRST | **IGCSE**

30 [3.08] Now listen again and answer the questions. Write no more than three words for each answer.

1 A Where does the boy want to go?
   B Which train can he travel on?
2 A What does the girl ask for?
   B What is she told not to do?
3 A What is Kim doing tonight?
   B What does Kim suggest that Mandy does?
4 A What is Emma trying to do?
   B Does Toby think she's right?

GRAMMAR GUIDE

Permission and obligation: *can / can't, be allowed to, let, be supposed to*

Permission: you have / don't have permission

- *You **can** / **can't take** your bike.*
- *Eating **is** / **isn't allowed** in here.*
- *You **are** / **are not allowed to eat** in here.*
- *My parents **will** / **won't let** me **go out**.*

Obligation: you are expected (not) to do it

- *I **am** / **am not supposed to stay** at home.*

➡ See **GRAMMAR REFERENCE** Workbook page 127

31 Transform the sentences so that the second sentence means the same as the first. Use the verbs in brackets.

0 Do not walk on the grass! (*allowed*)
   Walking ..*on the grass is not allowed*.. .
1 We should do at least two hours' work every evening. (*supposed*)
   We ....
2 They don't let us use our phones. (*allowed*)
   We ....
3 You shouldn't really wear jeans to an interview. (*supposed*)
   You ....
4 We don't let people bring dogs into the restaurant. (*can't*)
   You ....
5 I have permission to take photos. (*allowed*)
   I ....

32 SPEAKING Discuss the question in pairs.

Look at the list of things that can be bad for us. Should we be allowed to do them as much as we like, or should they be regulated?

- drinking sugary drinks
- sunbathing
- listening to very loud music
- eating junk food
- going to bed late

Writing a conclusion

LEAD IN

33 Look at the titles of essay questions below and the notes. Tick (✓) the items that should be in the final paragraph (the conclusion) of each essay.

1 'War is never justified.' Do you agree?
- ☐ your opinion
- ☐ other viewpoints
- ☐ arguments for and against
- ☐ a reference back to the first paragraph (the introduction) and / or the title
- ☐ examples and details
- ☐ a summary of points

2 Write about your favourite place.
- ☐ a detailed description
- ☐ reasons why you like it
- ☐ memories of the place
- ☐ a summary
- ☐ a reference back to the first paragraph (the introduction) and / or the title

3 Write an article about sports facilities in your town.
- ☐ a summary
- ☐ explanation of who uses them
- ☐ details about the good points and bad points
- ☐ your own viewpoint

ACADEMIC STRATEGY

The conclusion of an essay should contain a brief summary of the main points, and your personal opinion with a quick justification for it. It does not have to be more than a few sentences long.

- Useful phrases for the beginning of the concluding paragraph include: *to conclude*, *in conclusion*, *to sum up*. Note: Do *not* begin the conclusion with *Finally*, … (this goes in the main part of the essay, when you state your last point).

- These words and expressions are also useful in a conclusion: *in my opinion*, *I think*, *I believe*, *on the one hand … on the other hand*, *however*, *but*, *although*, *even though*, *while*, *despite*, *moreover*, *therefore*, *for this reason*.

- If appropriate, try to *echo* what you have written in the opening paragraph, and / or the title of the essay.

B2 FIRST | **IGCSE** | **IELTS**

PRACTICE

34 Look at the title, introduction and conclusion below. Complete the gaps with words and expressions from the strategy box.

'WAR IS NEVER JUSTIFIED.' DO YOU AGREE?

Introduction
It is easy for ordinary people to say that war is never justified, but it's much harder for the people who have to make the decisions. However, even though there are a lot of strong arguments in favour of going to war in some circumstances, I still believe it is never right.

Paragraph 2 …
Paragraph 3 …
Conclusion
¹ ...., I believe that war can never be justified. War makes things worse and more people die. ² ...., although many people disagree with me, ³ ...., killing people is always wrong.

35 WRITING Complete the following tasks in pairs.

1 Read the essay title below and the first part of the *Introduction*.
2 Make some notes for the rest of the *Introduction* and then try and complete it.
3 Then make notes for paragraphs 2 and 3.

Title: Do video games have a bad effect on teenagers? What do you think?

Introduction: Many people say that video games are bad for teenagers, for lots of reasons. On the other hand, there are plenty of people who believe that adolescents can benefit from them. […]

Paragraph 2 …
Paragraph 3 …

36 WRITING Now write the conclusion of the essay in exercise 35. Follow the steps below.

1 Think of your main points.
2 Give a short summary.
3 Express your own viewpoint.

REVISE AND ROUND UP

1 Choose all the correct options.

0 Tom's forgotten .... his wallet again!
We'll have to pay for his meal.
(A) to bring   **B** bringing

1 I think I'll stop .... now and go to bed.
A to read   **B** reading

2 Emma doesn't really like .... She prefers
....
A to sing   **B** to dance
C singing   **D** dancing

3 Do you regret .... that email?
A to send   **B** sending

4 My laptop has stopped .... I've tried .... it
off and on again, but it's no good.
A to work   **B** to switch
C working   **D** switching

5 Please remember .... your phone before you
go out.
A to charge   **B** charging

6 I really hate .... in public but I'll try .... a
short speech.
A to speak   **B** to make
C speaking   **D** making

2 Report the direct speech, using the prompts.

0 'Stop!'
police officer / driver / order
The police officer ordered the driver to stop.

1 'Please don't tell anyone!'
Jess / me / ask

2 'Oh, go on! Ask Tess out!'
Tom's friends / him / persuade

3 'Don't go too near the cliff edge!'
guide / us / warn

4 'Follow me!'
officer / soldiers / command

5 'Remember to take your key!'
my mother / me / remind

6 'Don't write in your books!'
teacher / us / tell

**3 Complete the sentences with the correct form
of the verbs in brackets.**

0 The sign warned people **not to swim** (not / swim)
in the sea.

1 I'm sure I remember .... (meet) you
before.

2 Please stop .... (drop) litter on the grass.

3 Let's ask Harry .... (come) to the party.

4 I'll never forget .... (see) the sea
for the first time.

5 We all tried .... (understand) the story
but we gave up!

6 I told Jack .... (not / be) late.

**4 Read the sentences and complete the replies.
Use *have* or *get something done*.**

0 'There's something wrong with my bike.'
'You'd better .... **have / get it fixed** ....'

1 'My hair's too long!'
'Well, why don't you .... ?'

2 'Wow! Did you make that cake yourself?'
'No! I ....'

3 'Those trousers are too long for you.'
'I know. I'll ....'

4 'There used to be an old house there.
What's happened to it?'
'The council ....'

5 'Where's your phone?'
'I've ....'

6 'Sue's hair didn't use to be blonde!'
'I know. She ....'

5 Correct the mistakes.

0 We tried to ~~not~~ make a noise but it was impossible.
not to

1 I had to stop to play football when I hurt my leg.

2 Does anyone remember to learn to walk?

3 My brother has a tooth taken out yesterday.

4 My sister had made her wedding dress
by a professional dressmaker.

5 Nobody reminded to get a ticket, and I forgot to do it.

6 Choose the correct option.

0 We're under 18 so we *mustn't* / *(don't have to)* pay
full price.

1 Our car broke down but fortunately my dad *was
able to* / *could* fix it quite fast.

2 Ssssh! You *mustn't* / *don't have to* talk!

3 It's not fair. Nobody *should* / *must* work all day
without a break!

4 You *have to* / *should* show your passport before
you get on the plane.

5 Children *couldn't* / *shouldn't* be rude to their
parents.

7 Complete the sentences with the correct form of the verbs in brackets.

0   Before I went on holiday, I **had to buy** some new clothes. (*must / buy*)

1   In the future, ... all diseases? (*doctors / can / prevent*)

2   I .... a coat with me – I'm cold. (*should / bring*)

3   Luke .... out last night, he .... his essay. (*can / not / go – must / finish*)

4   I hope one day I .... several languages fluently. (*can / speak*)

5   My mother .... time off work when my sister was ill last week. (*must / take*)

8 Use the prompts to write deductions.

✓ sure it's true
✓ sure it isn't true **?**
✗ maybe it's true
✗ maybe it isn't true **?**

0   Sara didn't come to my party.
    (**? ✗** get the invitation – **? ✓** know about it)
    She might not have got the invitation.
    She can't have known about it.

1   We went to meet Lucy at the station, but she wasn't there.
    (**? ✓** catch the right train – **✗** decide not to come)

2   Rick's dad drives a very expensive car.
    (**✓** be rich – **✗** be a bank robber!)

3   Oh no! I haven't got my sandwiches!
    (**✓** leave them on the kitchen table – **✗** have to borrow some money)

4   Tom dropped a heavy book on his foot and now his toe has gone black. (**✓** hurt it! – **✗** break it)

5   It's 1:30 pm and Andy's very hungry.
    (**? ✗** have breakfast – **? ✓** have lunch yet)

9 Complete the missing words.

0   Walk! Running ....**is not**........ allowed.

1   They won't .... us eat in the classroom.

2   Sssh! We are .... to talk.

3   Yes, of course you .... borrow this book.

4   .... we allowed .... use dictionaries?

5   Yes, cycling .... in here, it's fine.

Reading and Use of English

10 Rewrite the sentences so that the second sentence means the same as the first. Use the words in brackets but you must not change them. Write between two and five words.

0   You mustn't dive into the pool. (*not*)
    Diving ...**isn't allowed**... in the pool.

1   A nail technician painted her nails for her. (*got*)
    She .... at a nail bar.

2   I wish I hadn't eaten that huge meal. (*regret*)
    I .... a huge meal.

3   Running is not allowed in the building. (*run*)
    You .... inside the building.

4   She knows the rules so there's no need to explain them. (*have*)
    We .... the rules to her because she already knows them.

5   I don't think you are telling the truth – it's impossible. (*be*)
    What you said ...., in my opinion.

6   The strong wind blew down a tree. (*had*)
    We .... by the wind.

7   Students shouldn't really wear jeans to school. (*not*)
    At our school, students .... jeans.

8   'We'd rather not go out this evening.' (*prefer*)
    They said they .... out that evening.

9   'Don't forget to take an umbrella when you go out.' (*me*)
    She .... my umbrella when I went out.

10 It wasn't Tom you saw yesterday because he's on holiday. (*have*)
    Tom's on holiday so you .... yesterday.

11 They think the burglar entered through one of the flat's windows. (*into*)
    It is thought the burglar .... through a window.

12 Lois took out a loan with a bank to start her business. (*from*)
    Lois .... a bank when she set up her business.

The play

LEAD IN

1 Have you ever been to the theatre or seen film versions of plays? Were they comedies or tragedies? Which characters do you remember?

The Importance of Being Earnest (1895)

by Oscar Wilde

This play is a comedy that satirises various aspects of Victorian society. In this scene, Algernon Moncrieff is talking to his best friend, Jack Worthing. Algernon has always thought that Jack's name was Ernest.

from ACT I

Algernon	Now, go on! Tell me the whole thing. I may mention that I have always suspected you of being a confirmed and secret Bunburyist; and I am quite sure of it now.
Jack	Bunburyist? What on earth do you mean by a Bunburyist?
Algernon	I'll reveal to you the meaning of that incomparable expression as soon as you are kind enough to inform me why you are Ernest in town and Jack in the country. 5
Jack	My dear fellow, there is nothing improbable about my explanation at all. In fact it's perfectly ordinary. Old Mr. Thomas Cardew, who adopted me when I was a little boy, made me in his will[1] guardian[2] to his grand-daughter, Miss Cecily Cardew. When one is placed in the position of guardian, one has to adopt a very high moral tone on all subjects. It's one's duty to do so. And as a high moral tone can hardly be said to conduce very much to either one's health or one's happiness, in order to get up to town I have always 10 pretended to have a younger brother of the name of Ernest, who lives in the Albany, and gets into the most dreadful scrapes[3]. That, my dear Algy, is the whole truth pure and simple.
Algernon	The truth is rarely pure and never simple. Modern life would be very tedious[4] if it were either, and modern literature a complete impossibility!
Jack	That wouldn't be at all a bad thing. 15
Algernon	Literary criticism is not your forte, my dear fellow. Don't try it. You should leave that to people who haven't been at a University. They do it so well in the daily papers. What you really are is a Bunburyist. I was quite right in saying you were a Bunburyist. You are one of the most advanced Bunburyists I know.
Jack	What on earth do you mean?
Algernon	You have invented a very useful younger brother called Ernest, in order that you may be able to come up to 20 town as often as you like. I have invented an invaluable[5] permanent invalid[6] called Bunbury, in order that I may be able to go down into the country whenever I choose. Bunbury is perfectly invaluable. If it wasn't for Bunbury's extraordinary bad health, for instance, I wouldn't be able to dine with you at Willis's to-night.

(abridged excerpt)

1. **will**: a legal document that says who inherits a person's money when they die
2. **guardian**: a person legally responsible for a child
3. **scrapes**: trouble, problems
4. **tedious**: boring
5. **invaluable**: extremely valuable
6. **invalid**: someone who is very sick (old-fashioned)

PRACTICE

2 [3.09] **PAIRWORK** Read and listen to the scene. Discuss the questions with your partner.

1 What is a Bunburyist?
2 Why does Algernon accuse Jack of being a Bunburyist?

3 Read the scene again. Decide if the sentences are true (T) or false (F). Correct the false ones.

1	Jack is called Ernest in the country.	T	F
2	Jack was adopted as a child.	T	F
3	Jack is Cecily's grandfather.	T	F
4	Algernon thinks having a 'Bunbury' is essential.	T	F
5	Algernon's friend is very sick.	T	F

4 [3.10] Listen to the exchange between Jack, Gwendolen, Algernon and Algernon's aunt, Lady Bracknell. What surprising discovery do they make?

5 [3.10] Listen again and answer the questions.

1 Was Jack happy when he found out that he had a brother?
2 What did Jack and Algernon's father do?
3 Why doesn't Algernon remember his father's name?
4 Where does Jack find his father's name?
5 Did Lady Bracknell like her brother-in-law, the general?

6 Choose one of the following tasks.

1 Do you think people associate character traits with names? Choose three names and make a list of character traits for each.
2 In groups of three, Jack (Ernest), Gwendolen and Algernon, write your own short final scene for the play.

7 Critical thinking Read the questions below and discuss in groups.

1 How is going to the cinema different from going to the theatre? Think about:
  - the type of people who go
  - the way people dress and behave
  - the cost and getting tickets
2 Is the theatre an elitist art form? How could more people be encouraged to go to the theatre?

8 **PAIRWORK** Here are some films that were originally plays. Find out who wrote the plays and if the films and plays have the same name.

  - *My Fair Lady* (1964)
  - *Amadeus* (1984)
  - *Romeo + Juliet* (1996)
  - *Driving Miss Daisy* (1989)
  - *Finding Neverland* (2004)

9 **RESEARCH** Choose one of the films and find out how different it is from the original play. Think about:

  - setting
  - main story
  - characters

10 Find a review of one of the films and a review of the original play and compare. Was the film or the play more successful?

> ## COMPETENCY SKILLS

  - Collaborating and participating (ex 7)
  - Identifying links (ex 7)
  - Communicating (ex 8)

The science-fiction novel

LEAD IN

1 Inventions like the printing press and the internet have changed our lives dramatically. What invention would you like to see in the future?

The Time Machine (1895)
by Herbert George Wells

In this novel H. G. Wells popularised the idea of travelling into the past and the future. The main character is called simply the Time Traveller and in this excerpt, he is telling a group of friends about his first trip nearly a million years into the future.

1. **dials** : parts of a machine that you turn to operate
2. **levers** : handles that you push or pull to make a machine work
3. **twilight** : the time just before it becomes completely dark in the evening

from CHAPTER XI

I have already told you about how confusing travelling on the Time Machine is and how it made me feel ill. For an indefinite time I hung on to the machine as it vibrated violently. I looked at the control dials[1] and I was amazed to find where I had arrived. One dial records days, and another thousands of days, 5 another millions of days, and another thousands of millions. I pushed the levers[2] forward and saw that the thousands dial was moving round as fast as the seconds hand of a watch — into the future.

As I drove on, everything started to look different. There seemed 10 to be an eternal twilight[3], a twilight only broken now and then when a comet flew across the sky. The sun did not set any more — it simply rose and fell in the west very quickly, and grew wider and redder and the moon had completely disappeared. At last, the sun, red and very large, stopped motionless on the 15 horizon. The earth had come to rest with one face to the sun, just as in our own time the moon faces the earth. I decided to slow down and pulled back the levers. The machine started to go slower and slower until a desolate beach grew visible.

I stopped very gently and sat upon the Time Machine, looking 20 round. The sea stretched away to the south-west but there were no waves because not a breath of wind was stirring. Only a slight rise and fall like a gentle breathing showed that the eternal sea was still moving and living. And along the beach there was a thick incrustation of salt — pink under the lurid sky. There was 25 a sense of oppression in my head, and I noticed that I was breathing very fast.

(abridged excerpt)

PRACTICE

2 [3.11] Read and listen to the extract. Does the Traveller feel better at the end of the text? Explain your answer.

3 Read the extract again and order the events.

a ☐ The Time Machine slowed down.
b ☐ The Time Traveller felt sick because of the vibrations.
c ☐ The Time Traveller pushed the levers forward.
d ☐ The Time Machine landed on a beach.
e ☐ The Time Traveller was breathing quickly.
f ☐ The sun didn't set.
g ☐ The sun stopped moving.

4 [3.12] Listen as the Traveller continues his journey into the future. Which adjective best describes his vision of the future?

5 [3.12] Listen again. Match the adverbs and adjectives to the nouns.

1 ☐ bitterly	a	silence
2 ☐ bright	b	fingers
3 ☐ chilling	c	cold
4 ☐ complete	d	hills
5 ☐ distant	e	stars
6 ☐ great	f	wind
7 ☐ frozen	g	darkness

6 Choose one of the following tasks.

1 Imagine you are an anthropologist in the year 3017. What four objects best represent society in 2017? What do they tell you about the way life is lived in 2017?

2 Choose a year: 817, 1117, 1517, 1817 or 3017. You are 16 years old. Write a short account of your daily routine. Say where you are living.

RESEARCH SKILLS

7 **Critical thinking** Choose one of the questions below and discuss in groups.

1 Imagine that you are in a classroom in a hundred years' time. In what ways will classrooms be different from today?

2 Was the quality of people's lives better in the past when they didn't have the internet or smartphones or has technology made our lives more interesting and fun?

8 **PAIRWORK** Do some research to find out how far in the future these well-known sci-fi books and films are set.

- *The Martian Chronicles* (1950)
- *Dune* (1965)
- *Blade Runner* (1982)
- *The Matrix* (1999)
- *Inception* (2010)
- *Independence Day: Resurgence* (2016)

9 **RESEARCH** Choose a sci-fi book or film and find out what technological or scientific innovations are described.

10 Which aspects of the fictional world in the film / book do you think will become reality in the future? Give reasons for your answers.

COMPETENCY SKILLS

- Acting autonomously and responsibly (ex 7)
- Communicating (ex 8)
- Learning to learn (ex 10)

The detective story

LEAD IN

1 **GROUPWORK** As a class, brainstorm a list of fictional detectives (e.g., Hercule Poirot, Montalbano, Sherlock Holmes).

2 **GROUPWORK** Choose one detective, describe them and say what qualities they have which help them to solve crimes. Share your ideas with the class.

The Adventure of the Priory School (1904)

by Arthur Conan Doyle

This is a short story featuring the world-famous detective, Sherlock Holmes. Holmes has been called to the Priory School to investigate the disappearance of a young pupil, Arthur, the son of the Duke of Holdernesse. In this excerpt the head of the school is explaining what happened.

On May 1st Arthur arrived, at the start of the summer term[1]. He was a charming boy, and he soon settled in. I can tell you that he was not very happy at home. It is an open secret that the Duke's marriage had not
5 been a happy one. It ended in a separation and the Duchess went to live in the south of France. What we do know is that the boy's sympathies were strongly with his mother. It was for this reason that the Duke wanted to send him to my school. After a
10 couple of weeks the boy was quite at home with us and was apparently absolutely happy.
He was last seen on the night of Monday, May 13th. His room was on the second floor beside a larger room, in which two boys were sleeping. These boys
15 saw and heard nothing. His window was open, and there is a strong ivy plant leading to the ground so we are almost certain that he escaped through the window and climbed down the plant.
His absence was discovered at seven o'clock on Tuesday morning. His bed had been slept in. He had
20 dressed himself fully, before going off, in his usual school uniform of black jacket and dark grey trousers. There were no signs that anyone had entered the room, and it is quite certain that there was no struggle or shouting because Caunter, the
25 boy in the next room, is a very light sleeper.
When Arthur's disappearance was discovered, I immediately assembled the boys, the masters, and the servants. It was then that we found out that he had not been the only person to disappear.
30 Heidegger, the German master, was missing. His room was also on the second floor but at the other end of the building. His bed had also been slept in, but he had apparently gone away partly dressed, since his shirt and socks were lying on the
35 floor. He had also climbed down the ivy, for we could see the marks of his feet where he had landed on the ground. His bicycle was kept in a small shed[2] and it also was gone. Two days later Heidegger's body was found about a mile away from the school
40 but there is still no sign of Arthur.

(abridged excerpt)

1. **term** : one of the periods of time that the school or university year is divided into
2. **shed** : a small building used to store things such as tools

PRACTICE

3 🔊 **[3.13]** **PAIRWORK** Read and listen to the excerpt. Why do you think Arthur ran away? Compare your ideas.

4 Read the excerpt again and answer the questions.

1 Did Arthur like his mother or father best?
2 Was it hard for Arthur to start a new life at the Priory School?
3 How did Arthur get down to the ground from the second floor?
4 Does the headmaster think that Arthur had to leave very quickly? Why?
5 Does the headmaster think that Mr Heidegger left very quickly? Why?

5 🔊 **[3.14]** Listen to Arthur's father as he explains what happened. Order the events.

a ☐ James and Hayes kidnapped Arthur.
b ☐ The Duke got married.
c ☐ James wrote a letter to his father.
d ☐ Arthur was born.
e ☐ James was born.
f ☐ The Duke sent Arthur to the Priory School.
g ☐ Hayes was sent to prison.

6 🔊 **[3.14]** Listen again and answer the questions.

1 Why did the Duke send Arthur to the Priory School?
2 Why did Arthur go to meet James?
3 Why did Heidegger follow Arthur?
4 Who killed Heidegger?
5 What happened to Hayes?
6 What punishment did James accept?

7 Choose one of the following tasks.

1 Write the letter that James sent to his father after he had kidnapped Arthur.
2 In pairs, Student A is Sherlock Holmes and Student B is James. Write Holmes' interrogation of James after Arthur has been found.

RESEARCH SKILLS

8 **Critical thinking** Choose one of the questions below and discuss in groups or with a partner.

1 Is it easier to solve crimes today than it was in Sherlock Holmes' days? What technology and devices help detectives in their work?
2 Can crime fiction encourage people to commit real crimes? Can you find any examples of this happening?

9 **PAIRWORK** Do some research to find out the name of the detective in these well-known novels.

- *The Big Sleep* (1939)
- *A Murder is Announced* (1950)
- *The Girl with the Dragon Tattoo* (2005)
- *The Private Patient* (2008)
- *The Wrong Side of Goodbye* (2016)

10 **RESEARCH** Choose one of the novels and design a mind map to show the crime, suspects and motive.

11 Choose a TV crime series (e.g., *CSI*, *Bones*, *Sherlock*). Prepare a report including:

- a description of the main characters
- the time and location
- your opinion of the series

COMPETENCY SKILLS

- Collaborating and participating (ex 7)
- Communicating (ex 8)
- Learning to learn (ex 9)

The fantasy novel

LEAD IN

1 *Alice in Wonderland* is a well-known fantasy novel. As a class, brainstorm what you already know about this famous work.

Alice in Wonderland (1865)

by Lewis Carroll (Charles Lutwidge Dodgson)

Alice in Wonderland *is the story of a young girl, Alice, who dreams of incredible adventures. In this excerpt we find out how Alice's adventures began.*

from CHAPTER I

Alice was beginning to get very tired of sitting beside her sister and of having nothing to do: once or twice she had looked into the book her sister was reading, but it had no pictures or conversations in it, 'and
5 what is the use of a book,' thought Alice, 'without pictures or conversations?'
So she was considering, in her own mind (as well as she could, for the hot day made her feel very sleepy and stupid), whether she should pick some daisies
10 and make a daisy-chain[1], when suddenly a White Rabbit with pink eyes ran close by her.
There was nothing so *very* remarkable in that, nor did Alice think it so *very* strange to hear the Rabbit say to itself, 'Oh dear! Oh dear! I shall be late!' (when she
15 thought it over later, it occurred to her how strange that was, but at the time it all seemed quite natural); but when the Rabbit actually *took a watch out of its waistcoat-pocket*, and looked at it, and then hurried on, Alice jumped to her feet, for it flashed across her
20 mind that she had never before seen a rabbit with either a waistcoat-pocket, or a watch to take out of it, and burning with curiosity, she ran across the field after it, and fortunately was just in time to see it pop down a large rabbit-hole under the hedge.

In another moment down went Alice after it, never 25 once considering how in the world she would get out again.
The rabbit-hole went straight on like a tunnel for some way, and then dipped suddenly down, so suddenly that Alice had not a moment to think about 30 stopping herself before she found herself falling down a very deep well[2].
Down, down, down. Would the fall *never* come to an end? 'I wonder how many miles I've fallen by this time?' she said aloud. 'I must be getting somewhere 35 near the centre of the earth. Let me see: that would be four thousand miles down, I think — yes, that's about the right distance — but then I wonder what Latitude or Longitude I've got to?' (Alice had no idea what Latitude was, or Longitude either, but thought 40 they were nice big words to say.)

(abridged excerpt)

---

1. **daisy-chain** : a string of daisies (small white and yellow flowers) connected together like a necklace
2. **well** : a deep hole in the ground from which you can get water, oil, or gas

PRACTICE

2  **[3.15]** **Read and listen to the extract. Do you think Alice is frightened or excited by her strange adventure?**

3 **Read the extract again and answer the questions.**

1 Why didn't Alice want to read with her sister?
2 What seemed natural to Alice at the time that later seemed strange?
3 What did the Rabbit do that really surprised Alice?
4 Where was the rabbit-hole?
5 How far did Alice think she was falling?
6 What did Alice like about the words *longitude* and *latitude*?

4 **[3.16]** **Listen to the continuation of the story. Why is Alice feeling frustrated?**

5 **[3.16]** **Listen again. Decide if the sentences are true (T) or false (F). Correct the false ones.**

1	The long hall was very dark.	T	F
2	The table had four legs.	T	F
3	Alice was able to open one of the doors.	T	F
4	She saw a beautiful forest.	T	F
5	She had a telescope.	T	F

6 **Choose one of the following tasks.**

1 Make a list of the things in the two excerpts which are not realistic and which help to make *Alice in Wonderland* a fantasy novel.
2 Through a small door Alice saw 'the loveliest garden'. In pairs, try to imagine what was in the garden.

7 **Critical thinking** **In groups, choose one of the questions below and discuss.**

1 'Imagination is the only weapon in the war against reality', is a quotation from *Alice in Wonderland*. What do you think it means?
2 Why are fantasy books and films so popular today? Which type of fantasy appeals most to your age group? Discuss.

8 **PAIRWORK** **How many of the fantasy works below have you heard of, read or seen? Compare your answers.**

- *The Chronicles of Narnia* (1950)
- *The Fellowship of the Ring* (1955)
- *His Dark Materials* (1995)
- *A Game of Thrones* (1996)
- *Harry Potter and the Philosopher's Stone* (1997)

9 **RESEARCH Choose one of the above and write a short summary of the plot.**

10 **These songs were inspired by *Alice in Wonderland*. Find out what the connection between one of the songs and the novel is. Present your findings to the class.**

- *Alice* (Avril Lavigne)
- *Queen of Hearts* (Saxon)
- *Pulk / Pull Revolving Doors* (Radiohead)

COMPETENCY SKILLS

- Planning and prioritising (ex 6)
- Communicating (ex 8)
- Learning to learn (exs 9, 10)
- Problem solving (ex 10)

LITERATURE SKILLS 5

The stoic poem

LEAD IN

1 **PAIRWORK** Read this quotation from the writings of Marcus Aurelius. What do you think it means?

If you are pained by any external thing, it is not this thing that disturbs you, but your own judgment about it. And it is in your power to wipe out this judgment now.

– *Marcus Aurelius*, *Roman Emperor and Stoic philosopher*

If—(1895)
by Rudyard Kipling

If— is a poem by English Nobel Laureate Rudyard Kipling, written circa 1895. It is a literary example of Victorian-era stoicism and is written in the form of paternal advice to the poet's son, John.

If you can keep your head when all about you
Are losing theirs and blaming it on you;
If you can trust yourself when all men doubt you,
But make allowance for[1] their doubting too;
5 If you can wait and not be tired by waiting,
Or, being lied about, don't deal in lies,
Or, being hated, don't give way to[2] hating,
And yet don't look too good, nor talk too wise;

If you can dream—and not make dreams your master;
10 If you can think—and not make thoughts your aim;
If you can meet with triumph[3] and disaster
And treat those two impostors[4] just the same;
If you can bear to hear the truth you've spoken
Twisted by knaves[5] to make a trap for fools,
15 Or watch the things you gave your life to broken,
And stoop[6] and build 'em up with wornout tools;

If you can make one heap[7] of all your winnings
And risk it on one turn of pitch-and-toss,
And lose, and start again at your beginnings
And never breathe a word about your loss;   20
If you can force your heart and nerve and sinew
To serve your turn long after they are gone,
And so hold on when there is nothing in you
Except the Will which says to them: "Hold on";

If you can talk with crowds and keep your virtue,   25
Or walk with kings—nor lose the common touch;
If neither foes[8] nor loving friends can hurt you;
If all men count with you, but none too much;
If you can fill the unforgiving minute
With sixty seconds' worth of distance run—   30
Yours is the Earth and everything that's in it,
And—which is more—you'll be a Man, my son!

stoicism *noun*
the quality of experiencing pain or trouble without complaining or showing your emotions:
He endured the pain of his wounds with great stoicism.

1. **make allowance for**: prepare for the possibility of
2. **give way to**: surrender to. accept
3. **triumph**: victory; success
4. **impostors**: things that deceive you
5. **knaves**: dishonest men (old-fashioned)
6. **stoop**: bend your body over
7. **heap**: large amount
8. **foes**: enemies

PRACTICE

2  **[3.17] Read and listen to the poem. Decide if the words below are nouns (N), verbs (V) or adjectives (A). Then match the words to the correct definition.**

1 ☐ lies
2 ☐ wise
3 ☐ fools
4 ☐ tools

a experienced and mature
b equipment or instruments
c things that aren't true
d silly people

3 **Read the poem again and answer the questions.**

1 Which phrase means 'stay calm'?
2 What, according to the poem, should you do if people tell lies about you?
3 Why do you think Kipling calls 'triumph' and 'disaster' imposters?
4 What does he advise doing if you lose everything?
5 What do you is the meaning of the phrase 'lose the common touch'?
6 What personality characteristics alluded to in the poem express stoicism?

4 **[3.18] Listen about the life of Rudyard Kipling. How do the events in his life relate to the poem If—?**

5 **[3.18] Listen again and match the information to the name.**

1 ☐ Rudyard Kipling
☐
☐
2 ☐ Josephine Kipling
3 ☐ John Kipling

a … wrote a very popular poem.
b … died during the war.
c … died as a child.
d … studied away from home.
e … lost all his money.

6 **Choose one of the following tasks.**

1 Imagine you are an old man / woman. Write a letter / email to your grandchildren telling them what lessons you have learned in life.
2 With a partner, make a list of all the difficulties people experience in life. Can anything positive ever come out of bad experiences?

7 **Critical thinking** **Discuss these statements in groups.**

1 Human beings are by nature positive, so they will always try to overcome hardships and make the best out of life.
2 If more people were stoic, we'd live in a happier world.

8 **GROUPWORK** **Look at the list of characters in modern day films. In what way are they stoic?**

- Andy Dufresne in *The Shawshank Redemption* (1994)
- Maximus Decimus Meridius in *Gladiator* (2000)
- Yoda in the *Star Wars* series

9 **RESEARCH** **Choose one of the films above and do some research to find out:**

- the plot of the film
- the main characters and how the hardships in life affect them

10 **Choose one of the poems below and prepare a fact file including information about the author, the protagonist described and the meaning of the poem itself.**

- *The Old Stoic* (1846) by Emily Bronte
- *Baby Tortoise* (1909) by D.H. Lawrence

COMPETENCY SKILLS

- Identifying links (ex 8)
- Acquiring and interpreting information (ex 9)
- Learning to learn (ex 10)

CLIL A

Science

Germs and resistance

In this Module, we will plan a publicity campaign to raise people's awareness of infectious diseases.

1 LEAD IN Read the descriptions of four videos designed to show how infectious diseases can spread. Which do you think is the most effective?

> Infectious diseases spread when pathogens such as bacteria and viruses are transferred from the body of an infected organism into another body.

Video 1 – Five friends are exercising. When they stop, they pick up one bottle of water and they all drink from this bottle. A close-up of the bottle and a slogan appears on the screen.

....

▶ ⏸ 3:00 ━━━━━━━━━●━━━━ 🔊━●

Video 2 – Many people are walking along the street and a person sneezes freely and does not cover his mouth. The people walking *into the sneeze* are disgusted and a slogan appears.

....

▶ ⏸ 3:00 ━━━━━━●━━━━━━ 🔊━●

Video 3 – Four scenes in sequence:

1 A close-up of a man's hand holding the handrail of an escalator in a metro or bus.
2 The man runs to the door of a restaurant and we see his hand opening the door.
3 The man rushes to the table where three friends are already eating, they shake hands.
4 The man sits and we see his hands taking some bread and putting it into his mouth.

A slogan appears on the screen.

....

▶ ⏸ 3:00 ━━━━━━━━━━●━━ 🔊━●

Video 4 – Four scenes in sequence:

1 A cute dog is retrieving a Frisbee from the edge of a stream and sees a sick-looking rat. The dog **nudges** the sick rat.
2 A close-up shows **fleas** jumping from the rat into the hairy coat of the dog.
3 The dog runs back to his best friend and they run home.
4 Later the two are sleeping in bed and a flea bites the boy's arm which is hugging the dog.

A slogan appears on the screen.

....

▶ ⏸ 3:00 ━━━━━━━━━●━━━ 🔊━●

2 Decide which of the slogans below would conclude each video most effectively. Write these slogans in the spaces provided. There are three extra slogans.

1 Sneezing is a problem if you have an allergy.
2 Sneeze it, share it! Don't infect the world … trap your germs in a tissue!
3 Don't wash your hands before you eat? Yummy … you are eating everything that you have touched.
4 Great to share time with friends … NOT great to share pathogens.
5 Your pets are innocent but the **bugs** they may carry can be dangerous.
6 Always use a tissue when you open doors.
7 Dogs … man's best friend.

3 [3.19] **Why should we not overuse antibiotics? Complete the text with the words and phrases below. Then listen and check.**

> antibiotic resistance ▪ genetic diversity ▪ germ theory of disease ▪
> overused, abused and misused ▪ pasteurisation ▪ penicillin

In 1546, Girolamo Fracastoro suggested that diseases are carried by microorganisms that are too small to see with the naked eye. It took another 300 years before Fracastoro's [1]........................ was accepted in the late 1800s, when Louis Pasteur and Robert Koch demonstrated the relation between microorganisms and disease. Pasteur showed that heating beer and wine stops their degradation because high temperatures kill the microorganisms. Today, we still use [2]........................ to eliminate bacteria such as *Salmonella* and *E. coli* found in raw milk.

In 1928 Alexander Fleming found that [3]........................, a substance produced by a **mould** (*Penicillium notatum*), could stop bacterial growth. The discovery of penicillin is recognised as one of the greatest moments in medicine. However, Fleming also warned against *resistance*. He noted that if too little penicillin was used or if the treatment time was too short to eliminate most of the bacteria, the bacteria developed [4]........................ .

Why does resistance develop? Bacteria divide in a way that makes them slightly different, genetically. This [5]........................ within a population of bacteria allows some of the cells to survive the antibiotic treatment if the treatment is not strong enough. When these surviving cells then replicate, the next generation of bacteria is genetically more resistant to that antibiotic. What is worrying is that resistance can form against all antibiotics. Unfortunately, since their discovery, antibiotics have been [6]........................ . The World Health Organisation (WHO) warns that, if we are not careful, we might find ourselves with superbacteria, against which we have no antibiotics.

4 GROUPWORK Work in groups of four and prepare a leaflet for your campaign. Follow these steps.

1 Choose one message from the text above that the campaign should communicate to the public. Here are some examples:
  - High temperature can kill bacteria.
  - Always finish a course of antibiotics.
  - Pathogens can become resistant to antibiotics and develop into *superbugs*.
  - Using antibiotics too often helps pathogens to become resistant.

2 Now try and think of a slogan, like the ones in exercise 2, for your leaflet. Present your leaflet to the class. The class can vote on the best one.

5 REAL-LIFE TASK In groups of four, create a video storyboard.

1 Use the video descriptions in exercise 1 to help you generate ideas.
2 Divide your video into scenes and decide what will happen in each scene.
3 Draw each scene and write a caption underneath describing what is happening.
4 Present your ideas to the class. Act out the scene, record it and play your video to the class.

Glossary

bugs : insects
fleas : small, jumping insects that feed on the blood of animals

mould : a soft growth that develops on old food or on objects that have been left for too long in warm, wet air
nudges : pushes gently

Populations and epidemics

History

In this Module, we will understand how infectious diseases have shaped populations and affected the survival of different peoples.

1 LEAD IN In pairs, think of your friends and family.

1 Who always / never gets sick?

2 What about you? How frequently do you get sick?

> Pathogens such as viruses or bacteria make us ill and can transmit a series of illnesses from fever, coughs, and diarrhoea to pneumonia. However, some people seem to get sick all the time while others are always healthy.

2 Look at the captions (1–6) below and match them to the appropriate picture (A–F).

1 Homozygous twins.
2 Genetic information is used in legal cases.
3 Genetic diversity is seen through hair and skin colour.
4 Genetic differences affect how well intestines absorb nutrients.
5 Infective pathogens are transmitted by insects.
6 Some people get sick more than others.

A

B

C

D

E

F

3 PAIRWORK Read and complete the text with the linking words / phrases below.

- although
- are therefore
- for example
- these resistant genes
- these survivors
- this pathogen

GENETIC DIVERSITY, SELECTION AND SURVIVAL

Since we are slightly different from each other genetically, infectious pathogens do not affect everyone in the same way. [1] ...., between 1346 and 1353, the bubonic plague bacteria *Yersinia pestis* eliminated one-third of the population in Europe. [2] .... more than 100 million people across the world died from this **pandemic**, many survived. [3] .... were probably genetically more resistant to the plague bacteria. Epidemics [4] .... a form of genetic selection, since survivors of a given epidemic are genetically more resistant to that pathogen. **Offspring** of these survivors inherit [5] ...., and in the future they would probably be less severely affected by this pathogen than someone who had never been in contact with it. (Unless [6] .... also experiences genetic selection and becomes more infectious!)

4 PAIRWORK Look at each statement about infectious diseases and match it to the correct picture.

1 In crowded living conditions, a pathogen can spread much more quickly and affect many more people. Those who survive are genetically more resistant to that pathogen.

2 Where population density is low and people live in open fields, pathogens are less likely to spread since people can easily isolate themselves from infected individuals. However, this means that there is less *genetic selection* and the population remains more susceptible to future pathogens.

3 People who have never been exposed to a certain pathogen will be easily infected if they come into close contact with that pathogen, which could be carried by populations that have become less susceptible.

A ☐ In the Old World: densely populated and crowded European cities and slums.

B ☐ In the New World: Native Americans meeting the Europeans.

5 REAL-LIFE TASK In groups of four, investigate one of the following points. Prepare a presentation for your class.

1 There have been several epidemics and pandemics in history. Some have been recurrent and others have not. Investigate one of them and explain how it influenced historical events.

2 Before understanding the existence of pathogens, people thought that bad smells caused diseases. Investigate why this theory might make sense. Then prepare a report on the events that led to the understanding that infectious diseases were transmitted by microorganisms. How did society change because of these findings?

3 In some religions, you must wash your hands before eating. Find out how this helped people survive epidemics. Choose one particular period in history, like for instance the one of the Black Death, and find out if this religious practice reduced deaths in the population.

4 Investigate how **smallpox** played a part in helping the Europeans conquer Central America in the 1500s.

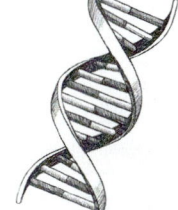

Glossary

offspring : a person's children (formal)

pandemic : existing in almost all of an area

smallpox : an extremely infectious disease that can cause fever and spots and often death

CLIL C

Travel and health

Geography

In this Module, we will reflect on how mobility has changed and what this means for the management of disease control today.

1 LEAD IN In pairs, examine the maps and, also using the scales, decide if the sentences are true (T) or false (F). Correct the false ones.

1   This family is originally from the UK.   T   F
2   The family roots are in the town of Leeds.   T   F
3   The farthest the grandfather had travelled to was Ilkley.   T   F
4   The father was the first generation to leave the UK.   T   F
5   The son has travelled as far as Australia.   T   F
6   The farthest the great-grandfather travelled was ca. 100 km from home.   T   F
7   The son has not been to Africa.   T   F
8   The farthest the father had travelled to was Corsica.   T   F
9   The first trains were probably invented when the son was a boy.   T   F
10   The son was probably the first in his family to travel by plane.   T   F

The images illustrate the distances travelled by four generations of a certain family.

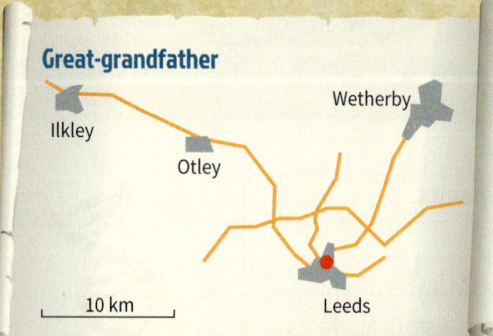

Great-grandfather
Wetherby
Ilkley
Otley
Leeds
10 km

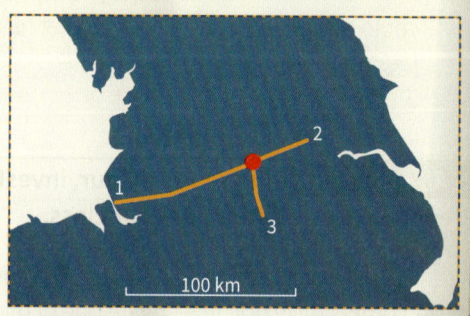

Grandfather
1 Liverpool
2 York
3 Sheffield
100 km

Father
1,000 km

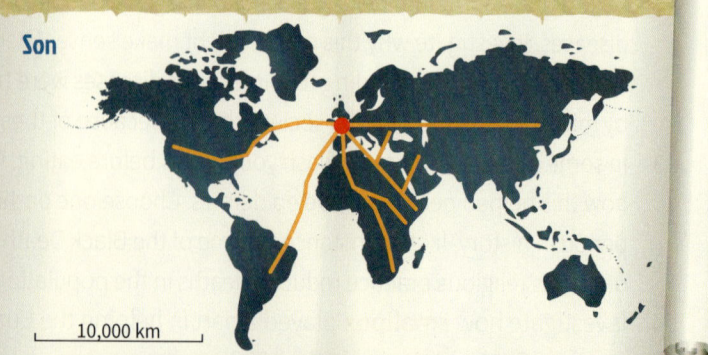

Son
10,000 km

2 [3.20] **Look at the letter below from an insurance company and put the sentences in order. Use the words in bold to help you. Then listen and check.**

Dear **Traveller**,

You have received this letter because you are about to go on holiday to an exotic country. It is really important that you read this information and comply with the instructions.

a ☐ **As an infected tourist**, you must remember that you have three responsibilities when you return. To start with, you must notify the infective disease officer at the airport on arrival, even if you no longer have any symptoms.

b ☐ **In preparation for this trip**, you have received the necessary injections. However, you could still become infected by one of the many pathogens present in the country you are visiting. For some pathogenic infections, the symptoms are immediate, such as diarrhoea or stomach ache.

c ☐ If you experience **such symptoms**, please

FLIGHT

contact the local hospital immediately and present the insurance card enclosed with this letter.

d ☐ **Lastly**, if you notice any people around you becoming ill with the same symptoms, alert them of your experience and encourage them to seek medical attention.

e ☐ **Once again**, enjoy your trip. Please comply with this strong recommendation. It is crucial to maintain public health and prevent the spread of highly infectious and fatal diseases.

f ☐ **Then**, as soon as you get home, you should visit your local **GP** so that they can monitor any abnormal developments.

If you have any questions, please do not hesitate to contact us.

3 **Critical thinking** **In pairs, discuss the problems of disease control. Why are these points of concern?**

1 Pathogens often have an incubation period, which means symptoms do not appear until some weeks after the traveller has returned home.

2 Some travellers could be resistant to the pathogen and may only be slightly ill or show no symptoms at all of being infected. They are still carriers, however, and can infect others around them with the disease.

3 Travel to distant places often requires stopovers at crowded airports.

4 Some people insist on taking their pets with them on holiday. How would this contribute to the transmission of pathogens through fleas and **lice**?

4 **REAL-LIFE TASK** **In groups of four, choose one of the following diseases to investigate.**

- SARS (Severe Acute Respiratory Syndrome)
- avian flu
- swine flu
- Zika virus

Find out:

1 What do epidemiologists believe is the origin of this disease?

2 How has long-distance movement of people and agricultural products affected this disease?

3 What are the ways we can stop or control the spread of the disease?

Use your findings to produce a health information leaflet for travellers to help prevent the spread of the disease.

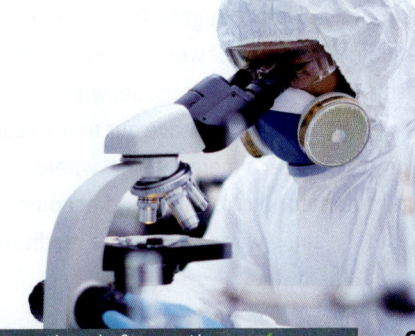

Glossary

GP (general practitioner) : a doctor who provides general medical treatment

lice : small insects that live on the bodies of people or animals

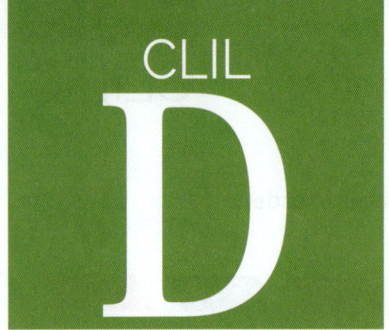

CLIL D

Art

Art and health

In this Module, we will see the positive effects that art can have on our mental and physical health.

1 LEAD IN Work in pairs to answer the questions

1 Look at the images below. What types of art can you see?
2 Have you tried doing any of these types of art? Which would you like to try?
3 Do you consider yourself to be artistic? Why / why not?

2 PAIRWORK Read at the statements below and decide if they are true (T) or false (F). Then read the text and check if your guesses were right.

		T	F
1	Anyone can create art.	T	F
2	Painting is the only form of art that can relieve stress.	T	F
3	You have to be good at something to benefit from it.	T	F
4	The average person has 6,000 thoughts per day.	T	F
5	Our brain can get stuck thinking the same thing over and over.	T	F

The benefits of creating art

Some people have a natural talent for singing, writing, or acting, but the truth is most of us don't. The same is true for art. For the majority of people, the art world seems like a very exclusive club. It only seems to be open to two groups of people: the few talented artists who create great works of art and to the even fewer experts who appreciate these works. But the truth is, we all need to express ourselves. And besides, you don't have to be good at something to benefit from it.

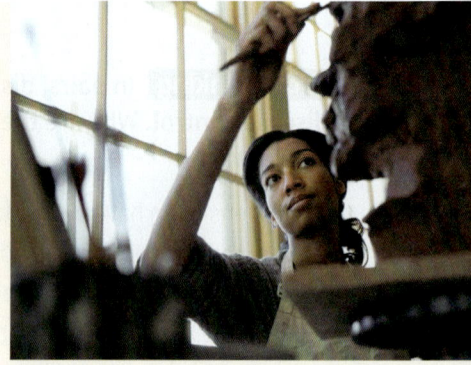

Even though most of us are not natural-born artists, we can still get a wide range of benefits from actually doing art. It's one of the many ways that we can effectively communicate our feelings and help ourselves **unwind**. This is not limited to just painting—printmaking, sculpture, ceramics and design are equally relaxing activities, and can lower stress levels and leave you feeling happy and calm.

But how does this happen? Well, creating art helps our brain escape from the routine of our everyday thoughts. On average, we have 60,000 thoughts per day, 95 per cent of which are repeated. Our brain essentially gets 'bored' thinking the same things. So, when we concentrate on creating art, we **unconsciously** leave our uninteresting thoughts and anxieties behind. We enter a mental 'zone' where we feel free. We are able to **flee** our monotonous routines and become happier, healthier people, much in the same way as if we were meditating.

3 Look at the images and match the images to the paragraphs of the text.

4 [3.21] Read and listen to the lecture about art therapy and answer the questions.

1 Where did the idea of adult colouring books come from?
2 What is the aim of adult colouring books?
3 Why are some people critical of colouring books?
4 How do we know that colouring books are popular?

Can colouring books really make you happier?

1 Colouring books are strictly for children, right? Wrong. Few people realise that there are in fact colouring books for adults and that they might be a worthwhile way of **relieving** stress, at least according to some reports. The trend first started in France, where **consumption** of antidepressants, tranquillizers, and sleeping pills is very high. The colouring books were designed to help adults reduce feelings of anxiety and stress, without having to resort to taking prescription **medication**.

2 However, some researchers argue that colouring books don't really improve mental health. They say that this only happens when people are asked to create art from scratch, guided by a **therapist**. This practice is known as art therapy. At first some people feel nervous at having to create art, especially if they don't consider themselves to be artistic, but overcoming this fear is part of the process and leads to a sense of achievement.

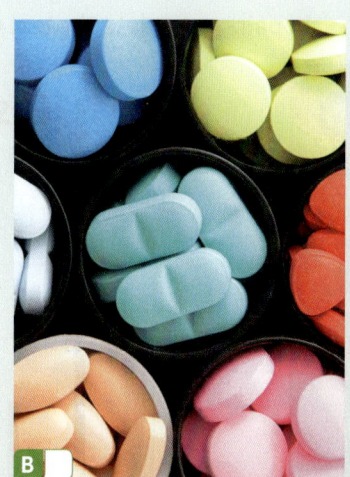

3 Overall, both creating art in a guided therapy session and filling in colouring books at home surely have their benefits. How successful each one is at making us feel better depends on the individual. And despite the arguments against colouring books as therapy, you cannot argue that they haven't been successful. In 2015, approximately 12 million adult colouring books were sold in the US alone. This trend even caused a global coloured-pencil shortage!

5 **REAL-LIFE TASK** In groups of four, find out more about art therapy.
Follow the steps below.

1 When did this practice begin?
2 Who can it help?
3 How is it carried out?
4 What kind of results can be obtained?
5 Prepare a presentation to share your findings with your class.

Glossary

unconsciously : without thinking
flee : escape
unwind : relax
relieving : making something better or less severe
consumption : quantity used
medication : drugs used to treat an illness
therapist : a professional who treats illnesses

Epidemiology through numbers

In this Module, we will study epidemics through graphs and maps and learn how to record data about the antibiotic industry.

1 LEAD IN The following text summarises the information in the graph. In pairs, complete the text with the phrases provided.

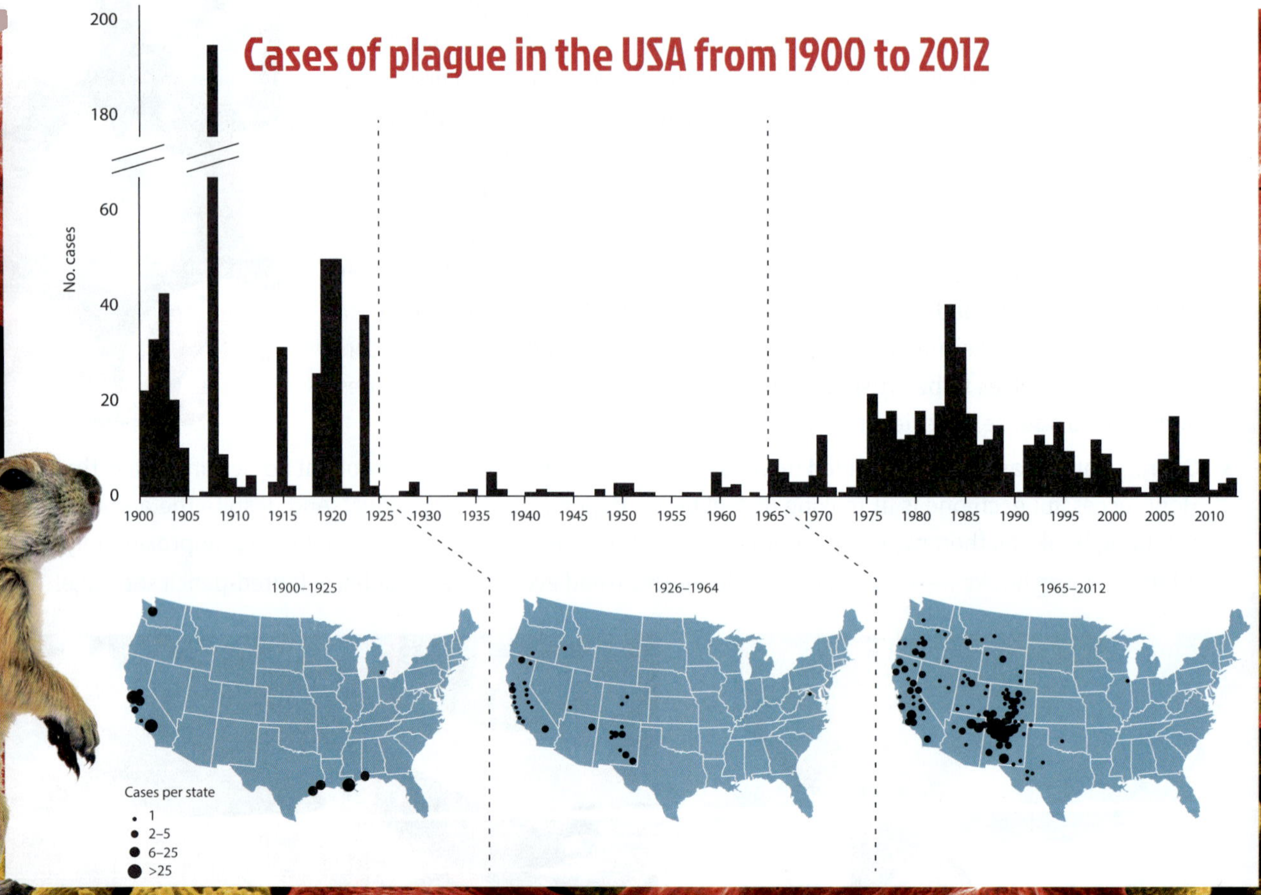

Cases of plague in the USA from 1900 to 2012

No. cases

1900–1925 1926–1964 1965–2012

Cases per state
- 1
- 2–5
- 6–25
- >25

and 1964 ▪ by rats transported in ships ▪ disease has evolved ▪ carriers of the plague bacterium ▪ exposed to infected fleas ▪ in densely populated port cities ▪ much farther inland ▪ very few in 1906

Between the years of 1900 and 2012 the US recorded three eras of plague **outbreaks**. In the first era (1900–1925) 496 cases were reported, but only [1]........................ . This is similar to how the Black Death (bubonic plague) entered Europe in 1346; [2]........................ . Although there were no cases reported in 1905 and [3]........................, the greatest number of cases in history was reported in 1907, with 191 infections. However, after the outbreak in 1924 in Los Angeles, there were only 42 cases for the next 38 years, between 1926 [4]........................ . This is the second era of the plague in the US. However, what is interesting about this second era is that some cases were found [5]........................ This reflects the migration of the plague bacterium. In fact, different species of **rodents** such as squirrels, prairie dogs and chipmunks had become [6]........................ . Since these rodent species are indigenous to the North American continent, their infection with a foreign pathogen explains how the [7]........................ in the third era (1965–2012). In fact, the 468 cases recorded for this era mainly occurred inland and also involved individuals from **affluent** areas who were probably [8]........................ through domestic pets or while attending to their gardens.

2 [3.22] **PAIRWORK** Study the table of new drugs approved by the Food and Drug Administration (FDA) between 1999 and 2005 and listen to the information. Then answer the questions.

1 Which of the illnesses cited in the table are acute (normally cured within a month) and which are chronic (normally take much more time, sometimes never cured)? Complete the table with *c* = chronic or *a* = acute.

2 The problem with illnesses caused by pathogens such as bacteria or viruses is that, in time, these pathogens can become drug-resistant. This means that old drugs are no longer effective. Put a tick (✓) next to the illnesses caused by pathogens that can develop resistance.

3 How many drugs were developed for chronic illnesses?

4 How many drugs might become less effective because of pathogens developing drug resistance?

5 What do you think motivates drug companies to develop new pharmaceuticals?

Category of 95 new drugs approved by the FDA between 1999 and 2005			
Drug type	Number of drugs approved	Duration (chronic / acute)	Develop resistance? Yes / No
Antibiotics for bacterial infections	11		
Medications for neurological disease (depression, psychiatric disorders, Alzheimer's, multiple sclerosis, Parkinson's, migraine)	22		
Oncological therapeutics (for cancer treatments)	22		
Medications for cardiovascular problems (including medicines for managing cholesterol)	16		
Medications for diabetes	9		
Treatment for respiratory problems (asthma, emphysema)	4		
Medications for viral infections (coughs, colds) and others	11		

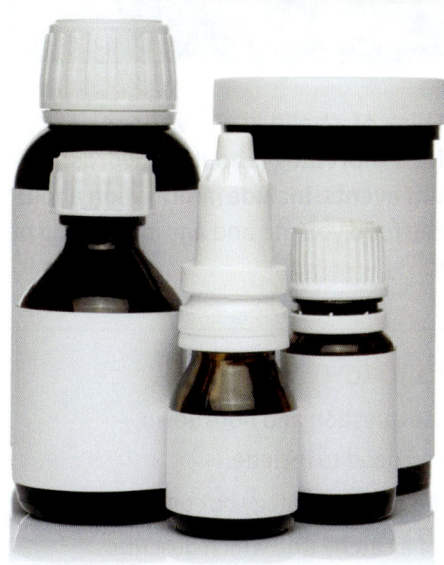

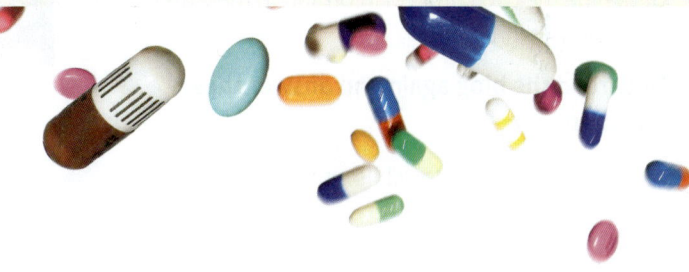

3 **REAL-LIFE TASK** In groups of four, research one of the following points and present your findings in tables, graphs and other effective visuals such as maps.

1 The cost of researching a new drug is from $800 million to $1.7 billion. Research one pharmaceutical company and find out how much they spend to produce different drugs. Which drugs bring them more profit (the money they get from the sale of the drug is higher than the money they spend to produce it)?

2 Why don't pharmaceutical companies invest in antibiotics? Research a pharmaceutical company. Look at how much money they spend to produce an antibiotic drug. Then research how much they sell it for. Are they making a profit? Compare this data with another drug they produce. What conclusions can you draw?

Glossary

affluent : rich, wealthy

migraine : a type of headache

outbreaks : a time when a disease suddenly begins

rodents : mice, rats, etc

A travel blog

Question

Travel blogs wanted

We are looking for travel blogs for our new online English-language magazine for teenagers.

Your blog must begin with this sentence: *We got here this morning. What an amazing place!*

Your blog must include: • The sea • Food

Write your blog.

Answer

Barcelona: dream city

We got here this morning. What an amazing place! Luckily, I'd managed to get a window seat on the plane, so I was watching as we landed. I could see the beaches clearly (it felt like we were heading straight for them!). There were rows of colourful umbrellas and the sea was sparkling blue (not like the sea back home in Britain!). Maybe because Barcelona is quite a big city, I hadn't imagined anything so beautiful.

It took ages to collect our bags and get out of the airport, but the metro was easy to work out. I practised my GCSE Spanish (grade A last year!) and managed to get directions to the hotel. It's quite small and friendly, very modern with bright colours everywhere, and a wonderful smell of coffee!

The first thing we did was eat. There was a tapas bar next to the hotel. There was lots of weird-looking sea food, which I avoided (I will try it before we leave, honestly!) so I stuck with things that looked familiar – it was delicious. Then we hit the tourist trail!

1 Read the question and the answer.

Underline the two pieces of information the writer needed to include.

2 Now read the blog again and answer these questions.

1 Where was the writer while writing the blog?
2 How did they travel?
3 Why was the writer surprised?
4 What were their first impressions of the hotel?
5 What kind of food did the writer *not* eat?
6 What does 'we hit the tourist trail' mean?

3 PAIRWORK What does the blog tell you about the writer? Answer these questions.

1 Has the writer ever been to Barcelona before?
2 Where does the writer come from?
3 Roughly how old is she / he?
4 Which of these words best describe her / him? Why do you think so?

☐ fearless   ☐ adventurous
☐ excited   ☐ lazy
☐ enthusiastic   ☐ unimaginative
☐ nervous   ☐ inquisitive

4 TASK Think of a holiday you've been on and write a short blog (about 150 words) to recount events. Include information about your travel, the food you ate and any interesting people you met.

Steps to follow

1 Read the question and note down what you need to include.
2 Read the Writing strategy box on page 17 again.
3 Think of a catchy title which describes the events.
4 Ensure your writing style is informal. Include abbreviations, slang expressions and contractions.
5 Do a rough draft. Check spelling, punctuation and grammar.
6 Write a final draft.

A formal email

Question

You recently ordered a book online. It was a birthday present for a friend. The order arrived but there were certain problems with it. Write an email to the Customer Services department complaining about the service you have received. Inform them of the problem with your item. Make sure you ask the company to respond to your complaint and provide some compensation (like refund you the money or send an alternative book).

- **order number:** ADX 00325738
- *Green Living*, **by David and Sarah Masters (paperback)**
- **£8.50**
- **next day delivery**

Answer

To:	Customer Services
Object:	Order number ADX 00325738

Dear Sir or Madam,

I am writing to complain about a book which I recently bought from your website. The title of the book is *Green Living*, by David and Sarah Masters.

The main issues I have are these. Although you told me that it would arrive the next day, it actually took a week. Moreover, when it finally arrived the package was wet and torn open and the book was damaged. The book was supposed to be a present, but it was so badly damaged, I had to buy something else.

I would therefore like a refund. Could you also let me know how to return the damaged book free of charge? I look forward to hearing from you as soon as possible.

Yours faithfully,
Joe Simpson

---

1 Read the question. Underline all the information the writer needs to include.

2 Now read the email. Then answer these questions.

  1 Does the writer know who he is writing to? How do you know?

  2 The writer makes two complaints. What are they? Which word links them?

  3 What does the writer want the company to do?

  4 How does the writer ask for his money back?

  5 How does the writer ask for more information?

  6 How does the writer show that he would like a quick reply?

3 **TASK** Write an email to the Customer Services department complaining about something you have just bought online. Think about these questions and include this information in your email.

- What is the item?
- Why are you disappointed? (e.g., Did they send the wrong thing? Is it broken? Was it described badly?)
- What do you want – your money back (a refund), or a replacement?

Steps to follow

1 Read the question and note down what you need to include.

2 Make sure you start with a formal greeting.

3 Remember to state the problem at the start of your email.

4 Remember the rules for formal language (avoid contractions and informal expressions).

5 Make sure you end with a formal salutation and request that the company provides some resolution to your problem (you should indicate what you want them to do).

6 Write in full sentences and make sure you check your spelling and grammar.

7 Write your first draft. Write about 100–120 words.

8 Check your work again and then write a final draft.

An opinion essay

WRITING EXPANSION

QUESTION

In your English class you have been talking about food waste.
Now, your English teacher has asked you to write an essay. Write an essay answering the question below, using all the notes and any extra ideas you can think of.
Give reasons for your point of view.

Every year the UK throws away 15 million tonnes of good food, but thousands of people are hungry. What do you think is the solution to this problem?

NOTES – Write about:

1 sharing food
2 restaurants that recycle food
3 (your own ideas) *governments — control waste, help the poor*

ANSWER

It is shocking that British people throw away 15 million tonnes of good food every year. Meanwhile, thousands of people do not have enough to eat. What can we do about this?

5   There are several local answers. First, communities could share food by having a community fridge and donating leftover food and taking what they need. This is a great idea, although it depends on people's generosity. In addition, some people could take food when they do not really

10 need it. Secondly, restaurants could recycle food that shops and other restaurants don't need. There are already some cafés like this and they are popular. On the other hand, they also depend on people's good will to survive. A third idea is that the government should act to control food waste and help the poor. For example,

15 they could fine people who throw away good food. They could also give more financial help to the poor, so that nobody is hungry.

   In my opinion, although local projects help with food waste and hunger, they are not enough by themselves. I believe that government action is the only way to solve the problem properly.

---

1   **Read the question. What is the essay about?**

2   **PAIRWORK** **Read the answer and discuss these questions.**

1   How does the writer show that he / she has read the question carefully?
2   What is the purpose of each paragraph?
3   What phrases does the writer use to link ideas?
4   How do we know when the writer is stating his / her own opinion?

3   **Use some of the linkers below to complete these sentences.**

(On the one hand …) on the other hand · However, … ·
… although … · so (that) · because (of that) · therefore ·
for this reason · Firstly / First of all, … · Secondly, … ·
Finally, … · In addition, … · Moreover, … ·
Not only that, … · For example, …

There are several possible solutions to food waste. [1]........................., we could buy less food. [2]........................., we could store it better.
[3]........................., we could share it with other people.
We live in a rich country. [4]........................., a lot of people go hungry every day. [5]......................... many people don't even have anywhere to live.
There are poor people in our town. [6]........................., a man sometimes sleeps in the street outside the supermarket.
[7]......................... we are raising money to help the homeless.

4   **TASK** **Write an opinion essay to answer this question. Use the notes and your own ideas. Write about 140–190 words.**

What is the best way to help poor people in developing countries? Write about:

1   raising money for charity
2   philanthropy
3   (your own ideas)

● **Steps to follow**

1   Read the question carefully.
2   Brainstorm ideas and add to the notes.
3   Plan your paragraphs, making sure each one has a clear purpose.
4   Make sure you state the question in the introduction in your own words, and summarise your points in the conclusion.

WRITING EXPANSION

An informal letter

1   Read the question. Where is Sara from?

Question

You've just returned from a week in London with a host family. Write a letter to thank them. In your letter:

- say what you enjoyed the most
- say what you will always remember – and why
- send them greetings from your family and invite them to visit you

Write at least 150 words. You do *not* need to write any addresses.

Answer

Dear Mr and Mrs Jackson,

I'm writing to say a big thank you for giving me such a great time in London. You were very kind to me and I really enjoyed it.

I think my favourite day was when we went on the Millennium Wheel and saw that fantastic view of London.

I thought I was going to feel sick because it went up so high, but it wasn't scary at all! It was fun walking along the side of the river and I liked the art gallery, too. I'd never seen art like that before!

I'll always remember your English breakfasts! They seemed very strange at first but I liked them very much. Oh, and I'm sorry I laughed when you drank cappuccino in the afternoon. (We never do that here in Italy!)

My parents send their best wishes. They would like to welcome you here one day.

I'd better go now. My mum's calling me.

Thank you again,

With love, Sara

2   PAIRWORK   Read the answer and reply to these questions.

1   What phrase does Sara use instead of 'thank you very much'?
2   What form of the verb comes after 'thank you for …'?
3   What did they do on her favourite day?
4   What does she apologise for? Do you think it was a very serious matter?

3   PAIRWORK   Read the letter again and discuss these questions.

1   Does the writer answer the question properly (think of the points she had to insert)?
2   What is the purpose of each paragraph?
3   What phrases does the writer use to start and end the letter?

4   TASK   Your British exchange partner is coming to stay with you for a week. You have already been to stay with her / him, so you know each other. You have decided to write to her / him in preparation for the visit.

In your letter:
1   ask how she / he is and give some news about yourself
2   explain some plans for the week
3   ask what she / he would like to do
4   send greetings to her / his family

Write at least 150 words. You do *not* need to write any addresses.

Steps to follow

1   Read the question carefully, especially the points the writer needs to include.
2   Brainstorm ideas and make notes.
3   Refer back to the Writing strategy box on page 43.
4   Plan your paragraphs, making sure each one has a clear purpose (introduction, middle, end).
5   Make sure you begin and end your letter appropriately.
6   Check your spelling, punctuation and grammar (think of the main tense you will use).
7   Write your first draft. Write about 140–190 words.
8   Check your work again and then write a final draft.

5

A news report

1 Rearrange the paragraphs to make a news report. Write 1, 2, 3 and 4.

☐ Witnesses described him as about 16 years old, white, and skinny. He was wearing a blue hoodie which hid his hair and face. He ran off in the direction of the bus station before anyone could stop him.

☐ Police spokesman **PC** Burns praised Mr Turner for his quick thinking and public-spirited attitude. He appealed to anyone who could help identify the culprit to contact the police on 07834893.

Police Constable

☐ Mr Turner, who was inside the shop at the time, noticed a youth behaving suspiciously. When the youth put his hand into 18-year-old Elisabeth Jones's bag, Mr Turner shouted 'Stop!'. This frightened the thief, who dropped the purse and ran out of the shop.

☐ On Monday 17 January at 10:15 am there was an attempted robbery in the Quickstop Shop on Lansdowne Road. The attempt failed thanks to 79-year-old Jack Turner.

2 Answer these questions.

1 Where did the incident happen?
2 What did Mr Turner see?
3 What happened next?
4 Who was nearly the victim of the crime?
5 What have the police requested?

3 TASK You are a journalist for a local newspaper. Read the situation and the notes, then write a report. Write between 140 and 190 words. Follow the order given in the notes.

Closed Circuit TV

A group of school children have been shoplifting sweets from several shops near where you live. Police have **CCTV** images of them, but their faces are not visible because of their hoodies.

- 8 incidents 8th-15th May: 4 in Mega Supermarket (London Road), 2 in Lindy's Sweets (also London Road) and 2 in Mazda's Newsagent's (Cliff Street)
- 2 boys, 2 girls, approx. 12/13 yrs old, wearing hoodies
- spokesman from Mega Supermarket said extra store detectives on duty
- Lindy Pearce from Lindy's Sweets: blamed parents ('They should control their kids – it's a disgrace')
- police: asked public to report suspicious behaviour: telephone number 0304388

Steps to follow

1 Read the task carefully, and make sure you cover all the points.
2 Refer back to the Writing strategy box on page 53.
3 Plan your paragraphs.
4 Use formal language (except in direct quotations).
5 Write your first draft. Write about 140–190 words.
6 Check your work again and then write a final draft.

A summary

- Indiana Jones – hero of series of films
- Created by George Lucas (also created Star Wars)
- Director: Steven Spielberg
- Star: Harrison Ford
- Archaeologist and explorer – exciting and romantic adventures
- First film: *Raiders of the Lost Ark* (1981)
- series popular ever since then

1 Indiana Jones, who is one of my favourite film characters, is the hero of a series of amazing films created by the famous filmmaker George Lucas. He also created *Star Wars*, another top film series. Steven Spielberg directed the Indiana Jones films, so that's why they're so great. Harrison Ford is the star, and he's brilliant. He plays an archaeologist who has exciting and romantic adventures. The first film in the series is called *Raiders of the Lost Ark* and it was released way back in 1981. They've been incredibly popular ever since.

2 Indiana Jones is the hero of a series of films created by George Lucas, who also created *Star Wars*, and directed by Steven Spielberg. The film series stars Harrison Ford in the role of an archaeologist, who has exciting and romantic adventures. It has been popular ever since 1981, when the first film, *Raiders of the Lost Ark*, was released.

1 PAIRWORK Look at the notes of an article on Indiana Jones and then read the two summaries. Which one is better? Why?

2 Now look at the notes on Petra. Fill in the gaps to form a summary.

- in Jordan – ancient city – carved out of rock
- called the Rose City – pink rock
- dates back to approx. 312 BCE – named as a wonder of the world 2007
- still being excavated – 2016 important new discoveries
- site very popular with tourists – too much tourism a threat – damage to environment

3 TASK Look again at the text on page 61. Then look at the notes and headings from exercises 11 and 12 on page 60. Write a summary of the text. Use about 80 words.

Steps to follow

1 Read the text carefully and check your notes cover all the points.
2 Use the headings to help you.
3 Refer back to the Writing strategy box on page 61.
4 Make sure you don't include unnecessary information or direct speech.
5 Use linkers and relative clauses to link points.
6 Remember that style and accuracy are as important as content.
7 Write your first draft. Write about 80 words.
8 Check your work again and then write a final draft.

Petra, ¹......................... is in Jordan, is ²......................... ancient city carved out of rock. It is often called *the Rose City* ³......................... of the rock's pink colour. The city, ⁴......................... dates back to ⁵......................... 312 BC, was named as a wonder of the world ⁶......................... 2007. Petra is still being excavated, ⁷......................... in 2016 ⁸......................... important new discoveries were made. The site is ⁹......................... popular with tourists, although too much tourism is creating a threat ¹⁰......................... it causes damage to ¹¹......................... environment.

An online review

YOU SEE THIS ANNOUNCEMENT ON A WEBSITE

Have you eaten out recently? What was it like? We'd love to hear from you! Write a review and post it here. Tell us about the food, the atmosphere, the service, the prices – in fact share the whole experience!

Write your answer in 140–190 words in an appropriate style.

Answer

The Fig Tree, Birmingham

A group of us went there last Saturday to celebrate my friend's 18th birthday. It was my first time there but I liked it straight away. The staff were really friendly and they'd even decorated our table with balloons. Most of us ordered pizzas and they tasted great – they obviously use fresh ingredients – although they weren't very big, and if you wanted salad, you had to order it separately. My friend's lasagne wasn't very impressive – it'd been reheated in a microwave, and she said it was a bit dry and tasteless. Most people had ice cream for dessert and said it was excellent. I had tiramisù and it was to die for! The service was fast – maybe even a bit too fast! The final bill was a bit pricey, but we all enjoyed the evening and would go again.

So, I'd definitely recommend it, but I'd go for a pizza if I were you, and keep away from the lasagne!

Stella, Birmingham

1 Read the question and the answer. Would you like to eat at The Fig Tree? Why / Why not?

2 PAIRWORK Now read the answer and discuss the questions.

1 Does the writer cover all the points in the question?
2 What was Stella's first impression of the restaurant? Underline the parts of the text that tell you.
3 What was good about the food, and what was not so good?
4 What do we learn about the waiters and waitresses?
5 Did Stella like her tiramisù? Which phrase tells us?
6 Did she think the restaurant was good value? How do you know?
7 What advice does she give to potential customers?

3 PAIRWORK Which sentence (A or B) is more appropriate for an online review? Why?

1 A I am writing this review in order to recommend it – we thoroughly enjoyed our evening there.
  B I'm happy to recommend this place – we had a great evening.
2 A The service was a bit slow but apart from that it was all good.
  B Unfortunately the slow service spoiled what was otherwise a pleasant experience.

3 A The fish was pretty good, but the chips were rather disappointing.
  B The French fries were sub-standard, although the fish was satisfactory.
4 A The ambience and decor were not to my taste.
  B I wasn't too keen on the style, personally.

4 TASK You are going to write your own answer to the question in exercise 1.

Choose a café or restaurant you have been to recently. Make sure that you include the sections mentioned in the question. Consider these things too:

- Would you recommend it? Why / Why not?
- Do you have any tips or advice for potential customers?

Steps to follow

1 Read the question carefully.
2 Make sure you include the areas the question talks about (there are usually three or four).
3 Brainstorm ideas under these headings and make notes.
4 Refer back to the Writing strategy box on page 71.
5 Use an informal style, but check your spelling, punctuation and grammar.
6 Write your first draft. Write about 140 and 190 words.
7 Check your work again and then write a final draft.

A story

Question

You have seen this announcement on your school notice board.

English Story Competition

The winning story will appear in the school magazine. This is your last chance to enter! Your story must begin with this sentence: I thought I was dreaming …

Write your story. Use between 140 and 190 words.

1 PAIRWORK Read the question, and look at the incomplete answer. Suggest words to complete the gaps. There are lots of possible answers. Think about these things:

- What kind of word is it (adjective or adverb)?
- Which words would fit the context and *feel* of the story?

2 PAIRWORK Now answer the questions.

1 What time of day was it?
2 At the beginning of the story, what was the narrator looking at? How do you know?
3 What happened then?
4 What was *the news* the following morning?
5 How did he know he hadn't been dreaming?
6 Is the phone message explained? What do you think happened?

3 PAIRWORK Answer the questions.

1 Which tenses are used
  - to set the scene?
  - to show sequence of events?
2 Look at the direct speech in paragraph 3. Do you think it would be better as reported speech? Why / Why not?
3 What do you think of the ending? How would you have ended it?

4 TASK Write a story (140 and 190 words) that begins with these words: *Nobody ever believed me.*

Answer

I thought I was dreaming. I was walking home, late at night, through the dark and ⁰ ~~quiet, silent, empty, lonely~~ street, when ¹ .... there was a / an ² .... flash of light in the sky. I looked up from my phone. For a few seconds, I saw something that looked like a / an ³ .... plane, but it wasn't moving.

Then the sky was ⁴ .... again. It happened so ⁵ .... that I thought perhaps I had imagined it. By next morning I had ⁶ .... forgotten all about it – but not for long.

'Have you heard the news?' my sister asked at breakfast time. 'People are saying they saw a UFO last night. How stupid! They watch too many sci-fi films.' I didn't say anything. Is that what I'd seen? I tried to remember exactly what had happened. My sister was staring at me. 'What's the matter?' she asked, 'You look ⁷ .... You don't believe in that rubbish, do you?'

I felt too ⁸ .... to reply. I was saved by a message on my phone. I picked it up ⁹ .... There was the proof that I hadn't been dreaming. I held up the phone to show my sister – a / an ¹⁰ .... thing in the shape of a plane, but with no wings, right above our house.

Steps to follow

1 Read the question carefully. Remember to include the sentence you are given. Do you have to put it at the beginning or at the end?
2 Make sure your story fits well with the sentence.
3 Brainstorm your story:
  - what kind of story is it? Scary, sci-fi, funny, …?
  - who are the main characters? What are their names?
  - is your story in the first person (*I*) or in the third person (*he / she*)?
  - what is the sequence of events?
  - how can you make it interesting?
4 Plan three or four paragraphs. Think about which tenses to use. Consider using direct speech.
5 Remember to use adjectives and adverbs to add colour – but not too many.
6 Refer back to the Writing strategy box on page 79.
7 Use an informal style, but check your spelling, punctuation and grammar.
8 Write your first draft. Write about 140 and 190 words.
9 Check your work again and then write a final draft.

An article

Have you already experienced the world of work? What did you do? What was it like? What did it teach you? Has it helped you decide what career you'd like?

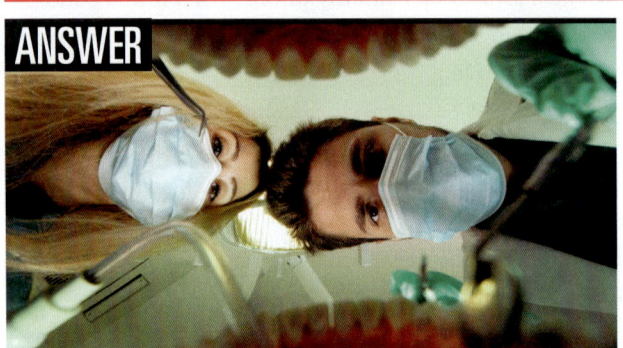

ANSWER

OPEN WIDE! MY WEEK AT THE DENTIST'S

1 It wasn't even 9:00, and already I was staring into a stranger's mouth, wondering if I really wanted to be a dentist. It was the first day of my work experience and I wasn't sure I'd survive the morning, never mind a whole week.

2 I'd had no idea that dentists started work so early – until I was told to turn up at 7:45 sharp. My job was mostly to go into the waiting room and call the next patient. Then I had to stand back and observe. It doesn't sound difficult, and I suppose it wasn't, but I learnt so much!

3 I hadn't realised how kind and sensitive a dentist has to be. Some of the patients were clearly terrified, but she always managed to calm them down with a friendly word and maybe a joke. I could see them relaxing. One woman was so scared she asked me to hold her hand. She thanked me afterwards and said it had helped. I felt really proud.

4 Although I'd wondered how I'd get through the week, I was sad when Friday came. Do I still want to be a dentist? Definitely!

---

1 PAIRWORK Read the question, and look at the answer. Discuss the questions.

2 Now answer these questions.

1 What did the writer have to do?
2 What surprised the writer?
3 Why did the writer feel proud?
4 What are the key facts in the first paragraph, that set the scene?
5 The third paragraph has six adjectives in it. What are they?
6 How does the last paragraph link to the first paragraph?
7 Have all the parts of the question been answered properly?

3 TASK Choose one option. You can either answer the question in exercise 1 or answer this question. Write between 140 and 190 words.

QUESTION ARTICLES WANTED FOR OUR STUDENTS' MAGAZINE

Tell us about something new that you recently experienced. For example, it could be a new sport or hobby, a new place you visited or a new TV show you'd never seen before.
Explain: Why did you do it? How did you feel at the beginning? What was it like? How did you feel at the end?

Steps to follow

1 Read the question carefully. Make sure you answer all the parts.
2 Brainstorm what to include in your article – try to include some interesting details as well as more general information.
3 Think of an eye-catching title and opening sentence.
4 Plan three or four paragraphs. Try to link the conclusion with the opening.
5 Use linking words and phrases, and a variety of tenses, to show the sequence of events; include some interesting details and use adjectives and adverbs (but not too many) to give colour.
6 Refer back to the Writing strategy box on page 89.
7 Use an informal style, but check your spelling, punctuation and grammar.
8 Write your first draft. Write about 140 and 190 words.
9 Check your work again and then write a final draft.

Comment online

1 PAIRWORK Read the conclusion to an article, and two comments. Then answer the questions.

In conclusion, although it is not politically correct to say that little boys are more aggressive than little girls, in my opinion it is true. Of course girls can also be aggressive, but generally speaking, boys are more likely to get into fights than girls. They might not be born like it, but for whatever reason, that's the way they are.

 JD Sorry, but I completely disagree. Aggression doesn't just mean physical fighting. Little girls can be really nasty, and so can little boys. It's nothing to do with their gender.

 NJW Here here! It depends on how they are brought up. You can't generalise.

1 What do you think the article is about?
2 What is the writer's opinion?
3 Which part of the conclusion does JD disagree with?
4 Who does NJW agree with?
5 Who do you agree with?

2 Place the comments into the correct category below.

1 (Sorry, but) I completely disagree.
2 Absolutely!
3 Here, here!
4 I completely agree.
5 I don't agree at all.
6 I don't think you're right.
7 I partly agree.
8 I quite agree!
9 I see what you mean, but …
10 I think some of that is true, but …
11 That's true, but on the other hand …
12 Well said!

Agree: Absolutely!,
Disagree:
Arguments on both sides:

3 Read the conclusion to another article. What was the article discussing?

To sum up, in my opinion war is never justified. It simply makes things worse, and kills more people. I strongly agree with the proverb 'Two wrongs do not make a right'. Instead of fighting, we should talk more and try to understand each other better.

4 TASK Write your own comment. Write three or four sentences.

5 PAIRWORK Read your partner's comment and respond to it with another comment.

Steps to follow

1 Read the conclusion carefully.
2 Consider your own opinion – do you agree or disagree – or do you think there are two sides to the argument?
3 Think about ways to express your response clearly — see exercise 2.
4 Refer back to the Writing strategy box on page 97.
5 Use an informal style, but check your spelling, punctuation and grammar.

Word building

1 **verb ➝ noun**

1 Look at the spelling columns below. Change these verbs into the names of jobs and add them to the correct lists.

assist ▪ build ▪ compose ▪ consult ▪ design ▪ direct ▪ entertain ▪ interpret ▪ invent ▪
lecture ▪ manage ▪ narrate ▪ navigate ▪ produce ▪ sail ▪ translate

verb + -er		verb + -or		verb + -ant
report**er**	paint**er**	act**or** conduct**or**		attend**ant**
read**er**	sing**er**	**But**		
But		decorat**e** ➝ decorat**or**		
writ**e** ➝ writ**er**	driv**e** ➝ driv**er**			
danc**e** ➝ danc**er**	blo**g** ➝ blo**gger**			

2 **noun ➝ noun**

2 Look at how these nouns changed into the names of jobs. Change the nouns below the same way and add them to the correct lists.

violin ▪ cartoon ▪ library ▪ mathematics ▪ history

+ -ist			+ -ian	
journal**ist**	novel**ist**		music**ian**	
art**ist**	guitar**ist**		technic**ian**	
But			**But**	
saxophon**e** ➝ saxophon**ist**	pian**o** ➝ pian**ist**		comed**y** ➝ comed**ian**	
econom**ics** ➝ econom**ist**	dram**a** ➝ drama**tist**		polit**ics** ➝ politic**ian**	

3 Change the head words into the name of a job. Then name famous examples.

0 compose   *composer* : *Verdi*

1 music   .... : ....

2 comedy   .... : ....

3 act   .... : ....

4 write   .... : ....

5 dance   .... : ....

6 art   .... : ....

7 blog   .... : ....

8 politics   .... : ....

9 design   .... : ....

🌐 WORD STRATEGY

Occupations

Many words that refer to jobs and occupations are both verbs and nouns. In these cases, the spelling usually changes.

VOCABULARY EXTENSION

Strong adjectives and intensifiers

WORD STRATEGY

Intensifiers

To make adjectives stronger, we use intensifiers:
very, really, extremely, incredibly, exceptionally.

> It's **very** cold today.
> I'm **really** tired.
> That's an **extremely** difficult puzzle.
> The result was **incredibly** surprising.
> The film is **exceptionally** interesting.

When we have extreme adjectives, these are already strong:

> exhausted = very tired
> astonished = very surprised

In this case, we do <u>not</u> use *very* but we can still use *really, extremely, incredibly* and *exceptionally*. We can also use *absolutely, totally, completely*. Note: we don't use these intensifiers with normal adjectives.

> I'm **really** starving!
> I'm **absolutely** exhausted.
> It's **totally** freezing today.
> That's a **completely** impossible puzzle.

1 Complete the diagram with the intensifiers from the strategy box.

Normal adjectives	Both	Strong adjectives
		absolutely
	really	4 ....
	1	5 ....
very	2	
	3	

2 Match the normal adjectives to the strong adjectives.

0	*e* cold		a	impossible
1	☐ tired		b	boiling
2	☐ difficult		c	tiny
3	☐ surprising		d	fascinating
4	☐ angry		e	freezing
5	☐ hungry		f	gorgeous
6	☐ hot		g	extortionate
7	☐ clean		h	furious
8	☐ small		i	awful
9	☐ silly		j	delicious
10	☐ big		k	exhausted
11	☐ interesting		l	terrifying
12	☐ pretty		m	spotless
13	☐ expensive		n	skinny
14	☐ bad		o	astonishing
15	☐ scary		p	filthy
16	☐ thin		q	starving
17	☐ funny		r	brilliant
18	☐ dirty		s	huge
19	☐ clever		t	ridiculous
20	☐ tasty		u	hilarious

3 **PAIRWORK** Brainstorm strong adjectives. For example, there are several more words that mean *very bad*.

4 **PAIRWORK** Choose five things, places or people and describe them using intensifiers and adjectives. Use the ideas below or your own ideas.

- chocolate
- Ferraris
- the English language
- mosquitoes
- Mark Zuckerberg
- Istanbul
- the Antarctic
- mangoes
- the Sahara Desert
- opera
- politics
- ice cream
- sharks
- Einstein

Chocolate is incredibly delicious.
My brother's / My sister's bedroom is totally filthy.

5 **PAIRWORK** Change partners. Take turns to describe what you chose – but don't name them. Can your partner guess what they are?

It's incredibly delicious.
It's totally filthy.

Stem words

1 PAIRWORK Complete the tables. Use a dictionary for any words you don't know.

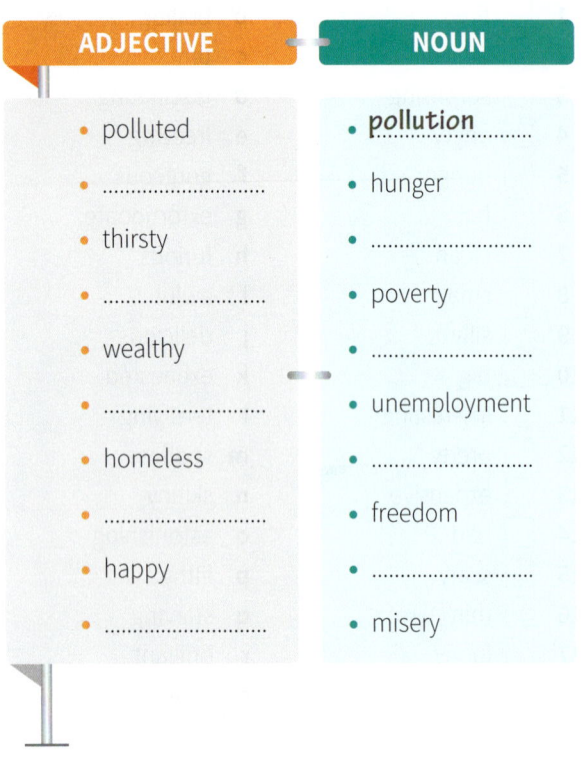

ADJECTIVE	NOUN
• polluted	• pollution
•	• hunger
• thirsty	• ....
•	• poverty
• wealthy	• ....
•	• unemployment
• homeless	• ....
•	• freedom
• happy	• ....
•	• misery

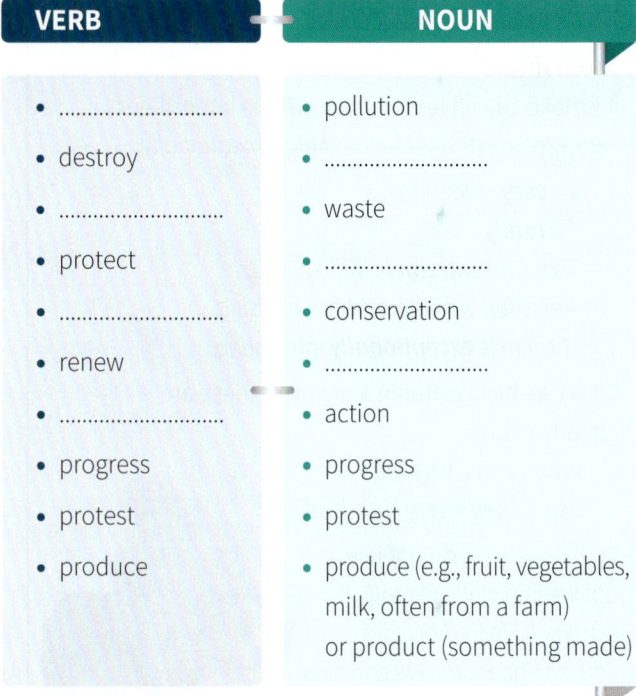

VERB	NOUN
•	• pollution
• destroy	• ....
•	• waste
• protect	• ....
•	• conservation
• renew	• ....
•	• action
• progress	• progress
• protest	• protest
• produce	• produce (e.g., fruit, vegetables, milk, often from a farm) or product (something made)

2 Practise saying these sentences. The letters in bold show where the word stress lies.

1   Medical research is making great pr**o**gress.
Medical research continues to progr**e**ss.
2   There was a pr**o**test about tuition fees yesterday.
Students often prot**e**st about tuition fees.
3   We sometimes buy fresh pr**o**duce from the farm shop.
The farmers prod**u**ce fresh food for the shops.

3 PAIRWORK Say how we can describe:

0   people with no homes: _the homeless_
1   people who are sick: ....
2   people with disabilities: ....
3   people with no jobs: ....
4   elderly people: ....
5   hungry people: ....

4 Make sentences with similar meanings. Complete the second sentence with words from exercises 1 and 3.

0   The number of homeless people is a big problem.
Homelessness is a big problem.
1   A lot of people in our town suffer from poverty and hunger.
A lot of people in our town are .... and ....
2   Food banks support people who don't have much money. They often don't have jobs.
Food banks support the .... .They are often ....
3   I sometimes buy things that developing countries make.
I sometimes buy .... from developing countries.
4   We must stop people destroying the rainforests. It's vital to conserve them.
We must stop the .... of the rainforest
Their .... is vital.
5   Some people have been complaining about cuts in government help for old people.
There have been some .... about cuts in government help for the ....

Formal and informal verbs

1 Read the strategy box and match the verbs to their equivalent.

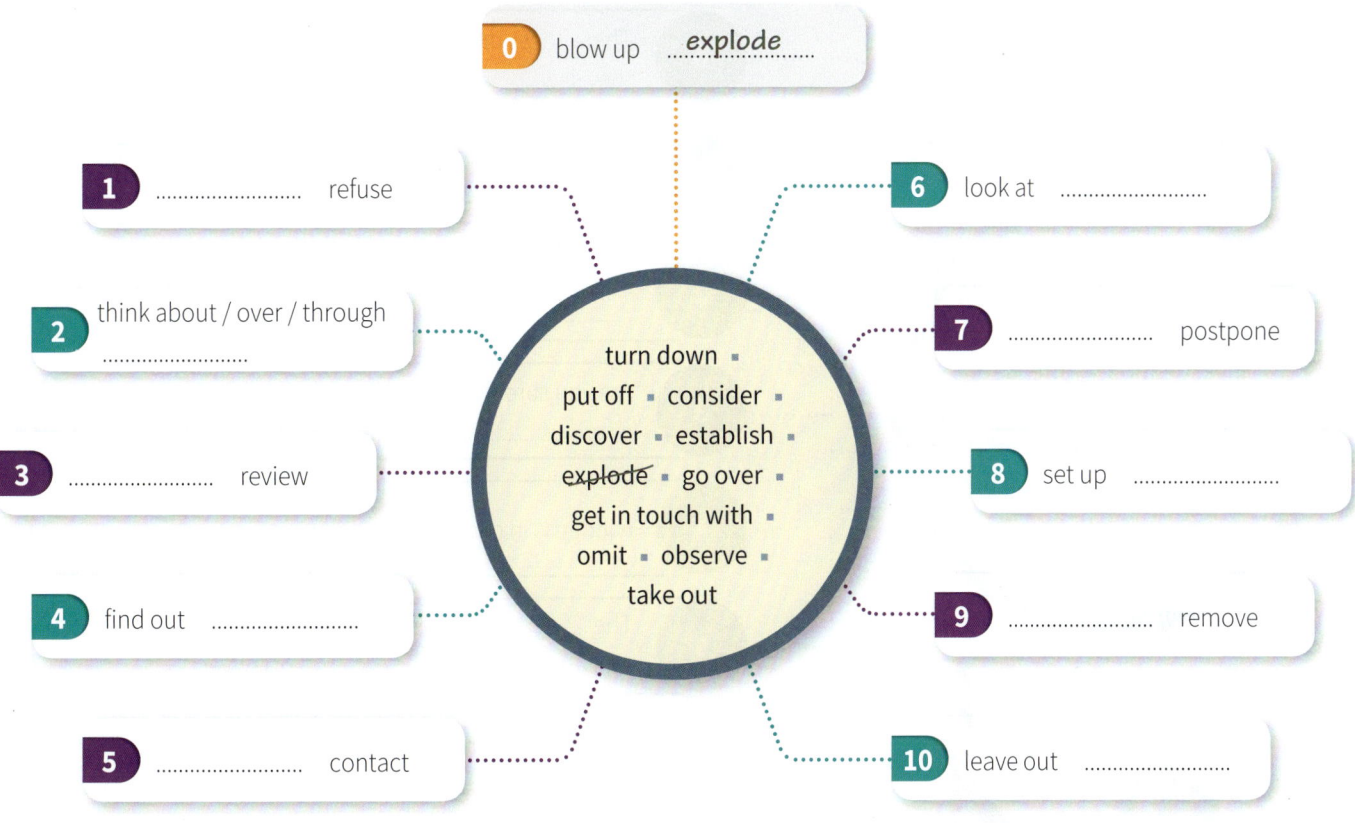

0 blow up ....*explode*....

1 .... refuse

2 think about / over / through ....

3 .... review

4 find out ....

5 .... contact

6 look at ....

7 .... postpone

8 set up ....

9 .... remove

10 leave out ....

(central box:) turn down · put off · consider · discover · establish · explode · go over · get in touch with · omit · observe · take out

2 Complete the sentences with words from exercise 1. Write one word in each gap.

0 Don't put ....*off*.... your decision – act now!

1 Perhaps one day we will .... new colonies on Mars.

2 Powerful telescopes allow us to .... distant galaxies.

3 Please, ... everything through carefully before you decide.

4 Are aliens trying to .... us? Perhaps we will never .... the answer.

5 Remember to include all your data – don't .... anything out.

6 Driverless cars will .... the need to take a driving test!

7 Please, take great care. Otherwise, the experiment might .... up.

8 If you had the chance to live forever, would you turn it ...., or say yes?

WORD STRATEGY

Formal and informal verbs

There are often formal and informal ways of saying the same thing. Phrasal verbs tend to be less formal, and words with Latin or Greek roots tend to be more formal.

e.g., *explode — blow up*

3 Rewrite the sentences in exercise 2, using the alternative verbs.

0 *Don't postpone your decision – act now!*

Crime and the justice system

1 Complete the sentences with the nouns given. Check a dictionary for words you don't know.

accusation ▪ defence ▪ defendant ▪ investigation ▪ offence ▪ penalty ▪ prosecution ▪ rehabilitation ▪ ~~statement~~ ▪ suspect ▪ trial

0 The witness must make a **statement** about what they saw.

1 The .... for a speeding .... is usually a fine.

2 Education and training are part of the prisoners' ....

3 Are you sure that boy stole your phone? That's a serious ....

4 A judge is in charge of the ....

5 The .... lawyer defends the ...., and argues with the .... lawyer.

6 After a thorough .... the police arrested their ....

2 **PAIRWORK** Make pairs of words and expressions that mean the same.

~~accused~~ ▪ against the law ▪ crime ▪ criminal ▪ ~~defendant~~ ▪ evidence ▪ illegal ▪ innocent ▪ interview ▪ jail ▪ not guilty ▪ offence ▪ offender ▪ prison ▪ proof ▪ question

accused → defendant

3 Use words from exercise 2 to complete the sentences.

0 If the **accused / defendant** is found ...., he / she is free to go.

1 The police need .... before they arrest their suspect and .... him / her.

2 Serious ....s go to high-security ....s.

3 Dangerous driving is a serious ....

4 It's .... to text and drive.

Descriptive adjectives

1 PAIRWORK Use a dictionary to complete the diagram and check the meanings.

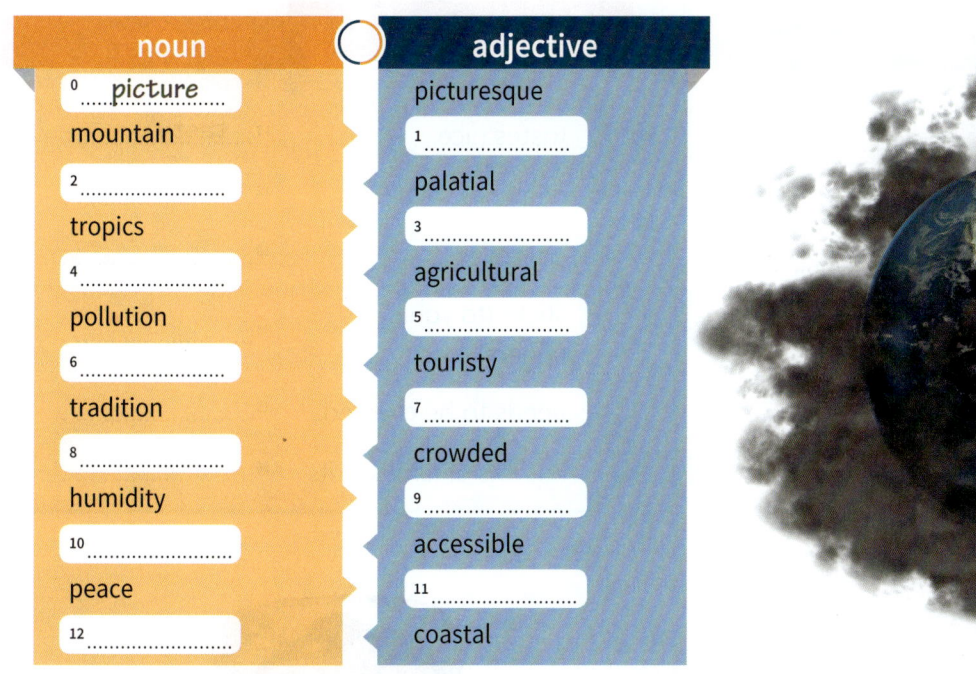

noun	adjective
0 *picture*	picturesque
mountain	1 ....
2	palatial
tropics	3 ....
4	agricultural
pollution	5 ....
6	touristy
tradition	7 ....
8	crowded
humidity	9 ....
10	accessible
peace	11 ....
12	coastal

2 Look at the adjectives in the list below.
They have the opposite meanings to the adjectives
in the diagram above. Find the opposites.

1	clean	*polluted*
2	deserted	....
3	dry	....
4	flat	....
5	industrial	....
6	inland	....
7	modern	....
8	polar	....
9	noisy	....
10	remote / off the beaten track	....
11	sleepy / unspoilt	....
12	tiny	....
13	ugly	....

3 Use words from this page to complete
the sentences.

0 There's no one here. It's completely **deserted** !

1 Some people dislike 21st-century architecture
and prefer more .... styles.

2 There's no phone signal here, it's
too ....

3 There are lots of hotels and souvenir shops in Bath
because it's quite ....

4 There aren't enough houses for everyone.
The town is too ....

5 John's got a huge house, it's really ....
My house, on the other hand, is so small,
it's ....

6 There are too many cars and factories in London.
The air is ....

7 Switzerland is popular with climbers and skiers
because it is so ....

8 I can't sleep. It's too .... outside.

9 The ice caps in .... regions are melting
because of global warming.

10 Tourists like to pose for photos in front of the Blue
Mosque because it's so ....

11 When the sea is at high tide, some ....
areas can be affected by flooding.

12 Clouds are formed when .... air rises.

Taste and texture

1 PAIRWORK Use a dictionary to complete the diagrams and check the meanings.

There's a lot of …	**It tastes …**
salt.	0 _salty_ .
1	peppery.
water.	2 ....
3	spicy.
milk.	4 ....
5	greasy.
cream.	6 ....
7	sugary.
oil.	8 ....
9	juicy.
butter.	10 ....

It …	**It's …**
tastes nice.	11 _tasty_ .
crunches.	12 ....
crumbles.	13 ....
sticks (to your fingers).	14 ....
needs to be chewed.	15 ....
has lots of lumps in it.	16 ....

2 Make pairs of opposites. Use a dictionary where necessary.

- bland
- crisp
- delicious
- dry
- fresh
- hard
- hot, spicy
- light
- lumpy

- moist
- rich
- smooth
- soft
- soggy
- sour, bitter
- stale
- sweet
- tasteless

bland - hot, spicy

3 GAME In pairs, do the tasks below.

1 Choose six things from the list below and match them to adjectives from this page.

- custard
- strawberries
- chocolate
- curry
- porridge
- toast

- toffee
- crisps
- apples
- chips
- biscuits
- bananas

- lemons
- coffee
- lettuce
- rocket
- cheese
- pizza

2 Read your adjectives to another pair. Can they guess the food?

A   Delicious, sweet, sticky.

B   Chocolate!

VOCABULARY EXTENSION

8

Idioms with *mind*

1   PAIRWORK
Match the meanings to the correct expressions.

0	**d**	have a mind of your own
1		keep / bear something in mind
2		have something on your mind
3		change your mind
4		be / go out of your mind
5		give someone a piece of your mind
6		be in two minds (about something)
7		have / keep an open mind
8		make up your mind
9		take your mind off something
10		have something in mind
11		speak your mind
12		have a lot on your mind

a	decide something, then decide something different
b	not decide anything – keep thinking about something
c	make a decision
d	be an independent thinker
e	be thinking about something all the time
f	say what you think
g	be worried about a lot of things
h	be unsure what to do
i	be / go crazy
j	have a plan
k	make a note of something, remember it
l	tell someone why you're angry with them
m	take a break from worrying

2   Read the expressions from exercise 1 and complete the missing words.

0   I keep thinking about it. It's ....**on**.......... my mind.
1   I think I'll watch a film. It'll .... my mind .... my problems.
2   It's a difficult decision. I'm .... two .... about it.
3   Thanks, that's useful information. I'll .... it .... mind.
4   I didn't sleep well last night. I have a lot .... my mind.
5   I don't need advice, thanks. I .... a mind .... my own.
6   I know what I'm going to do. I've .... my mind.
7   I'm going to give my opinion. I'll .... my mind.
8   I'm terribly worried. I'm going .... my mind.

3   PAIRWORK Discuss these questions.

1   Look at the expressions again. How do you say them in your language?
2   Which ones are the closest to your language?

Business

1 Match the phrasal verbs for business to the correct definitions.

1	c	carry out	a	establish, start (a business)
2		take off	b	test
3		weigh up	c	perform, do
4		try out	d	succeed
5		set up	e	resolve
6		give up	f	think of (a plan, an idea)
7		think over	g	put an end to (a business)
8		sort out	h	look at both sides
9		come up with	i	stop trying
10		close down	j	consider thoroughly

2 Complete the sentences with the phrasal verbs from exercise 1.

0 The police will **carry out** an investigation into the bank fraud.

1 I'd like to .... my own business one day.

2 When did Mark Zuckerberg .... the idea of Facebook?

3 Please .... your plan again and check everything.

4 I need to .... all my options and then I'll decide.

5 I hope my new business will .... and make me rich.

6 The business didn't do well so we had to .... it ....

7 Try not to .... if your plan doesn't work first time. Try again!

8 Let's discuss the problems and .... a solution.

9 We should .... the product first, to see if it works properly.

3 Complete the sentences with the words below.

> carry ▪
> close ▪ come ▪
> give ▪ out ▪ over ▪
> set ▪ sort ▪
> take ▪ weigh ▪
> with

If you [0] **come** up [1] .... a great idea, you might want to [2] .... up your own business. Before you do, you should [3] .... out lots of research, think it [4] .... carefully and [5] .... up the pros and cons. Then your business is more likely to [6] .... off. However, if it doesn't succeed, don't [7] .... up and [8] .... it down. Instead, [9] .... out the problems or try [10] .... something new!

Idioms with *battle*

1 Match the sentences to the explanations. Then check the meaning of the idioms with a dictionary.

1	**d**	You have to learn to fight your own battles.
2	☐	You should learn to choose your battles. You can't argue about everything!
3	☐	The contestants battled it out in the final.
4	☐	The workers who went on strike got a pay rise, but six months later they were sacked. They won the battle but lost the war.
5	☐	Nobody was willing to change their mind. It was a battle of wills.

a	Both sides competed seriously.
b	They had a short-term victory but it didn't last long.
c	It was a test of determination and will power.
d	Don't rely on other people – be assertive.
e	Focus on the things that really matter.

2 Match the idioms in exercise 1 (1—5) to the situations below (a—e). Use the idioms to answer the questions.

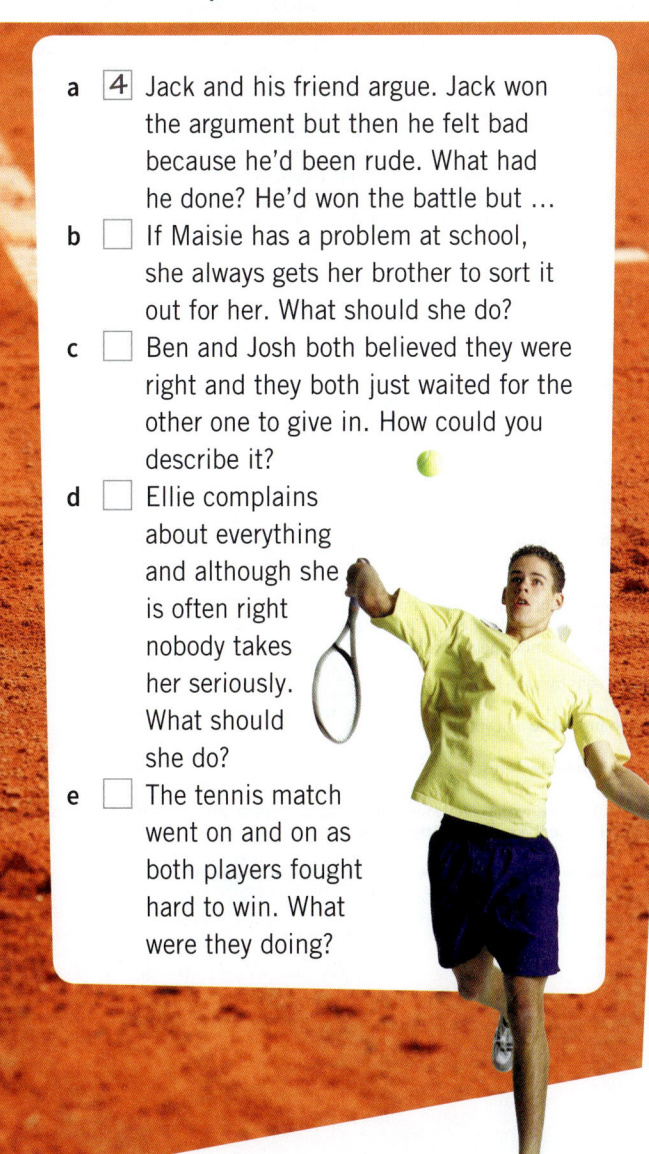

a **4** Jack and his friend argue. Jack won the argument but then he felt bad because he'd been rude. What had he done? He'd won the battle but …

b ☐ If Maisie has a problem at school, she always gets her brother to sort it out for her. What should she do?

c ☐ Ben and Josh both believed they were right and they both just waited for the other one to give in. How could you describe it?

d ☐ Ellie complains about everything and although she is often right nobody takes her seriously. What should she do?

e ☐ The tennis match went on and on as both players fought hard to win. What were they doing?

3 Complete the sentences with the idioms below. Check a dictionary to find out what they mean.

a losing battle ▪ an uphill battle ▪
~~a battle of wits~~ ▪ a running battle ▪
half the battle

0 It was the final of the chess competition. It really was *a battle of wits* .

1 We didn't manage to persuade Tom to come with us – he really didn't want to. We were fighting ....

2 We had to overcome a lot of obstacles before we finally managed to solve the problem. It was ....

3 The mobile phone company keeps sending me the wrong bill. It's been going on for months. We're fighting ....

4 When you're learning a new language, self-confidence is ....

4 PAIRWORK Discuss these questions.

1 Which of the idioms in exercises 1 and 3 are similar in your language?

2 Can you think of other idioms in your language on the theme of battles?

🌐 WORD STRATEGY

Battle can be a verb or a noun.

THANKS AND ACKNOWLEDGEMENTS

The authors and publishers acknowledge the following sources of copyright material and are grateful for the permissions granted. While every effort has been made, it has not always been possible to identify the sources of all the material used, or to trace all copyright holders. If any omissions are brought to our notice, we will be happy to include the appropriate acknowledgements on reprinting and in the next update to the digital edition, as applicable.

The publishers are grateful to the following for permission to reproduce copyright photographs and material:

Key: T = Top, TL = Top Left, TR = Top Right, CL = Centre Left, CR = Centre Right, C = Centre, B = Below, BL = Below Left, BR = Below Right, L = Left, R = Right, Ex = Exercise, B/G = Background, U = Unit.

Text

Maps on p. 118 adapted from Andrew Cliff & Peter Haggett, 'Time, travel and infection', British Medical Bulletin Vol. 69, Issue 1, by permission of Oxford University Press.

Photo

Cover Title: Lostanastacia

Cover Image: GlobalP

All photos are sourced from Getty Images.

p. 4 (Top B/G): C Brandon/Redferns; p. 4 (Centre B/G): Cofotoisme/iStock; p. 4 (music): Proksima/iStock; p. 5 (design): Drafter123/Digitalvision Vectors; p. 5 (CR): Visitbritain/ Grant Pritchard; p. 5 (BR): Jeff J Mitchell; p. 6 (BG): Aetb/iStock; p. 6 (TR): Tom Dulat; p. 6 (CL): Buda Mendes; p. 6 (swimming): Cajoer/iStock; p. 6 (climbing): Appleuzr/Digitalvision Vectors; p. 6 (running): Cajoer/iStock; p. 6 (diving): Cajoer/iStock; p. 6 (skiing): Cajoer/iStock; p. 6 (football): Cajoer/iStock; p. 6 (horse Riding): Cajoer/iStock; p. 6 (rowing): Cajoer/iStock; p. 6 (cycling): Cajoer/iStock; p. 6 (skating): Cajoer/iStock; p. 6 (basketball): Cajoer/iStock; p. 6 (tennis): Cajoer/iStock; p. 7 (BR): Aeduard/E+; p. 7 (CR): Sylwia Duda/ Moment; p. 8 (BG): Str/Afp; p. 8 (camp): Kutluhan Cucel; p. 8 (boy): Ismailciydem/E+; p. 9: Ridofranz/iStock; p. 10 (cow): Bartco/E+; p. 10 (Engineer Training): Monkeybusinessimages/iStock; p. 10 (construction site): Bartco/iStock; p. 10 (CL): David Schaffer/Caiaimage; p. 10 (CR): Mikecherim/E+; p. 10 (C): Education Images/Universal Images Group; p. 10 (Tablet): Blackred/E+; p. 11 (cap): Ihorzigor/iStock; p. 12 (B/G): Majority World/ Universal Images Group; p. 12 (CR): Artur Widak/Nurphoto; p. 12 (CL): Stephen Zeigler/ The Image Bank; p. 12 (seal): Aquir/iStock; p. 12 (browser template): Tovovan/iStock; p. 13: Pugping/iStock; p. 14 (Man shooting): Roberto Machado Noa/Lightrocket; p. 14 (screen): Vertigo3D/iStock; p. 14 (radio): Mgkaya/E+; p. 14 (B/G): John Lamb/Digitalvision; p. 14 (phone): Seewhatmitchsee/iStock Editorial; p. 14 (CR): Beeandbee/iStock Editorial; p. 15 (newspaper): Vladwel/iStock; pp. 16-17 (blog): Mikko Lemola/iStock; p. 18 (CL): Di_Studio/iStock; p. 18 (TR): Fandijki/Digitalvision Vectors; p. 20 (TR): Jag Images/Image Source; p. 20 (TL): Echo/Juice Images; p. 20 (BR): Dan Sipple/Ikon Images; p. 21 (photo 1): Thomas Tolstrup/Taxi; p. 21 (photo 2): David Burch/Uppercut Images; p. 21 (photo 3): Eric Audras/Onoky; p. 22 (TL): Moodboard/Cultura; p. 22 (TR): Bellurget Jean Louis/Stockbyte; p. 22 (C): Classen Rafael/Eyeem; p. 22 (cola): Adyna/DigitalVision Vectors; p. 23 (T): Alashi/Digitalvision Vectors; pp. 24-25: Visitbritain/Joanna Henderson; p. 24 (pod): Obeonline/iStock; p. 25 (dubble bed): Visitbritain/Joanna Henderson; p. 26 (CR): Vgajic/E+; p. 26 (BR): Payaercan/Digitalvision Vectors; p. 26 (BG): Liuzishan/ iStock; p. 29 (BR): Andresr/E+; p. 29 (icons): Krizzdapaul/iStock; p. 32 (T): Isci/iStock; p. 32 (BR): Afp; p. 33: Artqu/iStock; p. 34 (B/G): 31Moonlight31/iStock; p. 34 (shop): Peopleimages/Digitalvision; p. 35 (TL): Indiapictures/Universal Images Group; p. 35 (TR): Justin Sullivan; p. 35 (BL): Christianchan/iStock; p. 36 (photo a): Ted Russell/Photographer'S Choice; p. 36 (photo b): Hero Images; p. 36 (photo c): Mrpliskin/iStock; p. 36 (B/G): Bluelela/iStock; p. 36 (bread): Dmitriykazitsyn/iStock; p. 38 (photo a): Justin Sullivan; p. 38 (photo b): Hero Images; p. 38 (photo c): Hero Images; p. 38 (photo d): Hero Images; p. 38 (BG): Subjob/iStock; p. 39 (students): Colorblind Images/The Image Bank; p. 39 (BR): Sorbetto/Digitalvision Vectors; p. 39 (abstract): Shuoshu/Digitalvision Vectors; p. 39 (newspaper): Vladwel/iStock; p. 40 (book): Michael Freeman/Corbis Documentary; p. 40 (CL): Bettmann; p. 41 (TL): Atomic Imagery/Digitalvision; p. 41 (BR): D-Base/Digitalvision; p. 42 (BL): Ileximage/E+; pp. 42-43: Scott Peterson; p. 44 (CR): Jim Watson/Afp; p. 44 (TR): Pinkypills/iStock; p. 46 (TL): Christian Mueller/iStock Editorial; p. 46 (CR): Visitbritain/Chris Renton; p. 46 (TR): Cybrain/iStock; p. 47: Hero Images; p. 50 (header): Peter Dazeley; p. 50 (header): Spaces Images/Blend Images; p. 50 (T): Marco Di Lauro; p. 50 (CL): Marco Di Lauro; p. 50 (handcuffs): Theerakit/iStock; p. 50 (man with coffee): Marco Di Lauro; p. 51 (BR): Alashi/Digitalvision Vectors; p. 51 (T): Vicvic13/ iStock; p. 52 (canoe): Willard/iStock; p. 53 (police): Christopher Furlong; p. 53 (CL): Goldy/iStock; p. 54 (camera): Yoanna Boyadzhieva/Eyeem; p. 54 (interrogation): Richlegg/ E+; p. 54 (witness): Rubberball; p. 54 (fingerprint): Smile3377/iStock; p. 55 (B): Johavel/ iStock; p. 55 (silhouettes): Bearty/iStock Plus; p. 56 (TL): Brianajackson/iStock; p. 56 (BR): Lightcome/iStock; p. 57 (TL): Omgimages/iStock; p. 57 (TR): Denis Doyle; p. 58 (flood): Marco Secchi; p. 58 (boot): Delmethomasphotography/iStock; p. 58 (T): Valentinrussanov/iStock; p. 59: De Agostini Picture Library/G. Dagli Orti; p. 60 (BL): Ulimi/Digitalvision Vectors; p. 61 (Europe): Planet Observer/Universal Images Group; p. 61 (BG): Digital Vision; p. 62 (Mosque): Ron Dahlquist/Design Pics/Perspectives; p. 62 (Opéra Garnier): Serts/iStock Unreleased; p. 62 (Taj): Saiko3P/iStock; p. 62 (London): Olegalbinsky/ iStock; p. 62 (boot): Pierredesrosiers/iStock; p. 62 (belt): Sergey_Peterman/iStock; p. 62 (museum): Howard Kingsnorth/Photolibrary; p. 64 (swans): David Tipling/Lonely Planet Images; p. 64 (water): Danilovi/iStock; p. 65 (pie chart): Mathisworks/Digitalvision Vectors; p. 68 (BL): Dlerick/E+; p. 68 (BR): Thomas Tolstrup/The Image Bank; p. 68 (tomato): Anna1311/iStock; p. 68 (T): Clubfoto/iStock; pp. 70-71 (B/G): Dogayusufdokdok/iStock; p. 71 (Chef): Pier Marco Tacca; p. 71 (Johnny): Dougal Waters/Digitalvision; p. 71 (Kylie): Filadendron/E+; p. 71 (Greg): Justin Case/Digitalvision; p. 72 (crumble): Anjelagr/iStock; p. 72 (apples): Olyasolodenko/iStock; p. 74 (BR): Maxiphoto/iStock; p. 74 (BC): Lew Robertson/Digitalvision; p. 74 (TL): Jonathan Kantor/Digitalvision; p. 75 (BR): Sorbetto/Digitalvision Vectors; p. 76 (girl): Fizkes/iStock; p. 76 (header): Avava/iStock; p. 76 (digital clock): Kickstand/iStock; p. 76 (analog clocks): Rouzes/E+; p. 76 (BG): Mediaproduction/ iStock; p. 77 (B): Stevestone/E+; p. 78 (discussion): Youst/Digitalvision Vectors; p. 78 (newspaper): Don Farrall/Digitalvision; p. 78 (man): Dima_Sidelnikov/iStock; p. 78 (beach): Lisa-Blue/iStock; p. 78 (train): Nikada/E+; p. 79 (TL): Universal Images Group; p. 79 (woman): Aldomurillo/E+; p. 79 (BG): Ktsimage/iStock; p. 80 (BL): G-Stockstudio/iStock; p. 80 (B): Cecilie_Arcurs/E+; p. 82 (TL): Jetta Productions/Digitalvision; p. 83 (people): Skynesher/iStock; p. 83 (boy): Brand X Pictures/Digitalvision; p. 86 (ATM): Eclipse_Images/E+; p. 86 (header): Simon Dawson/Bloomberg; p. 86 (CR): Pepifoto/E+; p. 86 (coin): Alfexe/iStock; p. 86 (bill): John W Banagan/Photographer'S Choice Rf; p. 88 (BL): Hoaru/ iStock; p. 89 (BG): Fotokostic/iStock; p. 89 (dragon): Jpa1999/Digitalvision Vectors; p. 90 (photo 1): Solstock/E+; p. 90 (photo 3): Floresco Productions/Cultura; p. 90 (photo 2): Wavebreakmedia Ltd; p. 90 (CL): Scanrail/iStock; p. 92 (TL): Monkeybusinessimages/ iStock; p. 92 (market): Steve Ryan/Taxi; p. 92 (BR): A-Digit/Digitalvision Vectors; p. 93 (photo 1): Fangxianuo/E+; p. 93 (photo 2): Bartekszewczyk/iStock; p. 93 (CL): Kbeis/Digitalvision Vectors; p. 94 (TL): Win-Initiative; p. 94 (TC): Szabolcs Kiss/Eyeem; p. 94 (TR): Nicole Lienemann/EyeEm; p. 94 (Olive branch): Malerapaso/E+; p. 94 (wire): Fajrul Islam/Moment; p. 94 (CR): Bazilfoto/iStock; p. 94 (cranes): Diane555/iStock; p. 94 (TL): Afp; p. 96 (BL): Djvstock/iStock; pp. 96-97 (B/G): Incomible/iStock; p. 97 (teens): Gpointstudio/iStock; p. 98 (T): Frans Sellies/Moment; p. 98 (BL): Wastesoul/iStock; p. 101 (CR): Dea/A. Dagli Orti/De Agostini Picture Library; p. 101 (paper): Rustemgurler/E+; p. 101 (boy): Mediaphotos/iStock; pp. 104-105 (T): Robbie Jack/Corbis Entertainment; p. 105 (T): Robbie Jack/Corbis Entertainment; pp. 106-107 (T): Robert Downie/Eyeem; p. 108: Mspoli/iStock; p. 109: Archive Photos; p. 110: Fototeca Storica Nazionale/Hulton Archive; p. 111: Print Collector/Hulton Archive; p. 112 (TR): Fotogablitz/iStock; p. 112 (B/G): Michael Roberts/Moment; p. 113: Universalimagesgroup; p. 114 (CR): Peopleimages/ E+; p. 114 (BR): Avemario/iStock; p. 114 (BC): Goldfinch4Ever/iStock; p. 114 (Icons): Chengchilin/Digitalvision Vectors; p. 114 (music): Marsbars/E+; p. 114 (TR): Frank Bienewald/Lightrocket; p. 114 (player): Filborg/iStock; p. 115 (bacteria): Pasieka/Science Photo Library; p. 115 (capsule): Pbombaert/Moment; p. 116 (TR): Yuri_Arcurs/E+; p. 116 (photo a): Xixinxing/iStock; p. 116 (photo b): Uniball/iStock; p. 116 (photo c): Nechaev-Kon/iStock; p. 116 (photo d): Littlebee80/iStock; p. 116 (photo e): Chris Ryan/Ojo Images; p. 116 (photo f): Sankalpmaya/iStock; p. 117 (CR): Print Collector/Hulton Archive; p. 117 (CR): Mpi/Archive Photos; p. 117 (BR): Saemilee/Digitalvision Vectors; p. 117 (TL): Gregor Schuster/Photographer'S Choice Rf; p. 118 (BG): Chester Ong/Dorling Kindersley; p. 118 (TR): Kaupang/iStock; p. 118 (BL): Jakataka/Digitalvision Vectors; p. 118 (BR): Pasha18/iStock; p. 118 (walking): Time & Life Pictures; p. 118 (Cunard): Hulton Deutsch/Corbis Historical; p. 118 (UK A Map): Phototos2016/iStock; p. 119 (BL): Selektor/ E+; p. 119 (envelope): Coprid/iStock; p. 119 (logo): Serkorkin/iStock; p. 119 (boy): Mediaphotos/iStock; p. 120 (T): Chuvipro/Digitalvision Vectors; p. 120 (BL): Hero Images; p. 120 (BC): Jeff Greenberg/Universal Images Group; p. 120 (BR): Hill Street Studios/Eric Raptosh/Blend Images; p. 121 (photo A): Fotografiabasica/E+; p. 121 (photo B): Benjavisa/iStock; p. 121 (photo C): Kelsey Pangborn/iStock; p. 122 (K): National Institutes Of Health/Stocktrek Images; p. 122 (CL): Auscape/Universal Images Group; p. 122 (BR): Jane Burton/Nature Picture Library; p. 122 (map): Negoworks/iStock; p. 123 (CR): Brian Hagiwara/Photolibrary; p. 123 (CL): Tanuha2001/iStock; p. 124 (Barcelona): Tomassereda/iStock Editorial; p. 124 (object): Bombyx/iStock; p. 124 (circle): Weedezign/iStock; p. 125 (email): Aşkın Dursun Kamberoğlu/Digitalvision Vectors; p. 125 (B): Antoniokhr/ iStock; p. 126 (TC): Vuk8691/iStock; p. 126 (TR): 22Kay22/iStock; p. 127: Dobok/iStock; p. 128 (policeman): Andrew_Howe/E+; p. 128 (newspaper): Zerbor/iStock; p. 128 (notepad): Jaroszpilewski/iStock; p. 129 (Indiana Jones): Murray Close/Moviepix; p. 129 (CL): Peter Unger/Lonely Planet Images; p. 129 (frame): Hudiemm/iStock; p. 129 (BG): Vitalalp/iStock; p. 129 (paper): Ke77Kz/iStock; p. 130 (photo d): Littlebee80/iStock; p. 130 (laptop): Wabeno/iStock; p. 130 (coffee): Djgunner/ iStock; p. 130 (chef): Hero Images/Digitalvision; p. 131 (spaceship): Koya79/iStock; p. 131 (blackboard): Eli_Asenova/iStock; p. 132 (TL): 1001Nights/E+; p. 132 (woman): Izusek/E+; p. 133 (B): Lenanet/iStock; p. 133 (soldiers): Frank Rossoto Stocktrek/Digitalvision; p. 134 (BR): Savaryn/iStock; p. 135: Viktorcap/iStock; p. 137 (satellite): Claudioventrella/iStock; p. 138 (BL): Grinvalds/iStock; p. 138 (BR): Avosb/iStock; p. 139 (earth): Comotion_Design/E+; p. 140 (BC): Lew Robertson/Digitalvision; p. 140 (CL): Floortje/ E+; p. 140 (B): Malerapaso/E+; p. 141 (girl): Laflor/E+; p. 141 (head): Brainmaster/E+; p. 142 (man): Yuri_Arcurs/E+; p. 142 (bulb): Gorica/iStock; p. 143 (Tennis): Photodisc; p. 143 (court): Dkart/E+.

Photos from other sources:

p. 106 (CL): Pictorial Press Ltd/Alamy Stock Photo;

Video

All video content is sourced from Getty Images.
Please follow the link below for full details of all clips.
http://www.cambridgelms.org/talent

Illustrations by Damiano Groppi.

Music

All music is sourced from Getty Images.
Please follow the link below for full details of all clips.
http://www.cambridgelms.org/talent

Video stills by Lada films.

Video produced by Lada films.

CLIL Modules by Teresa Ting.

The publishers would like to extend a special thank you to all the teachers who helped shape the content of this book.